FAMILIES

WHAT THE
BIBLE SAYS
ABOUT
FAMILIES

Bill and Judy Norris

College Press Publishing Company, Joplin, Missouri

Copyright © 1985
College Press Publishing Company

Library of Congress Catalog Card Number: 85-071488
International Standard Book Number: 0-89900-099-1

Table of Contents

This manuscript might be termed "A Family Affair." Bill read every verse of Scripture from Genesis to Revelation, plus using the Analytical Bible and the Cross-Reference Bible for details on the background of each book. He also pored over various translations before completing his notes, trying to achieve the clearest meaning. We chose the New American Standard Bible for quotes with a few from the King James Version. Our choice of the NASB resulted from assurance of its faithfulness to the original languages plus its clarity of expression in our modern language.

As Bill completed his research on each book, he handed voluminous (And I do mean "voluminous!") notes to me. Before writing, I looked up each character in Hastings Dictionary of the Bible, adding interesting data found there.

Bill minored in Greek in the university but did not study Hebrew. I have no competence in either of these ancient languages. We purposely did not use them in the manuscript itself, preferring to make the book easily read and understood. Our aim was to write a practical book for family use, not especially a scholarly one.

But, in saying this, I want to note that any fear that our interpretation might conflict with those languages sent us to scholars. Old Testament inquiries resulted in a call to Dr. Robert Owens at Emmanuel School of Religion. Dr. Robert Hull from Emmanuel helped in some New Testament problems. Each of these men responded graciously, no matter what questions were asked. A couple of times Dr. Owens remarked, "Well, I never heard of that one before!" But he humored me.

We had a scholarly helper very close, too. Our son, Dr. Fred Norris, also an Emmanuel professor, listened to his mother at any hour of the day or night. Sometimes his father bent his ear. He frequently made suggestions we included. Since he was in the midst of writing a book, I am quite sure we occasionally interrupted his train of thought. Yet he graciously listened, critiqued, and even praised our efforts. (Perhaps taking his television away for a lengthy period when he sassed during childhood had a permanent effect!)

Seriously, we are most grateful for the assistance of these professors, both dedicated and learned, who offered not only their expertise but their loving friendship. We include our son in this. Shouldn't adult children be our friends? We inquired of Dr. Dean E. Walker, the dean of Christian Church scholars and our dear friend of many years standing, as to the possible meaning of one obscure passage. He, too, responded with interest and love.

We also spent much time in prayer, asking God's help for the project. Interpreting His Word strikes fear into the heart of a conscientious Christian. We pled for His guidance that the book might be helpful to Christian families, never hurtful.

We were married June 15, 1939. All those succeeding years have been a partnership in the service of God. When Bill preached, I directed choirs. When he led singing and sang solos, I accompanied him on the piano, even acting as his organist stateside when he served as a chaplain in World War II and in Korea. Although I am the writer, (Bill dislikes writing) much of the thought and research are his. We mulled over each page together; discussing proper phraseology, trying to decide the clearest way to state our sincere thoughts. This project seems to have been a culmination of the many other cooperative efforts we have experienced in our lives together with Him.

Perhaps we should make one final comment. We are still speaking! We loved doing this. We wish we had made the study thirty years ago. We might have improved our parenting!

Bill and Judy Norris
Johnson City, TN

INTRODUCTION

The family appears as the primary unit of society both in the Old and New Testaments. The Old Testament provides many stories of families. We found special interest as we assessed family problems of that era, discovering that the psychological, spiritual and material difficulties of our culture were pervasive in the ancient culture as well. That will be a thrust of this book. Similarity of problems of ancient polygamous households and modern divorce situations actually leaped at us from Old Testament Writ. Old Testament polygamy established several small families in one large household. Modern divorce and remarriage creates much the same sort of difficulty when people attempt to blend children united by one parent in common. Some families in the Old Testament managed to maintain a vestige of loving unity. Others

11

failed. We shall try to show a few reasons both for the successes and the failures.

In the Old Testament, polygamous households have all the pitfalls and emotional turmoil associated with that form of society. The polygamous family seems to have evolved as part of primitive culture. Perhaps it resulted from the need of the less muscular and smaller female for the protection of the larger, more aggressive male in civilization's infancy. At no point in the Old Testament does God command polygamy. His acceptance of the lifestyle appears to be part of His persuasion for His creation to possess free will even if that free will flouts His commands and leads humanity into devastating trouble. We find it significant that neither of the Genesis accounts of creation mentions God's making more than one woman for Adam. Had the great Creator deemed polygamy either essential or fulfilling, would He not have done so? One may trace several generations of Biblical families before finding any mention of polygamy. In fact, the first Biblical reference to two wives for one man appears in the genealogy of Cain. Lamech married two women, Adah and Zillah. Lamech was five generations beyond Cain, therefore six generations from Adam. We also pondered upon the meaning of finding polygamy first in the descendants of Cain, the one whose heart was not right before God.

Sibling rivalry resulted in the first murder. It still wreaks havoc today. Adulterous relationships of the ancients created broken lives and homes. We marveled at the ability of the Bible to reach into modern times with its detailed approach to marriage and family problems.

The first part of the book will attempt to describe and assess Old Testament families. The latter part of the Old

Testament division will go into the wisdom literature and its relationship to modern family life.

The second part of the book comes from the New Testament. The first section will discuss families and their lives as revealed in the New Testament itself. The second section will bring a discussion of the advice literature as it relates to family living. What do the letters really say about our families? How may we use the great wisdom found there in a totally different frame of reference such as our culture today? May we carry over the teaching without trying to transfer first century culture to our modern era? Can we distinguish between expediency for the New Testament age and commands for all time?

One of the things we noted continually through both the Old and New Testaments was God's emphasis upon unselfish love. We observed the effect of this type of love upon character development and its relationship to harmonious family living. We watched through the eyes of our minds while God personified love in action, dealing mercifully with His sinning children. Some learned. Some didn't. We became increasingly aware of the necessity for maturity before one really reaches the state of wisdom demanded of a true child of God.

We've learned much in preparation of this book. We hope it will help our readers to a closer walk with God and with each other.

THE OLD TESTAMENT

1

ADAM AND EVE

God's plan for the human family appears first in Genesis 1:26-31.

Then God said, "Let us make man in our image, according to our likeness; and let them rule over the fish of the sea and over the birds of the sky and over the cattle and over all the earth." And God created man in His own image, in the image of God He created him, male and female He created them. And God blessed them; and God said to them, "Be fruitful and multiply, and fill the earth, and subdue it; and rule over the fish of the sea and over the birds of the sky, and over every living thing that moves on the earth." Then God said, "Behold, I have given you every plant yielding seed; and it shall be food for you; and to every beast of the earth and to every bird of the sky and to every thing that moves on the earth which has life, I have given every green plant for food"; and it was so. And God saw all that He had made, and behold, it was very good. And there was evening and there was morning, the sixth day.

We thrill to the joys of that first honeymoon couple in the second chapter of Genesis. How easy it is to identify with Adam as he exclaims, "This is now bone of my bones, and flesh of my flesh; she shall be called Woman, because she was taken out of man." Then the Bible states, "For this cause a man shall leave his father and his mother, and shall cleave to his wife; and they shall become one flesh. And the man and his wife were both naked and were not ashamed" (Gen. 2:23-25).

As we read the account of the serpent's seduction of Eve, we identify characteristics few of us have conquered. Eve carefully explained how blessed she and Adam were in their paradise created by God. But the serpent was crafty.

"Can you eat everything here?"

One can almost feel Eve's hesitation as she answers, "Well, no. We can't eat from that one tree in the middle of the garden. God told us we'll die if we do."

Suddenly the garden wasn't such a paradise after all. The lovely trees from which they could eat receded into the background. The one forbidden fruit assumed monumental importance, just as Satan had known it would when he began his subtle seduction.

Then Satan played his trump card. He probably smiled enchantingly as he said, "Oh, you won't die. God knows as soon as you eat that fruit, you will be like Him, knowing good from evil." The inference was there. She couldn't have missed it. "God wants to keep all the special goodies for himself!"

Nowhere in the Biblical account did Satan say, "Go ahead and eat it." He simply used his knowledge of the desires of

18

human hearts to evoke certain reactions in Eve's mind. He applied seductive techniques. He made her more aware of denials than permissions, thus enhancing the attraction of forbidden fruit. He added an attack upon her ego. "You can be as important as God." So Eve made the fatal decision herself.

For centuries Biblical interpreters have judged Eve more evil than Adam. We believe careful study removes that premise. In Genesis 3:6, we read,

> When the woman saw that the tree was good for food, and that it was a delight to the eyes, and that the tree was desirable to make one wise, she took from its fruit and ate; and she gave also to her husband with her, and he ate. Then the eyes of both of them were opened, and they knew that they were naked; and they sewed fig leaves together and made themselves loin coverings.

The story reads like the tale of a couple of children. Eve liked the fruit, so she shared it. Adam loved his pretty bride, so he ate it. Suddenly their eyes were opened. The honeymoon was over. Their lovely garden was no longer a place of innocent love.

As soon as innocence disappeared, their walk with God went with it. When God came, they hid. When God called, they made excuses. Let's read the narrative.

> Then the Lord God called to the man, and said to him, "Where are you?"
> And he said, "I heard the sound of Thee in the garden, and I was afraid because I was naked; so I hid myself."
> And he said, "Who told you that you were naked? Have you eaten from the tree of which I commanded you not to eat?"
> And the man said, "The woman whom Thou gavest to be with me, she gave me from the tree and I ate." (Note the

double thrust here. "If you hadn't given me this woman, I wouldn't be in all this trouble! It's her fault for making me eat!" A far cry from his rapturous exclamation when God presented Eve to him. And not by any to be construed as courageous!)

Then the Lord God said to the woman, "What is this you have done?" And the woman said, "The serpent deceived me, and I ate" (Gen. 3:9-13).

An interesting sidelight may be observed here. Eve did not react angrily to the man's suggestion that it was her fault. She was willing to blame the serpent, but she made no accusations toward her husband. She might have said, "I didn't hold you down and shove it in your mouth!" Many modern women would have said just that, but Eve didn't. Some specialists in psychology say women are more realistic than men. Was this part of the evidence here? They had already destroyed their Eden. Eve knew it. What was the point? But she did tell on the serpent. She didn't love him!

The same behavioral characteristics continue in modern life, do they not? Cultures change. Human beings tend to remain the same, especially in the field of emotional reactions.

There follows in Genesis 3:14-19, God's curse upon the serpent first and then upon that honeymooning couple who had ruined everything for themselves and quite a few things for their descendants. The serpent was assigned to the lowest status among all the beasts of the field, condemned to eat dust as he crawled on his stomach the rest of his days. Not only that, but enmity was to exist between the serpent and the children of Adam and Eve. Eve's fate lay in the multiplication of her pain in childbirth. (The Bible doesn't say she wouldn't have had it anyway, but that it would be multiplied.) In spite of the pain of childbirth, she was to desire her husband; and because of that desire, he would have control over her. Then Adam's curse was stony, infertile ground, problem soil from which he would have to make a living. The beautiful, peaceful garden was gone forever.

As we assess this story, the central focus arising is the extent of their sin. Each person involved had put someone else ahead of God. Eve knew what God had said, but she listened to the serpent because she was more interested in her own importance than in God's commands. Adam knew the command also, but he was having such fun with the pretty little Eve that she assumed more importance than his dedication to the One who had provided her. Satan, of course, was still involved in the type of activity that got him kicked out of heaven in the first place.

So God removed the newlyweds from the garden. But not before He made them warm garments for a cold world they knew nothing about. The honeymoon had become a nightmare. However, they still had each other. They could make love. God had given them intelligent understanding, the ability to make a living. The cold world outside the garden was a challenge. It also had its rewards. Could they see that? Can we?

Chapter four records the fact that Adam and Eve had sex relations. Because no mention of this relationship occurs earlier, many people believe and teach that sex is an evil thing, only appearing after humanity's fall from grace.

That seems quite difficult to prove since the command, "Be fruitful and multiply, and fill the earth, and subdue it; . . ." appears in Genesis 1:28 before the Biblical writer records the sin of the first couple. Apparently the entire human family was not supposed to remain permanently in Eden. God planned for them to people the whole world. We may only conjecture, but was the complete globe a glorious Eden before God caused it to bear the thorns and thistles?

Since multiplying involves the sex act, God intended a sex relationship for His children. In fact, we may safely assume from this Genesis account that God placed His blessing upon marriage, ordaining the act that made one man and one woman one flesh before their Creator. Contrary to the belief that sexual relationships resulted from the fall, we think God permitted Adam and Eve to retain the relationship as a means of comfort in a difficult life. God, the Creator, understood human need for intimacy.

When we accept the philosophy that all sex is evil, we make God the originator of evil. The misuse of sex is soundly condemned in the Bible, but not sex in its proper place in marriage, not only for the procreation of the family, but also for the genuine happiness it establishes in the home. Much of what is taught today in some circles concerning the sex relationship originated with Augustine. He lived in the latter part of the fourth century and the beginning of the fifth. He, personally, had been a degenerate, and in his writing, he visits his own degrading behavior upon the entire sex relationship. God does not teach that in His Word.

Eve praised God following the birth of Cain, saying, "I have gotten a manchild with the help of the Lord" (Gen. 4:1). The next verse simply states, "She gave birth to his brother Abel." We chuckled a bit at this statement. How like us today! A complete photograph album of the first child while the second one barely has a picture or two in a drawer somewhere!

The Biblical narrative leads immediately into a sketchy description of Cain as a tiller of the ground and Abel as a shepherd. The two brothers brought separate offerings to God; Cain from the fruit of his labors as a farmer, Abel from the firstlings of his flock. God accepted Abel's offering but rejected Cain's.

When Cain erupted into anger, God scolded him, asking why he was so angry. "If you do well, will not your countenance be lifted up? And if you do not well, sin is crouching at the door; and its desire is for you, but you must master it" (Gen. 4:7).

The thoughtful reader ponders Cain's rejection. After all, he had brought an offering from his harvest. No command appears prior to the story for any specific type of offering. In fact, we read no command for offerings at all.

We must rely upon later Scriptures to clarify this point. In Hebrews 11:4 the author writes, "By faith Abel offered to God a better sacrifice than Cain through which he obtained the testimony that he was righteous, God testifying about his gifts, and through faith, though he is dead, he still speaks."

I Samuel 16:7 informs us, ". . . God sees not as man sees, for man looks at the outward appearance, but the Lord looks at the heart."

Verses 10 and 11 in Jude describe the way of Cain. "But these men revile the things which they do not understand; and the things which they know by instinct, like unreasoning animals, by these things they are destroyed. Woe to them! For they have gone the way of Cain. . . ."

We also find throughout the Old Testament, especially the prophets, many warnings about hypocritical offerings bearing an appearance of reverence without any involvement of the heart.

In any serious study of the life of Jesus, we are faced with more sober facts. Our Lord accepted the riffraff of humanity, the type of folk often rejected by others. Repentant sinners received a warm welcome from Him, much more so than those who pretended piety with no true emotional involvement.

So we may be assured that, although Cain went through all the proper motions, his heart was not right with God.

Genesis 4:8 tersely describes the first murder. "And Cain told Abel his brother. And it came about when they were in the field, that Cain rose up against Abel his brother and killed him."

We might wish for the Biblical account to tell us exactly what Cain said to Abel when he informed his brother of God's rejection of his offering. We might long to know how Abel responded. Did Abel lecture Cain about his relationship with God, urging greater closeness? Did Abel tell Cain to shape up and behave properly as Abel had? Abel might have suggested Cain improve his relationship with the heavenly Father. A heart right with God would have wanted his brother to have the same experience. We may be sure Abel didn't make the second statement. Had he harbored thoughts of superiority and been patting himself on the back for his admirable piety, Abel's gift would have been rejected also. No, we must assume Cain's jealousy of the gentle Abel and his relationship to God laid the groundwork for murder.

Here, for the first time upon the stage of history, sibling rivalry, with all its ugly aftermath, puts in an appearance. As we shall see in the pursuit of our research on Biblical families, it is certainly not the last time. One might wonder if Eve gave Cain less attention after Abel's birth, thus setting the stage for Cain's hatred of his brother. Was Adam more shepherd than farmer? Perhaps he spent more time with Abel? Psychologists could have a field day with the story, but the inspired writer simply states a fact with no emphasis upon causes or justification for Cain's behavior.

Then God moves into the account again. He asks Cain where Abel is. How defensively Cain replies! "Am I my brother's keeper?"

Cain learned the hard way that no one can evade God and His searching questions. He also discovered a fact we are still struggling to comprehend. No matter how hurt or angry he had been, no matter how rejected, no matter what faults might have existed in his rearing, he was held personally accountable for moral behavior toward humanity and spiritual response to God.

God's moral rectitude asserts itself with the first family again. Adam had been told he'd have to work hard to raise crops. Cain's curse went further. The ground would refuse to respond to his efforts, making him a "vagrant and a wanderer on the earth."

Cain cries out in anguish saying, ". . . My punishment is too great too bear! Behold, Thou hast driven me this day from the face of the ground; and from Thy face I shall be hidden, and I shall be a vagrant and a wanderer on the earth, and it will come about that whoever finds me will kill me" (Gen. 4:13, 14).

Again we see the mercy of God toward a frightened sinner as the pitying Father places a mark on Cain asserting that whoever killed him would receive sevenfold vengeance.

Right at the beginning of Genesis, we are forced to realize two major emphases pursued throughout the Bible. God had created humanity in His own image to be His companions. When they failed to rise to that beautiful concept of life, His righteousness forced judgment. However, His love and mercy for these bumbling, self-willed, sinful people always created a way out, a second chance. God could have executed Adam and Eve for their disobedience. Instead, He moved them to a different arena with another opportunity to achieve His hopes for them. When a jealous, angry, sinful Cain murdered his brother, God might have made him pay with his own life. But He didn't. He made existence difficult for Cain but refused to allow anyone to execute him. We see in the very beginning of God's Word a loving Father striving to help His willful children.

The second major emphasis we observe in this story is the devastating effect of guilt. When God rejected Cain's offering, He didn't say, "I want nothing to do with you, Cain. You're no good and you never will be." On the contrary, God advised Cain to master his sin before it mastered him. Cain heard only the rejection. He didn't listen to God's loving offer of a second chance.

After Cain's murder of Abel, God never said He would turn His face from Cain permanently. Only Cain said that. His guilt blinded him to every opportunity for repentance God provided.

The human race has reacted this way to intense guilt ever since. We tend to believe even today that God will not forgive. God forgives anything but permanent rejection of Him and His Son. Often it is we who cannot forgive ourselves. God doesn't turn His face from us. We hang our heads refusing to look up and see His mercy. Now, as in the beginning of history, our inability to deal with guilt wreaks havoc, not only in the individual spirit, but also in our families as it did with the first family.

Genesis 4:16 says, "Then Cain went out from the presence of the Lord, and settled in the land of Nod, east of Eden." The thoughtful reader again notes the wording. God didn't leave Cain. Cain left God.

Genesis 4:17 records Cain's sex relations with his wife, her conception and the birth of their son, Enoch. Where did Cain get his wife? Any answer to that old question would be pure conjecture, for the Bible doesn't say. The remainder of the fourth chapter of Genesis contains information of Cain's descendants.

The first mention of polygamy comes in Genesis 4:19 when Lamech, five generations away from Cain, took two wives. It is interesting to find the origin of polygamy among the descendants of the man who had gone out from the presence of God.

Genesis 4:23 records two more murders committed by Cain's polygamous descendant. Lamech killed a man who had wounded him and a boy who had struck him. Although the reader may experience a sense of sorrow for Cain, such feelings disappear in regard to Lamech. He boastfully claims, "If Cain is avenged sevenfold, then Lamech seventy-sevenfold."

Cain, at least, had known parents who walked with God. Lamech, five generations later, flouted God's mercy with his braggadocio. Separation from God had taken a terrible toll. The family was beginning to be torn apart by polygamous relationships, an exact reversal of God's original plan. Murder moved into the realm of the respectable among those who no longer cared what the Creator thought. Mankind was already hurtling along the road to destruction.

The Biblical narrative had relegated Adam and Eve to anonymity during its preoccupation with Cain and his sinful behavior. The writer fails even to describe their grief over Abel's death and Cain's sin. Our humanity makes us sure they felt it. At the close of chapter four, they reenter our story.

From the love of Adam and Eve came another son, Seth. Eve rejoiced for God had sent her a replacement for Abel. Seth must have possessed the same gentle spirit found in Abel, for the inspired reporter tells of the birth of Seth's son, Enosh, following this announcement with a simple statement, "Then men began to call upon the name of the Lord" (Gen. 4:26).

Adam and Eve had come full circle from a garden honeymoon; a sinful rebellion against God's commands; the tragic loss of both Cain and Abel, Abel through death and Cain through his rejection of all they held dear; to Seth and his son, Enosh, who found the relationship with God Adam and Eve had once lost.

Knowledge of people forces realization of the influence of Adam and Eve in all these events. Who hasn't seen couples beginning married life with great hope and promise, only to founder on some sinful problem, losing all they had in the process? Perhaps bitterness forced its way into their attitude toward living. One problem led to another. Even their children suffered. Then bitterness dissolved and they found their way back to God. Later children, entering a home of reverence and lovingkindness, cherished a faith not seen in those who were born during the parents' separation from God.

Cain, as the eldest son, may have been so angered by his parents' stories of their expulsion from the Garden of Eden that it resulted in his rebellion against God, leading to the first murder. This, again, must be conjecture. But such incidents do occur in the lives of families.

Sometimes loss of material blessings exacts its pound of flesh. During the world-wide depression of the 1930's, some men blew their brains out after losing their wealth and with it their standing in the community. Many homes and businesses disappeared as well. In a more primitive sense, this happened to Adam and Eve. We must admire our first ancestors for their eventual recovery from the results of their sin. Their son Seth seems to have been all God wanted him to be. Since we know children must be trained to have this sort of moral and spiritual fibre, Adam and Eve must have planted proper reverence and faith within the young boy's soul.

Genesis 5:1-3 helps us comprehend something of God's hopes for His people. It also enables us to see the transformation resulting in the lives of Adam and Eve because they faced the cold, hard world with courage.

> This is the book of the generations of Adam. In the day when God created man, He made him in the likeness of God. He created them male and female, and He blessed them and named them Man in the day when they were created. When Adam had lived one hundred and thirty years, he became the father of a son *in his own likeness, according to his image,* and named him Seth.

It took one hundred and thirty years, but Adam had matured through suffering and struggle. His son, Seth, the son of his image, called upon the name of the Lord. Seth provides living proof of Adam's transformation.

Another somewhat astonishing part of this story is Eve's attitude. As her children came, she always appeared grateful to God for giving them. What a far cry this is from the silly adolescent in the Garden of Eden who wanted to be a god herself! The Bible never quotes Adam during this period of travail, but it does reveal the humble heart of Eve. Her later years should have earned our admiration. Isn't it sad so few people note this part of the story? Everyone seems to recall her sin so vividly, but few notice the Biblical evidence of her return to God.

So, we have studied our first Biblical family. The earth was young. Humanity was still in its cradle as far as civilization was concerned. Yet we've listed a catalog of sins and virtues, the very same ones characterizing the human race today.

We've observed grass roots, so to speak, as Eve was seduced by the notion that "Grass is always greener on the other side of the fence," or the "Forbidden Fruit Syndrome."

We've watched lying create chaos, the competitive worship of self rather than God arise to plague our original ancestors. Pretended piety, sibling rivalry, anger and jealousy have already resulted in murder. At least one man in the line of Cain refused to be content with or faithful to one wife.

We've also seen humility and maturity developing as that first couple met the challenges of a hostile environment. As our story unfolded we've rejoiced to see good, gentle people emerge from its pages, people who walked with God. Most of all, we've seen the righteous judgment of God tempered by love and mercy. What a foundation for learning how to undergird our own family life!

2

DOES THE BIBLE TEACH
HEREDITARY GOODNESS?

The author of Genesis uses a single chapter, the fifth, to carry us through the families from Adam to Noah, ten generations. Cain and his descendants fade from view. The generations of Adam continue through the line of Seth. The Scripture reveals nothing of family life in this chapter. However, we do find noble character, something essential to our understanding of family influence. We also discover, as in many later stories, that the firstborn son is not always the one who excels, although much of the patriarchal family system is based on the supremacy of the firstborn son. The Bible does not name the children, but tells us Adam had other sons and daughters during the eight hundred years of his life following Seth's birth. In each instance, one name is recorded in the genealogy, apparently the most important one. Then follows the statement, ". . . and he had other sons and daughters." Let's trace the line.

Seth fathered Enosh; Enosh, Kenan; Kenan, Mahalalel; Mahalalel, Jared; Jared, Enoch; Enoch, Methusaleh.

Perhaps we should pause here to note the godly Enoch. Genesis five, after recording Methusaleh's birth and that of "other sons and daughters," makes a thought-provoking statement. "And Enoch walked with God; and he was not, for God took him" (Gen. 5:24). Another noble character from the line of Adam through Seth, who was born in his father's image! Further evidence of the first family's return to their Creator!

We continue the genealogy. Methusaleh fathered Lamech. Lamech became the father of Noah, the next person in our outstanding family series.

College psychology courses often include sections about apparent hereditary sources for good and evil. College students are faced with evidence of mental retardation and criminal inheritance tendencies. On the positive side in American history, we may follow the line of the Adams family producing leaders in all phases of national life. The Holmes family provides examples of outstanding participation in literature and jurisprudence. One of the most amazing illustrations of family influence in America comes from the line of Jonathan Edwards, that famous New England preacher. Generation after generation produced leaders in government, theology and education. Are such characteristics inherited or the result of environmental influence? We have argued this question for generations.

One might wonder if God includes genealogies in His Word for this very reason. We have discussed both Cain and Seth. Cain walked away from God. Through his line came polygamy and further murder. Seth and his son, Enosh, started men calling upon God again. Through Seth's descendants came the godly Enoch and the moral giant of Holy Writ, Noah, who saved mankind from extinction. Is this coincidence? Is it in the genes? Is it spiritual environment or lack of it?

If only Seth and Cain entered the picture, our decision would appear clear-cut. Cain's environment with parents who were struggling to exist after the shock of losing all they had originally possessed was inferior to that provided by the same parents at a calmer, more mature time. But that is not all the Bible describes for us. The godly Noah had one son who failed to have good moral and spiritual judgment. Noah himself was not without sin. As one continues to read the Bible, one discovers outstanding parents with children who refused to follow their precepts and example.

However, for the most part, Biblical genealogy teaches us godly homes produce godly people even if it takes them a while to get that way.

Let us continue our search.

3

THE FAMILY OF NOAH

We meet Noah in the last three verses of the fifth chapter of Genesis, introduced to us briefly as Lamech's son and the father of Shem, Ham and Japheth.

The beginning of the sixth chapter describes the attraction of the "sons of God" to the daughters of men resulting in giants or "Nephilim" as they are called in the New American Standard Bible. These offspring are also mentioned as "the mighty men who were of old, men of renown" (Gen. 6:4). God warns that His Spirit will not always strive with men. In fact, humanity had become so depraved that the Biblical writer states,

> And the Lord was sorry that He had made man on the earth, and He was grieved in His heart. And the Lord said, "I will blot out man whom I have created from the face of

the land, from man to animals to creeping things and to birds of the sky; for I am sorry that I have made them" (Gen. 6:6, 7).

Then we read the benediction of God upon Noah. "But Noah found favor in the eyes of the Lord" (Gen. 6:8). In verse nine, the sacred scribe gives us the reasons for God's favor: ". . . Noah was a righteous man, blameless in his time; Noah walked with God."

Nine generations had transpired since Adam walked with God in the garden. Noah, born from the line of Seth, was blessed by a great grandfather so close to God he never tasted death. Noah emerges in our story as a completely committed man of God.

An interesting sidelight here might be the Biblical meaning of generations as compared to our modern understanding of approximately thirty years. The Bible states that the children of Israel spent four hundred years, or four generations in captivity in Egypt. Obviously, they computed generations differently. So more years may have elapsed between these stories than a conservative estimate might indicate.

In our studies of families of the Bible, we note that each family remarkable enough to receive lengthy comment contained at least one very strong character, good or evil. In Noah's family, that person was Noah himself. In the Patriarchal Period, most of the strong heads of families were men. However, we shall see as we pursue the subject throughout the Old Testament, that some women, particularly widows, occupied the authoritative position in the family structure. The strengths of these women impress us especially because of the era in which they lived. With all the emphasis of their society directed toward the dominant male, they had to be outstanding, far above the average

36

woman of their day. This emphasis never arises in the family of Noah. The Genesis writer fails even to record the name of Noah's wife.

Noah was born only forty-six years after Adam's death, although he is the tenth recorded generation of humanity. Seth had died only fourteen years before Noah's birth. Noah's life span of nine hundred and fifty years made him a contemporary of Enosh for sixteen years. For the purpose of our study of family influence in Biblical times, we must deal with this extended life span among the ancients. Seth, a man of God, lived long enough to influence eight generations. Noah not only received moral and spiritual guidance from the good men who preceded him, but also survived to guide generations following him. This assumes particular importance when we reflect that five generations are unusual in our time.

Old Testament emphasis upon respect for the aged made the old men and women of families primary influences upon the young. Children since the beginning of time have loved stories. The ancients enjoyed telling them. As bodies aged in a primitive society and the hard work of that culture became impossible, the aged spent much time in reflection, meditation and story-telling. From this type of life, men like Adam, Seth, Enosh and Noah gave youth a sense of heritage and belonging. Strength arises from such influence if heeded. Nobility is permitted to flourish.

Another aspect of Old Testament family life comes to the forefront in the story of Noah. It was there all the time, but we see it more clearly in this account. In modern times, we have labeled it, "the extended family." God placed His blessing upon the concept when He said, ". . . you shall enter the ark—you and your sons and your wife and your sons' wives with you" (Gen. 6:18).

The extended family then, as now, provides dangers. Jealousies and bickering can and often do occur. However, the multi-generation family appears to render tremendous influence upon developing children. One observes this both positively and negatively. Again, let us refer to Cain. His descendant, Lamech, quoted him centuries later for evil. In the line of Seth, the effect of the wisdom of the ancients appears in Noah, the man whose goodness kept God from extinguishing the light of humanity from the face of the earth.

Noah walked so closely with God that God confided in him. God revealed His plan for the flood. Along with that revelation, God issued exact instructions to be followed if Noah's family were to survive. The sacred writer states the great man's reaction quite simply. "Thus Noah did; according to all that God had commanded him, so he did" (Gen. 6:22).

At the time of the flood, Noah was six hundred years old. He had lived a long time to absorb the testimony of his faithful ancestors. No callow youth was involved in this enterprise or flight of fancy as the neighbors might have imagined it. Do you suppose the surrounding people thought him senile? An ark sitting on the floor of a desert! Doesn't sound too sensible, does it?

Again we find evidence of the strong head of the family and the extended family. Shem, Ham and Japheth were no youngsters either. The Bible tells us Noah was five hundred years old at the time of their birth. That makes them one hundred when the flood came. How their friends must have derided them and their crazy old father! But they followed Noah's leadership, secure in their knowledge of his walk with God.

38

Noah's family climbed the gangplank into the ark. The inspired writer becomes poetic in the description of God's penalty for man's sin. "In the six hundredth year of Noah's life, in the second month, on the seventeenth day of the month, on the same day all the fountains of the great deep burst open, and the floodgates of the sky were opened" (Gen. 7:11). We may not understand exactly what the Bible means by the bursting open of the fountains of the deep, but the mental picture chills. We are told the water rose twenty-two and one-half feet above the level of the highest mountains.

Genesis 7:24 states, "And the water prevailed upon the earth one hundred and fifty days." How depressed we become when rain goes on and on for days! If it's very heavy with dark, dismal skies, how we long for the sun! Anyone who has reared a family knows family life tends to be just as dismal as the sky in such weather. We can easily imagine being shut up in a boat with eight people and a host of smelly animals in a pouring rain day after day. Wouldn't tempers fray?

The Bible is brutally frank. Lives of great men form a panorama before us; nothing masked, no cover-ups for sin. Yet, in this story of Noah's family, no mention of family quarrels fills the narrative. From what we may read, only gratitude for survival occupies their minds. The first thing Noah did upon leaving the ark was to build an altar of thanksgiving to God. From His delight in the faithfulness of one loving family, God promised Himself never to obliterate mankind again by flood.

Chapter nine begins, "And God blessed Noah and his sons and said to them, 'Be fruitful and multiply, and fill the earth.'" In this chapter we read, "Whoever sheds man's blood, by man shall his blood be shed, for in the image of God He made man" (Gen. 9:6). Had the Lord begun to despair of protecting murderers like Cain? Instead of gratitude, Cain had passed on his rebellious spirit through the generations following in his blood line. Did God decide at this point that some sort of legal system was mandatory to train His people? We cannot know the mind of God, but some law is laid down during this period of re-peopling the globe.

Another premise appears in this chapter, one that weaves a thread through the entire Bible. God tells Noah and his sons, ". . . I Myself do establish my covenant with you, and with your descendants after you" (Gen. 9:9). This is our first glimpse of the covenant-making Father, establishing covenants with earthly families. Simply restated, God told them what He had already promised Himself, that He would never again destroy the earth by flood. He placed the rainbow in the sky as a symbol of that covenant.

There is a good reason for mentioning the covenant-making Father in a book about families. Each time God made a covenant, He impressed His hearers with the fact that He was making that covenant with the family and all its descendants. One cannot miss the important emphasis the heavenly Father assigns to earthly families by this gesture. He had placed the original couple in the garden, planning for them an ideal family life, knowing that family is necessary for happiness in those He had created in His image. This lifts the family unit, this and the subsequent covenants, to spiritual unities, not to be dealt with lightly.

No mention of sin enters the story of Noah's family as long as they remained in the ark. One might say the family unit was completely protected from temptation in the ark.

Some of us still try to preserve our families by building walls around them instead of strength within them.

After leaving the ark, Noah started to farm, planted a vineyard and made some wine. He drank too much of the wine, became drunk and apparently stripped in his tent before sleeping it off. Ham saw his father's nakedness and told his brothers.

Was Ham a bit like some modern sons? Do you suppose he called his brothers, "Hey, Shem and Japheth, come look at the old man! He's drunk and naked as a jaybird!"

Respect for parents was a foundation stone for homes of the Patriarchal era. Search for understanding of Old Testament family life leads us to definite commands from God for children to obey and respect parental authority. Shem and Japheth refused to go along with Ham's suggestion, backing into the tent and covering Noah without looking at him.

When Noah awakened from his drunken stupor, he realized what Ham had done. He lost his temper, cursing Ham, declaring Ham and his descendants would be lowly servants for Shem and Japheth and their descendants. He blessed the two older brothers because of the respect they had shown for him.

In rereading this story, we experienced anew a sense of disappointment in this great man of God. Ham was wrong, of course. No one could deny that. But Noah was wrong also. If he had not drunk too much wine, lost his self-control and stripped off his clothes, his son would have had nothing about which to be disrespectful.

Noah was like many parents today. His personal guilt made his punishment of the son who took advantage of his failure much stronger than it might have been otherwise. We would have liked Noah better had he said, "I was wrong,

41

too, Ham." We also wonder if the succeeding story of Ham might have been different had Noah always proved worthy of respect.

There is much food for thought in this story as we rear our families today. Since the beginning of time parents have had to earn the respect of their children. True respect arises from the quality of life parents exhibit. Another problem surfaces here. Noah had earned Ham's respect by years of good behavior. One slip seems to have blown it. Both parents and children need to spend time thinking about this. Parents are not perfect, so one slip should not nullify years of good living, especially with an adult child such as Ham. On the other hand, parents need to realize the fragile quality of respect and guard it zealously. Years of careful family living may be destroyed with one careless action.

4

GENEALOGY OF NOAH'S DESCENDANTS

The entire tenth chapter of Genesis is devoted to genealogy of Noah's line. Some interesting facts come to light.

Obviously, the main Biblical emphasis falls upon the ancestral family of God's chosen people, the nation selected to give the Redeemer to the world. God doesn't forget the others, although they do recede into the background. As we noted in chapter five, complete genealogies seem unimportant to the purpose of God. Only the names and families significant to the redemption of mankind assume importance. Some historical analysis appears; but mostly, the Bible is single-minded. Mankind fell. Through these families, humanity will return to the Creator.

This chapter mentions no outstanding sons of Japheth. The name of Nimrod, Ham's grandson through his son

Cush, draws special attention in the list of Noah's descendants. The Bible describes him as a mighty hunter, the founder of the Assyrian Empire and several cities in Babylon.

Canaan, son of Ham, is recorded as the father of the tribes mentioned later in Biblical history of the land of Canaan when the children of Israel fled there from their captivity in Egypt.

No one name arises as outstanding at this point in the descendants of Shem. Their residence is noted as the hill country of the east.

Apparently all three families had settled in the plain of the land of Shinar following Noah's death. No one knows how long they remained. It was here they tried to build the tower of Babel. God confused their language and forced them to scatter to all corners of the earth.

Remember God's command to them to fill the earth after the flood? They hadn't obeyed. They had bunched together in one plain. Copying Eve's ambition to achieve godhood for herself and Adam, these later human beings collaborated to build a tower to heaven. Egotism destroyed them once again as God dispersed them and confused their language so they couldn't even understand each other.

For our purpose in studying what the Bible says about families, we note that the dispersion came about on a family basis. Even as He separated them, God emphasized the importance He placed upon the family.

The eleventh chapter of Genesis, following the story of the dispersion of the descendants of Noah, devotes itself to more genealogies, leading to the next important family man, the faithful and just Abraham, called the Father of the Hebrew nation. Abraham came from the line of Shem through Shem's son Arphaxad. Abraham is ten generations away from

Noah. One of the facts perhaps worthy of notice in this chapter is the shortening life spans of the people. They were having children younger and length of life decreased as much as five hundred years.

Also we are now introduced to the custom of naming the wives of men and the mothers of their children. Previously the only women named are Eve; Adah and Zillah, the two wives taken by Lamech in the line of Cain; and Zillah's daughter, Naamah.

Could recognition of the importance of women in the scheme of things finally be appearing? We do not know, but naming Sarai and Milcah introduces a whole new thought pattern after chapters recording unnamed wives and daughters. Did women occupy a respected role in the Old Testament family? Let's see.

PART II: THE PATRIARCHS

5

THE FAMILY OF ABRAHAM

The twelfth chapter of Genesis begins with a statement of God's covenant with Abram. The covenant promise bears conditions. To earn God's favor, Abram must leave his familiar country, even his relatives and his father's house, proceeding to a country God would show him. Following God's command would result in his being the father of a great nation in the land God would give him. God's blessing and sustenance were to be his in exchange for his obedience.

In our day of constant travel, excellent road maps, beautiful motels and super highways, this wouldn't be such a tall order. So the significance of Abram's unquestioning obedience often escapes us.

In Haran, Abram was an important man, descending from an eminent family heritage. Few people with such community standing throughout history have emigrated to a foreign land. Usually immigrants are suffering people seeking a better lot in life. Abram already had it made from a worldly point of view.

Abram was seventy-five years of age when he left Haran in response to God's command. What a caravan they must have made! The Bible tells us he took Sarai, his wife; Lot, his nephew; all the possessions they had accumulated; and the entire working staff required to run such a huge entourage. They set out for the land of Canaan, stopping in Shechem to erect an altar to worship God.

The first action of each of these great men of God upon entering a new area was the construction of some sort of worship center. This is another thread running throughout the entire Old Testament chronicles of families. Godly families made many mistakes. We find no element of perfection anywhere. But they were consistent in their emphasis upon putting God first in their lives. When they moved— and they were nomads for the most part—they either carried their worship center with them or built an altar upon arrival.

As Abram's family moved around the land of Canaan, a famine fell upon the land. So, Abram took his entire household to Egypt. This is the first place Abram shows weakness.

Sarai was a very beautiful woman. So Abram asked Sarai to lie, saying she was his sister. (This is a reversal of the sin of Adam and Eve in the early part of our family studies. In that story, the woman instigated the sin. In this one, the man did.) Apparently Egyptians were notorious for killing husbands to get their beautiful wives. Abram was scared.

Tales of Sarai's famous beauty echoed throughout the land. Pharaoh claimed her for his harem. Abram profited from all the gifts showered upon him by Pharaoh because of the king's infatuation for Sarai.

Again the heavy hand of the righteous God fell upon sinful men. The Bible doesn't tell us how Pharoah figured out that his problems originated from God's wrath over his possession of another man's wife. Somehow he learned of Sarai and Abram's lie. We must suppose Pharaoh did not order the couple killed because he feared vengeance from their God. At any rate, he commanded Abram to take his wife, his household and his possessions and leave.

We should pause here and assess the magnitude of this sin of Abram and Sarai. On the surface, it appears nothing but a lie rooted in fear. Actually, it was more than that.

God had promised Abram he would be blessed and sustained, that from his seed all nations of the earth would be blessed. Abram and Sarai had no children. God's promise had not been fulfilled. Would He not protect Abram and Sarai?

Abram's sin resulted from a temporary lapse of total faith in God's promise. Each time Sarai and Abram got into trouble, impatience with God's slowness to act coupled with anxiety to handle things themselves were the source. Sounds like us, doesn't it?

It is very difficult in the light of our modern knowledge to understand Abram's willingness to allow Sarai to enter an illicit sex relationship with Pharaoh to save his own skin and feather his nest. As we've explained before, the Bible states cold, hard facts about its heroes and exposes their lives to searching scrutiny, warts and all! The obvious disapproval of God appears in the narrative. Abram's actions were never condoned, only recorded. He was accepted because he kept on trying in spite of his mistakes.

The family returned to the original campsite in the land of Canaan. We are told Abram called on the name of the Lord.

Was it a call of abject repentance? Some evidence might be assembled for such a belief. Abram's next action was totally different from his behavior in Egypt.

When Abram's herdsmen and Lot's herdsmen began quarreling over who would graze their animals in the finest pasture, Abram gave Lot first choice. Was he ashamed of his self-serving tactics in Egypt? One might hope so. As the senior member of the family, the primary option was his.

Lot had learned a little about self-centeredness himself. Given the opportunity, he selected the fertile valley of the Jordan River near Sodom. His self-serving actions carried his family right into the sphere of influence of two cities that live in Biblically recorded infamy. In fact, Lot's greed was to cost him far more than he ever gained from the choice location. This should provide food for thought for those of us who consider material rewards to be essential for good family living.

The two families separated. When Lot journeyed into the area near the wicked cities, no mention is made of his building any kind of altar for the worship of God. But Abram moved to the country surrounding Hebron. The author of Genesis records, ". . . and there he built an altar to the Lord" (Gen. 13:18).

A group of kings named in Genesis fourteen made war upon the kings of Sodom and Gomorrah. They took all the goods and food from the two cities. They also captured Lot and all his household. One of Lot's servants escaped and fled to Abram for help.

Here again we find the extended family at work in a different way. Forgotten was Lot's selfishness. Abram might well have said, "He selected that part of the land because it was richer. Let him suffer from his own choices." Instead, Abram, family relationship uppermost in his mind, armed his people and pursued the conquering kings to Dan and Hobah. Abram's forces triumphed. The kings surrendered Lot and all his possessions.

This story reads a bit like the history of the clans in Scotland or the family feuds of the Appalachian Mountain region in America. The thoughtful Christian reader deplores bloodshed and hostility. However, one is forced to admire family loyalty.

Our first record of a tithing family appears in this story. Melchizedek, king of Salem, was a priest of God. Abram gave Melchizedek one-tenth of all he possessed.

In gratitude for the rescue, the king of Sodom urged Abram to return the people but to keep the goods for himself. Abram refused, saying he had made a vow to God not to profit from the enterprise. Is this more proof of Abram's sorrow for the profits he had derived from his sin in Egypt? Certainly it is evidence of his maturing in his understanding of God's requirements for His servants.

God reiterated His promise. This time Abram revealed his personal doubts. He insisted he had no children. Then he suggested the Lord might mean his steward, Eliezer of Damascus, one who had been born in his house and was his heir.

God insisted Abram's own personal descendants would be as numerous as the uncountable stars. The Bible says, "Then he believed in the Lord; and He reckoned it to him as righteousness" (Gen. 15:6).

Still Abram asked for proof. He experienced a vision, including prophecy of the captivity of his descendants in Egypt for four hundred years. Then God renewed His covenant and promised the land of Canaan to the family.

51

How characteristic of the human race Abram was! God had to repeat His promises over and over. Each time doubt crept into His servant's mind. Whenever doubt took control, Abram and Sarai committed some sin affecting them and their household. One of their sins still wreaks havoc upon the modern world.

How can we speak of a couple who made such earth-shattering mistakes as faithful? Yet the Bible does. If we were to promise someone something, we would be angry and discouraged with their lack of trust in our word. The Bible allows God's people to suffer for their silly mistakes and doubts, but God continues to forgive and accept those who rise above their own foolish errors and distrust. Abram was one of those. He was filled with faith, but his life also reflects times of severe uncertainty.

What hope there is for us in these stories of Biblical families! Doubt and sin do not alienate us from God unless we ourselves refuse to accept the hand He offers in mercy. Our families may and often do suffer from our lack of wisdom, but we may all be acceptable to God when we repent and return to stable faith.

Abram and Sarai waited ten years in the land of Canaan. Still Sarai was not pregnant. Almost anyone would have felt as Sarai did. A woman with deep faith might have questioned her own understanding of the Lord's will.

"Perhaps I misunderstood. Maybe only Abram is to be the founder of God's special nation. The promise might not have included me at all. After all, I'm almost too old to bear a child and Abram is eighty-five."

So Sarai took matters into her own hands. She had a young Egyptian maid Hagar. She approached Abram with the idea of his sleeping with Hagar. In the ancient patriarchal system, children born to slaves were the property of the

owners. "Perhaps these empty arms of mine may yet hold
a son. Hagar's son would really be mine." Was this the way
Sarai thought? The Bible seems to indicate it.

Abram certainly showed no reluctance. Had he, too, become concerned that the promise of God would never be
fulfilled through Sarai? Was Hagar especially lovely? The
Bible does not say. We are only told Hagar conceived and
then despised her mistress.

Did Hagar change from a fine servant to a conceited,
rebellious, lazy clod? From the vantage point of modern life,
one might excuse her if she did. What opportunity had
been presented to her to accept or reject Abram's attentions? She had been used by her master and mistress to
achieve their own ends. Perhaps Abram had shown compassionate tenderness toward the young girl. That would
coincide with what we know of his personality. Hagar might
have decided the master was going to replace the mistress
with her maid. Perhaps she even believed Abram had fallen
in love with her. Sarai could have feared the same thing.
All the Biblical narrative indicates women of that day considered themselves unworthy if they failed to conceive a
son. Sarai obviously loved Abram. She might have feared
the influence of the lovely young maid once she had borne
Abram's child. Whatever the reasoning behind it, conflict
arose between the two women.

Sarai's reaction was interesting. ". . . 'May the wrong done
me be upon you. I gave my maid into your arms; but when
she saw that she had conceived, I was despised in her sight.
May the Lord judge between you and me'" (Gen. 16:5).

The Bible reports no reaction on Abram's part such as
the reader might expect. Most men would have protested,
"Whose idea was this?" Instead of that, Abram said, "She's

your maid. Do as you please with her." He did suggest Sarai do what "was good" in her own sight with Hagar.

If Hagar had been experiencing delusions of grandeur, they soon evaporated. Sarai became a hard taskmistress, so difficult in fact that Hagar ran away.

Judged in this more enlightened day, Abram and Sarai collect no good conduct medals for their unkind use of Hagar. Judged in the context of their own cultures, they probably behaved better than most.

An angel of the Lord caught up with Hagar at a desert well and sent her back to Sarai. The angel assured the young maid things would be all right for her, insisting she return to her mistress and accept Sarai's authority. She did and bore Ishmael. Abram was eighty-six years old when Ishmael was born.

In chapter seventeen, God renews the covenant with Abram, changing his name to Abraham. God also commanded circumcision for all boys at the age of eight days. God promised Sarai, whose name was changed to Sarah, would bear a son.

Abraham reacted understandably to this. "Then Abraham fell on his face and laughed, and said in his heart, 'Will a child be born to a man one hundred years old? And will Sarah, who is ninety years old, bear a child?'" (Gen. 17:17). In the modern vernacular, we might say Abraham rolled on the ground laughing! Immediately he suggested Ishmael might please God.

How patient our heavenly Father is! Here was this man, so superior to most of his day, and yet doubting repeatedly when God made promises. As we read the story, we comprehend his feelings. Yet God's word is sure.

God reassured Abraham He had not forgotten Ishmael; that Ishmael would father twelve princes and become the forerunner of a great nation. We cannot escape the inference in the story that Abraham was again thinking he'd better handle things for the Lord. This time God was definite. "But my covenant I will establish with Isaac, whom Sarah will bear to you at this season next year" (Gen. 17:21).

Abraham obeyed God. All males in the household were circumcised immediately. He was circumcised himself.

God visited Abraham a second time promising Isaac's birth. This time Sarah, listening behind the door, laughed. God mentioned her laughter. She denied it, but God knew.

God appeared to Abraham as one of three men who came to Abraham's tent at the oaks of Mamre. Abraham entertained the strangers. As they left Abraham's camp, he accompanied them to a high point overlooking Sodom and Gomorrah. There God informed Abraham of His plan to destroy the wicked cities. Abraham pled for Sodom, finally exacting a promise from God to save Sodom if only ten innocent people could be found within its walls.

At this point in the narrative we discover a story no one wants to handle. Commentaries have terrible trouble with it. The two angels, dispatched by God to Sodom, met Lot at the entrance to the city. He offered them hospitality. While they were in Lot's home, the men of the city tried to batter down the door in order to have sex relations with the two visitors. Hence the origin of the word, "sodomy," for sexual practices between men.

Reading Lot's reactions sickens modern students. He pled for them to honor his guests. Then Lot offered that mob his two virgin daughters. He even said the men might do as they pleased with his daughters if they'd refrain from molesting visitors. No story in all of Holy Writ reflects the low status of women more than this one.

Granted that rules of hospitality among the nomads of the region demanded protection for guests, did not the father have responsibility to guard his daughters? Reflecting upon the situation, one might wonder if Lot were attempting to be shrewd in dealing with the dilemma. Women do not arouse confirmed homosexual men. Yet he had no way of knowing that none of the men were bi-sexual. Lot had lived there a long time. Perhaps he thought they would not molest his daughters. Even with the kindest possible interpretation of his actions, however, Lot presents a very ugly picture of fatherhood. One cannot help noting he did not offer himself in place of his visitors, only his daughters.

They refused his offer. They did attempt to attack Lot personally. The sacred writer records, "But they said, 'Stand aside.' Furthermore, they said, 'This one came in as an alien and already he is acting like a judge; now we will treat you worse than them.' So they pressed hard against Lot and came near to break the door" (Gen. 19:9).

The angels rescued Lot. In the process, they blinded the vicious men so they could no longer find the doorway. They also insisted Lot take his family and leave the doomed city.

Lot found the two young men who were engaged to his daughters and told them the story. Their reaction in modern language might be expressed as, "You've got to be kidding!" Lot himself seemed wandering in a daze. Finally the angels took Lot, his wife and his two daughters by the hand and led them away from the city. Lot asked permission to stay at a nearby village named Zoar. In the course of their flight, the angels warned them not to look back. Lot's wife didn't obey. She turned to see what she had left and was changed to a pillar of salt.

Any woman finds it easy to understand Lot's wife. They had lived in Sodom for a number of years when the destruction came. She had poured a lot of herself into her home there. Women seem especially tied to their homes, particularly those who have lived in one spot for a long time. Perhaps she just wanted one more nostalgic glance. But God had commanded her to look forward, not backward. Disobedience cost her the future with her family.

We all know this story appears in the Bible to show the danger of ignoring God's commands. But could its message be two-pronged? In clinging to the material possessions she left in Sodom, Lot's wife lost sight of a family who needed her. Is the message of the story also intended to point out to us that people are always more important than things? The people she loved were safe. Only things she had cherished were being destroyed.

Lot's daughters reflected their years spent in the wicked cities. While they dwelt in a cave in the mountains above Zoar, they got their father drunk and had sexual intercourse with him. Their incestuous relationships produced Moab and Ben-ammi, the father of the Moabites and Ammonites, both desert idol worshipers.

Lot's family, although part of the larger family of Abraham, illustrates a study in tragedy. As we follow Lot from his greedy selection of the best pasture to the city of Sodom, we observe several things.

One is the fact Lot worshiped Lot and his wants more than he worshiped God. No mention appears in the Bible of his building altars. He was hospitable, probably a nice fellow to meet, but God's Word mentions no worship in his life.

The second thing we can see in the story is the effect of environment even upon adults in a family. Lot's wife was tied to the luxuries of Sodom, ignoring the vice and corruption around her because she was so comfortable. She had not been accustomed to worship or concern for the commands of God. So she disobeyed and perished.

Lot's daughters, reared in a Godless city, thought more about self-preservation and the continuation of the family than the moral precepts of a God who had been a minimal part of their lives at best. Their father's denigration of them to such low estate may have figured in their decision that producing sons was of greater importance than the method of their conception.

This is the record of a family whose only apparent connection to God came through Abraham, Lot's uncle. Lot appears to have had some concern for righteous morality (II Peter 2:7-8), but he never developed much of a personal relationship with God. At least, none is recorded and this sort of thing usually is mentioned. This story shows the utter failure of inherited religion unless personally claimed. Parents must remember that religious faith is always just one generation away from extinction.

In the second chapter of Deuteronomy, we read God's command to the Hebrews that they not take the land of Moab. ". . . Do not harass Moab, nor provoke them to war, for I will not give you any of their land as a possession, because I have given Ar to the sons of Lot as a possession" Deut. 2:9). In Deuteronomy 2:19, the same command is issued in regard to the land of the descendants of Ammon, Lot's other son.

So, many years following the death of Abraham and Lot, God still honored His promise to Lot's family. We find this especially remarkable since worship of Jehovah was not the primary religion of Moab nor of Ammon. In their early history, the Moabites did worship one God but refused to deny the existence of others, an attitude expressly forbidden in the Ten Commandments. The Ammonite religion matched their reputation among the nations, cruel and barbaric.

The Biblical narrative returns to Abraham's immediate family. Abraham and Sarah traveled to Gerar where they repeated their mistake from Egypt. Fearing for his life because he thought the country of Gerar ungodly, Abraham asked Sarah to declare herself his sister again. (In the twentieth chapter of Genesis, we learn Sarah really was Abraham's half-sister and also his wife.) The fact still remains they handled the truth recklessly to achieve their own ends. One cannot help noting that sin originated in the human family with a lie and continues throughout history to be propagated in the same way.

Abimelech, King of Gerar, claimed Sarah but never had sex relations with her. God warned him in a dream, and Abimelech was a God-fearing man. Abraham had misjudged him.

A lesson in humanity's inability to pronounce judgment upon the faith of others appears here. Abraham sinned because he did not know another man's relationship to God and judged him to have none.

One marvels at God's patience with Abraham and Sarah. How often they failed to trust Him! Yet He rescued them and blessed them. Apparently their good points far outweighed the bad. They always asked God's forgiveness when they failed. Abraham lived a life of prayer. Surely we can learn from these stories of the ancients that our heavenly Father does understand and forgive when we fail. However, moral law exists. These records of Biblical families illustrate the way families also suffer for the waywardness of individual members.

Just as God had promised, Isaac arrived. Sarah's doubting laughter turned into the laughter of complete joy. The name,

Isaac, even means "laughter." Finally, Sarah's aching arms held her own baby boy.

Jealousy re-enters our story. The Bible reads,

> Now Sarah saw the son of Hagar the Egyptian, whom she had borne to Abraham, mocking. Therefore she said to Abraham, "Drive out this maid and her son, for the son of this maid shall not be an heir with my son Isaac." And the matter distressed Abraham greatly because of his son (Gen. 21:9-11).

Ishmael was entering adolescence at the time of Isaac's birth. How could he have helped noting his demotion in the family? How would it feel to be the son of the maid rather than the son of the wife? How would it affect a boy who had been the only son of his father suddenly to become the un-important one while everyone designated Isaac as the son of the promise? No wonder Ishmael mocked! He couldn't handle the situation. What fourteen year old could? Ishmael was jealous of his half-brother.

One must also try to understand Sarah. The whole rotten mess could be laid at her door. It was her idea in the first place. Abraham didn't have to concur, of course, but she originated the plan. Then Isaac, her precious only son, arrived. Women who are not selfish for themselves often become greedy for their children. She had waited so long! Sarah became the over-protective mother.

Another point arises in this story. Abraham truly loved Ishmael. He protested sending the boy away, carrying his personal grief to God. God assured Abraham He would make a great nation of Ishmael, too. God also saved Hagar and Ishmael as they wandered in the wilderness without water.

Abraham and Sarah, the main characters of this story, emerge in a most unusual way.

The Bible doesn't say how they happened to marry. However, they surely were deeply in love. They agreed on a singleness of purpose in serving God. Abraham and Sarah, both very strong personalities, are probably the first couple in Holy Writ to share the kind of intimate relationship causing them to speak with one voice even when they were wrong. Theirs obviously was an outstanding marriage. Had it not been, Abraham would have left Sarah when she failed to bear him a son, or at least have taken a second wife. Sons were more important than wives in their culture.

Most of the time Abraham and Sarah lived with a deep faith in God's promises. One might say with the old nursery rhyme, "When they were good, they were very, very good, but when they were bad, they were horrid."

Civilization ever since the day of this ancient couple has suffered from their sin. Conflict in the modern Middle East reflects it. The Israelis descend from Isaac, the Arabs from Ishmael, all tracing their ancestry to Abraham. Around the campfires of the Arabs for centuries, the tale of Ishmael's mistreatment at the instigation of Sarah has passed from generation to generation. They have neither forgotten nor forgiven. So the world suffers and they most of all.

Genesis 21:20 appears to have been ignored by those who have thought God loved only the Jews of the ancient world. Speaking of Ishmael, the Bible says, "And God was with the lad, and he grew; and he lived in the wilderness, and became an archer."

The Arabs worship one God, too, and claim Abraham as their spiritual as well as physical father. They call God "Allah" rather than "Jehovah" or "Jahweh," but they are not like others in the world who worship many gods, some of nature and others made by human hands. Just as generation following generation has been reared on tales of Sarah's treachery, Abraham's faith in one God has been passed from father to son.

The story of Abraham and Sarah, although a beautiful love story, reverberates also with pathos and sorrow as we shall learn as it continues. However, the Bible never again records doubt in these two great stalwarts of the faith. It seems the birth of Isaac in accordance with God's promise wiped out all insecurity and fear, for Abraham never faltered when God asked him to sacrifice Isaac. He unflinchingly told the young man as they climbed the mountain to the place of sacrifice that God would provide the lamb. By that time, his faith might be termed "unflappable." And he was right. God did provide the lamb.

In chapter 23 of Genesis, the Bible states, "Now Sarah lived one hundred and twenty-seven years, these were the years of the life of Sarah. And Sarah died in Kiriath-arba (that is, Hebron) in the land of Canaan; and Abraham went in to mourn for Sarah and to weep for her" (Gen. 23:1, 2).

In chapter twenty-five, the marriage of Abraham to Keturah is mentioned, also the children of that marriage.

> And Abraham breathed his last and died in a ripe old age, an old man and satisfied with life; and he was gathered to his people. Then his sons Isaac and Ishmael buried him in the cave of Machpelah, in the field of Ephron the son of Zohar the Hittite, facing Mamre, the field which Abraham purchased from the sons of Heth; there Abraham was buried with Sarah his wife.

It appears Isaac and Ishmael put away all animosities as they grieved for their father Abraham. How tragic it is that those animosities should have resurfaced to plague mankind!

Chapter 25 accords Ishmael's family respectful listing of his generations. Through Ishmael came twelve princes, heads over twelve tribes just as God had promised. The prophecy of the angel to Hagar in Genesis 16:12, "And he will be a wild ass of a man, his hand will be against everyone, and everyone's hand will be against him; and he will live to the east of all his brothers," is fulfilled as recorded in Genesis 25:18. "And they settled from Havilah to Shur which is east of Egypt as one goes toward Assyria; *he settled in defiance of all his relatives.*"

So the Bible offers space and consideration to Ishmael. Yet the Scripture is clear. No other child of Abraham was to supersede Isaac, the son of promise.

So we move to Isaac's family.

6

THE FAMILY OF ISAAC

Now Abraham was old, advanced in age; and the Lord had blessed Abraham in every way. And Abraham said to his servant, the oldest of his household, who had charge of all that he owned, "Please place your hand under my thigh, and I will make you swear by the Lord, the God of heaven and the God of earth, that you shall not take a wife for my son from the daughters of the Canaanites, among whom I live, but you shall go to my country and to my relatives, and take a wife for my son Isaac (Gen. 24:16).

Rebekah moves into our story in answer to the longing of Abraham and the prayer of his devoted servant. What better way could anyone find to select a wife? The Scripture describes her as "very beautiful, a virgin" (Gen. 24:16). She was the daughter of Bethuel, Abraham's nephew.

When Rebekah approached the well at the city of Abraham's brother, Nahor, the servant asked for a drink. She not only gave him water but offered to water his camels, the very sign he had specified in his prayer.

Thanking God for immediate answer to prayer, the servant followed Rebekah to her home. Laban, her brother, rushed outside to welcome the stranger and offer him hospitality. Refusing to eat before explaining his mission, the old servant informed Bethuel and Laban of Abraham's request, his promise, his prayer, his encounter with Rebekah, and Isaac's offer of marriage. Perhaps the most significant comment of the whole story comes in Genesis 24:50, 51. "Then Laban and Bethuel answered and said, 'The matter comes from the Lord; so we cannot speak to you bad or good. Behold Rebekah is before you, take her and go, and let her be the wife of your master's son, *as the Lord has spoken.*'" If the Lord had spoken, the faithful dared not disobey.

Chapter 24 ends, "And the servant told Isaac all the things that he had done. Then Isaac brought her into his mother Sarah's tent, and he took Rebekah, and she became his wife; and he loved her; thus Isaac was comforted after his mother's death" (Gen. 24:66, 67).

Rebekah remained barren. So Isaac prayed. God answered that prayer with twins. The Bible says the children struggled even while in Rebekah's womb, so much so that she inquired of God.

"And the Lord said to her, 'Two nations are in your womb; and two people shall be separated from your body; and one people shall be stronger than the other; and the older shall serve the younger'" (Gen. 25:23).

Isaac was forty years old when he married Rebekah, sixty when the twins were born. The first born was named Esau, the second Jacob. The Biblical scribe indicates fundamental differences in their personalities from birth. As they grew the comparisons appeared even greater. "When the boys grew up, Esau became a skillful hunter, a man of the field; but Jacob was a peaceful man, living in tents" (Gen. 25:27).

One simple statement in the narrative sets the stage for family discord. "Now Isaac loved Esau, because he had a taste for game; but Rebekah loved Jacob" (Gen. 25:28).

We are introduced to our first case of sibling rivalry precipitated by parental favoritism. One can scarcely think of a more shallow or perverse reason for preferring one child over another than "a taste for game." Was Isaac the spoiled child of Sarah and Abraham, giving his love only in response to self-centered satisfaction? The text certainly makes the reader wonder.

Then we must ponder upon the description of Jacob as peaceful, living in tents. Jacob emerges as the cerebral son rather than the macho one. Mothers love boys who take time to talk, including Mother in the conversation. However, that is scarcely a viable reason for showing favoritism either. In fact, favoritism in a family almost always results in heartache for all concerned.

Esau, son of a father whose love emerged from his tastebuds, sold his birthright for a mess of pottage. The Bible says, "Thus Esau despised his birthright" (Gen. 25:34).

Another famine drove Isaac's family to Gerar, the land of Abimelech, king of the Philistines. There God repeated the promise of Abraham to Isaac. In Gerar, Isaac reenacted the sin of his father Abraham by declaring Rebekah to be his sister. Abimelech caught Isaac in the lie but ordered the people to treat Isaac and Rebekah with courtesy. While in the land of the Philistines, Isaac amassed an even greater fortune than that left to him by his father. Envy made the Philistines drive Isaac's family from the land.

They went to Beersheba. Isaac, reflecting his espousal of his father's faith, built an altar at Beersheba to worship God. Building altars and digging wells became a way of life; one due to faith, the other showing desperate need for water in a dry land.

The 26th chapter of Genesis closes with two verses that are quite significant in our study of Biblical families. "And when Esau was forty years old he married Judith the daughter of Beeri the Hittite, and Basemath the daughter of Elon the Hittite; and they made life miserable for Isaac and Rebekah" (Gen. 26:34, 35).

In-law problems may have existed previous to our story of the family of Isaac, but they had never been noted before. The succeeding explosion of anger and envy may be traced in part to these two verses.

Esau was already in trouble with his mother. He preferred roving the fields to spending time with her. Then he added insult to injury. He brought home two wives neither of his parents could stand.

The Bible makes no explanation of the conflict's source. We might theorize a difference in culture since the young women were Hittites instead of Jews. There surely was a contrast of religion. Perhaps they simply did not like Isaac and Rebekah, and a classic personality conflict arose. At any rate, the household was thrown into chaos.

Chapter 27 records the collaboration of Rebekah and Jacob to deceive Isaac and defraud Esau. Isaac, believing Jacob to be Esau, gave Jacob the blessing intended for the first born.

One might wonder what had turned Rebekah, the gentle submissive girl who gladly gave of herself to Isaac, into the

68

cheat who used her knowledge of him to help Jacob deceive him. No one knows what happens in someone else's home. However, the angel had told Rebekah her elder son would serve the younger. Perhaps Rebekah had tired of people motivated primarily by physical needs with no emphasis upon thought. Did Jacob inherit his tremendous intelligence from his mother? There is more evidence in the Bibical story for that assumption than the other way around. Both Isaac and Esau are described as concentrating upon physical desires.

Finally Esau begins to understand the mammoth fraud perpetrated by Rebekah and Jacob. He weeps as he pleads for a blessing of his own. The Biblical writer arouses much sympathy for Esau as he records the genuine love and respect he bears for Isaac. "So Esau bore a grudge against Jacob because of the blessing with which his father had blessed him; and Esau said to himself, 'The days of mourning for my father are near; then I will kill my brother Jacob'" (Gen. 27:41).

One observes the complexity of Rebekah's nature when she sends Jacob away.

> Now therefore, my son, obey my voice, and arise, flee to Haran, to my brother Laban! And stay with him a few days, until your brother's fury subsides, until your brother's anger against you susbides, and he forgets what you did to him. Then I shall send and get you from there. Why should I be bereaved of you both in one day? (Gen. 27:43-45).

What motivated Rebekah's statement? Obviously fear for Jacob's life was one motivation, plus worry about Esau's becoming a murderer. One thing a thoughtful reader might note is the length of time Rebekah mentioned. "A few days" for stealing both Esau's blessing and his birthright? Was Esau such a man of action rather than thought that even serious anger, justifiable anger, if not acted upon immediately, soon disappeared from his mind?

We might also wonder whom Rebekah meant by "you both." Was she speaking of the impending death of Isaac or of the rejection she knew she'd meet from Esau after the truth of her conspiring against him became known? Did she love both sons in spite of seeing the superiority of the one? Was the family dedication to the promise so important even family relationships receded into the background?

Answers to all these questions remain in the realm of conjecture. However, we do know she sent Jacob away for two reasons; one, his safety and the other to keep him from marrying a Canaanite woman. "And Rebekah said to Isaac, 'I am tired of living because of the daughters of Heth; if Jacob takes a wife from the daughters of Heth, like these, from the daughters of the land, what good will my life be to me?'" (Gen. 27:46).

Isaac, always in love with the beautiful Rebekah, sent Jacob away with another blessing, charging him not to marry a Canaanite but rather someone from among his mother's people.

Another picture of differences between families arises here. When Abraham decided to secure a wife from his own people for Isaac, a servant was sent. Isaac was forty years old but the servant managed all the affairs of Abraham's household. Granting the fact that Jacob must flee from Esau's anger, wasn't Jacob being taught to be a stronger man? We see this in our society today. When parents over-protect children, weakness results. The Bible characterizes Jacob as very strong, while Rebekah seems the stronger in the home of Isaac. Isaac appears easily manipulated. For the sake of our study of families, perhaps we need to learn from this that children must bear responsibility for their own actions and be taught to make their own decisions if strength of character is to result.

We talk much of communication or the lack of it in families today. We see the effect of its lack in this story. Obviously, Isaac and Rebekah had not discussed their antipathy toward Canaanite ways with Esau. The Bible says Esau learned Jacob had obeyed his parents, going to Paddan-aram for a wife. He heard of his father's charging Jacob not to take a wife from the Canaanites. Chapter 28, verses 7 and 8 record, "So Esau saw that the daughters of Canaan displeased his father Isaac; and Esau went to Ishmael, and married, besides the wives that he had, Mahalath the daughter of Ishmael, Abraham's son, the sister of Nebaioth."

Was this a pathetic effort on the part of Esau to gain favor in his father's eyes by marrying a relative? If so, communication failed again for bad blood existed between Ishmael and Isaac.

Esau seems a tragic character. How could he not have known how his mother and father felt about his wives? Was Esau mentally slow, or did he just move in a world of his own, unconscious of emotions around him?

Who knows? But another Biblical family was split asunder by sibling rivalry, this time fostered by parental favoritism.

Isaac and Rebekah disappear from our account at this point except for the mention of Isaac's death in Genesis 35:29. Perhaps Rebekah paid dearly for her part in the deception of Isaac. She evidently lost the comfort of both sons in her old age.

The Biblical account turns to Jacob's family since that family inherits the promise. However, Genesis 36 records the generations of Esau, establishing him as the father of the Edomites. In his own way he appears to have had an element of greatness. When he and Jacob separated from each other in later life after their reconciliation, it was Esau who voluntarily left Canaan to establish himself in another land. By that time he had great possessions. Past animosities had disappeared. Apparently he had accepted the fact that the family of the promise received the land of Canaan. Great respect for the promise given to Abraham runs through each family. The years mellowed and strengthened Esau. He, too, came from great people and became the ancestral head of a nation.

One great lack in Esau's life attracts our attention. We never read of his erecting an altar or turning his life to God. Perhaps the eventual idolatrous worship engaged in by the Edomites may be traced to Esau's shallow thought.

For the purpose of study of the families of the Bible, however, we turn our attention to the family of Jacob.

7

THE FAMILY OF JACOB

One must wonder about the thoughts filling Jacob's mind as he fled from his father's house. Was he consumed by guilt? What about fear? The Bible doesn't tell us. However, God, who knows the minds and hearts of His creation, appeared to Jacob in a visionary dream, assuring him of his place in history and his security in the heavenly Father's care.

In Genesis 28, we find Jacob walking in the pathway blazed by his worshiping ancestors.

> Then Jacob awoke from his sleep and said, "Surely the Lord is in this place and I did not know it." And he was afraid and said, "How awesome is this place! This is none other than the house of God, and this is the gate of heaven." So Jacob rose early in the morning, and took the stone that

he had put under his head and set it up as a pillar, and poured oil on its top (Gen. 28:16).

We observe the spiritual side of Jacob beginning to emerge as he starts his lonely journey. Depth, not present in the purely physical Esau, surfaces in Jacob's personality. He has not conquered self-centered greed yet, but one can see a metamorphosis of character occurring in the thoughtful lad who valued both the birthright and the blessing. We might note for the sake of discouraged parents that aged saints don't come that way! It takes time. Not only did Jacob set up an altar, but he vowed allegiance to God and a tenth of his income. At this point, Jacob, alone and frightened, reached out for the hand of God.

Our story again centers around a well. As Abraham's servant found Rebekah, the shepherdess, at the well, Jacob found his cousin, Rachel, also a shepherdess, coming to water flocks. Apparently it was love at first sight, or at least physical attraction. Jacob immediately wanted to marry the beautiful Rachel.

Jacob, following an enthusiastic greeting by his Uncle Laban, stayed with the family one month. He must have worked hard for his board and room, for Laban insisted Jacob deserved a salary. He asked Jacob to quote his price. The young man asked for Rachel's hand in marriage although she was the younger of Laban's daughters. One verse in the Scripture arouses sympathy for Leah, the older daughter. "And Leah's eyes were weak, but Rachel was beautiful of form and face" (Gen. 29:17).

The ancients were not so different, were they? Remember the child who wore glasses in elementary school? "Four Eyes" became a derogatory nickname, thoughtlessly applied. Had Leah spent years squinting against the desert sun in an effort

74

to see? Had such squinting distorted her features or was she just the ugly duckling of the family? One's heart aches for Leah.

We might note another variation in this account from the trip of Abraham's servant to arrange for a wife for Isaac. The Bible tells of all the gifts the servant presented to Bethuel before he took Rebekah back with him to marry Isaac. This was the custom of the time. But as this story of Jacob unfolds, we learn that Jacob had nothing to offer but himself and his work potential. Obviously, his having to run from Esau's wrath and his father's disgust with his cheating tactics kept any money for gifts from being forthcoming.

Is there a lesson here for parents today? Jacob had to work for everything that eventually became his. The Bible leads us to believe him a stronger man than Isaac. Was this one reason why?

Another important attribute of character appears in the story. We were saddened by Rebekah's deception, but what a rank amateur she was compared to her brother! Laban agreed to allow Jacob to marry Rachel following seven years of service. The Biblical scribe reports, "So Jacob served seven years for Rachel and they seemed to him but a few days because of his love for her" (Gen. 29:20). Then Laban gave Leah to Jacob instead.

Did Jacob, overwhelmed by this deception, begin to understand Esau? Was suffering from fraud a necessary part of Jacob's growth and comprehension of life's values? At any rate, he protested, "What is this you have done to me? Was it not for Rachel that I served you? Why then have you deceived me?" (Gen. 29:25).

After one "bridal week" spent with Leah, Jacob was permitted to marry his beloved Rachel. Again Holy Writ

75

demonstrates the tragedy of sibling rivalry. Obviously Laban gave no consideration to the feelings of either of his daughters.

Let's look at Leah. Older sisters, especially unattractive older sisters, find acceptance of a beautiful younger sister difficult. When a desirable, marriageable male appears on the scene, emotions run even higher. How degrading to Leah's sense of self it must have been to be sneaked into Jacob's tent in the black of night and forced to pass herself off as her beautiful sister! Did Leah hope achieving a good sexual relationship with Jacob might win him over? Whatever her thought, and the Bible doesn't give us an inkling, losing her virginity to a man who screamed with anger because she wasn't her sister had to be devastating. Yet Leah played the role of dutiful wife. Did she continue to hope Jacob might be satisfied with her? No one knows; but, at the end of that first week, he walked away to Rachel.

Rachel, too, must have been furious with her father. Jacob was her man! He'd worked for her! Knowing he was sleeping with Leah couldn't have helped frustrating her. Frustration is probably a masterpiece of understatement.

> So Jacob went in to Rachel also and indeed he loved Rachel more than Leah, and he served Laban another seven years.
>
> Now the Lord saw that Leah was unloved (literally, "hated") and he opened her womb, but Rachel was barren. And Leah conceived and bore him a son and named him, Reuben, for she said, "Because the Lord has seen my affliction; surely now my husband will love me" (Gen. 29:30-32).

As we read the narrative, we note Leah's gradual change of mood from hope to acceptance. After her first son, she hoped for Jacob's love. Following the birth of her second son, Simeon, she repeats her hurt over being unloved.

76

Following Levi's birth, she opts for acceptance. Then came Judah whose birth she greeted by saying, "This time I will praise the Lord" (Gen. 29:35).

Had the lives of four little sons who loved her begun to compensate for a husband who didn't?

Chapter 30 begins with Rachel's jealousy. In a culture that not only prized sons but needed them for conducting the family work, a barren woman was despised as utterly useless by those around her. Even Jacob's single-minded devotion could not counteract the sense of deprivation she felt because of her inability to bear children. Beautiful women are not accustomed to negation. Here was a situation a lovely face and figure could not overcome.

> Now when Rachel saw that she bore Jacob no children, she became jealous of her sister; and she said to Jacob, "Give me children, or else I die."
> Then Jacob's anger burned against Rachel, and he said, "Am I in the place of God, who has withheld from you the fruit of the womb?" (Gen. 30:1, 2).

Perhaps Rachel believed she hadn't conceived because Jacob was not as enthusiastic in his lovemaking with her as he was with Leah. No scientific knowledge of fertility and infertility was available to women of that era. Rachel only knew she was miserable. She needed someone to blame. Finally, she gave her maid Bilhah to Jacob, for that culture gave the maid's children to her mistress. Bilhah bore Dan and Naphtali. Rachel's statement following Naphtali's birth lends insight to the ongoing struggle between the sisters. "With mighty wrestlings I have wrestled with my sister, and I have indeed prevailed" (Gen. 30:8).

But Leah was not to be outdone. She had quit bearing, but she, too, had a maid, Zilpah. So she gave Zilpah to

Jacob. Zilpah bore Gad and Asher. Another significant quote appears here. "Then Leah said, 'Happy am I! For women will call me happy'" (Gen. 30:13). Being identified as one who provided sons to her husband raised Leah's status among her peers. We note she no longer hopes for Jacob's love, only for status in the group. She doesn't say she is happy because of personal satisfaction but because other women will think she is. There is something almost pathetic about her statement.

> Now in the days of wheat harvest Reuben went and found mandrakes in the field, and brought them to his mother Leah. Then Rachel said to Leah, "Please give me some of your son's mandrakes."
>
> But she said to her, "Is it a small matter for you to take my husband? And would you take my son's mandrakes also?" So Rachel said, "Therefore he may lie with you to-night in return for your son's mandrakes."
>
> When Jacob came in from the field in the evening, then Leah went out to meet him and said, "You must come in to me, for I have surely hired you with my son's mandrakes." So he lay with her that night (Gen. 30:14-16).

One cannot help wondering how Jacob felt about all this infighting among his wives. Was he flattered to be the subject of such jealousy? Or was he inclined to want to run from the whole mess? Who made Rachel the one who decided with whom he would spend the night? What terrible negative emotions controlled the family of Jacob! Peace was certainly an unknown quantity.

This segment of the narrative seems highly significant in understanding the family unit and its internal conflicts. Mandrakes were beautiful, odoriferous plants considered love potions by the ancients. Since the Bible tells us Jacob served Laban twenty years before leaving and he served seven years before marrying Leah, a little simple arithmetic makes Reuben no more than ten or eleven years of age at the time he gathered the mandrakes for his mother. Had he listened to Leah bemoaning her unloved state? Was a devoted little boy bringing mandrakes to his mother so she might make a love potion to attract his father? Had the eldest son become his mother's confidant? Were all of Leah's sons deeply hurt by Jacob's obvious preference for Rachel? Did they feel like second-class citizens because their father, failing to love their mother, also, at least to a degree, rejected them?

Leah bore Jacob two more sons, Issachar and Zebulun, and a daughter, Dinah. Then the Bible records, "Then God remembered Rachel, and God gave heed to her and opened her womb. So she conceived and bore a son and said, 'God has taken away my reproach.' And she named him Joseph, saying, 'May the Lord give me another son'" (Gen. 30:22-24).

So Joseph arrived on the scene, probably welcomed by only two people, Jacob and Rachel. The atmosphere of jealousy and rivalry could only have intensified following his birth.

Jacob finally decided he had served Laban long enough. He yearned to return to his own country. Struggle arose in the separation. Laban's sons, jealous of Jacob's prosperity, turned their father against him. Obviously, Laban's own difficult and dishonest personality had its effect upon his children. Both Laban and Jacob tried to cheat the other and gain the upper hand. No mention appears of Laban's being a worshiper of God throughout those years Jacob and his family spent in the area. In fact, Laban's family must have been idol worshipers, for Rachel stole the household gods when she left. She deceived her father when he came to her tent looking for them. We see definite evidence of deception passing from generation to generation in this family. The inspired writer drops the story of the household gods after Jacob's family leaves the country. Did Rachel continue to deceive Jacob about stealing them? The author does not say. Of two things we are sure. Laban didn't exemplify virtuous living for his children to emulate. And Jacob, a novice in the art of deception, had paid dearly for his ill treatment of Esau.

Laban pursued Jacob but the two men made their peace. In Genesis 31:49, we find the famous Mizpah benediction, "May the Lord watch between you and me when we are absent one from the other." This statement, attributed to Laban, indicates he really did believe in God. Was he like many of us, only calling upon God in times of stress? Did his children reflect this concept, that God's presence was only needed in times of crisis? Such attitudes didn't build strong people then. They still don't.

When Laban departed without a battle, Jacob must have breathed a sigh of relief. Yet he knew he had to cross another barrier before he could find peace in his home country. What would Esau do? More than twenty years had elapsed. He had wronged his brother. Would Esau still seek Jacob's blood?

After dividing his people into companies hoping some would escape the slaughter he feared, Jacob met the crisis with prayer.

O God of my father Abraham and God of my father Isaac, O Lord, who didst say to me, "Return to your country and to your relatives, and I will prosper you," I am unworthy of all the lovingkindness and of all the faithfulness which Thou hast shown to Thy servant; for with my staff only I crossed this Jordan, and now I have become two companies. Deliver me, I pray, from the hand of my brother, from the hand of Esau; for I fear him, lest he come and attack me, mother with children. For Thou didst say, "I will surely prosper you, and make your descendants as the sand of the sea, which cannot be numbered for multitude" (Gen. 32:9-12).

Jacob had traveled full circle in character development. He used his own wits, but he also asked God's help. The cocky youth with all the answers had changed to the man who knew he had been blessed for the purposes of God and not because he really deserved it. Jacob had learned and deepened through suffering and responsibility.

When Jacob's family resumed their trek toward Canaan the next morning, Jacob carefully arranged his beloved family. The maids and their children took first place in the line, then Leah and her children, finally Rachel and Joseph. But Jacob placed himself at the head of the company, the most dangerous spot of all. Gone was the sly human being who valued things above relationships. All his children deserved his protection. He gave it.

Still one is made aware of the hurt Jacob again inflicted upon the children of Leah and the maids. His positioning of the family could only accentuate his evaluation of their worth. Rachel and Joseph were his favorites. Who could have missed that fact? Only maturity of spirit enables one to take last place with grace. These were youngsters. No mature understanding existed, only awareness of rejection and favoritism.

Imagine Jacob's joy when a forgiving Esau ran to meet him and embraced him, greeting his wives and children with loving appreciation. Jacob wasn't the only one who had grown up. Esau had accepted the fact that Jacob was the recipient of the promise. Relationships had assumed major importance to him also. He had achieved personal status among his peers, so he no longer felt the need to be most important in the family of his birth. Gone was the sibling rivalry, replaced by gratitude for kinship. The two quarreling boys parted as adult friends.

Human personality remains much the same as in Old Testament times. Many of us have experienced the same spiritual growth with our own siblings. Realization of personal worth ends numerous sibling rivalries even today.

One must also take into account the prayer Jacob uttered asking God for protection for his family, the family of the promise. Forgiveness and reconciliation motivated Esau's loving acceptance of his cheating brother. Such forces only come from God.

Deuteronomy 2 records an interesting sidelight both to this story and that of the conquest of Canaan.

> . . . "You will pass through the territory of your brothers the sons of Esau who live in Seir; and they will be afraid of you. So be very careful; do not provoke them, for I will not give you any of their land, even as little as a footstep because I have given Mount Seir to Esau as a possession. You shall buy food from them with money so that you may eat, and you shall purchase water from them with money so that you may drink. For the Lord your God has blessed you in all that you have done; He has known your wanderings through this great wilderness. These forty years the Lord your God has been with you; you have not lacked a thing." So we passed beyond our brothers the sons of Esau, who live in Seir, away from the Arabah road, away from Elath

and from Ezion-geber. And we turned and passed through by the way of the wilderness of Moab (Deut. 2:4-8).

Esau's animal appetites made him more open than Jacob to the secularization and immorality of life displayed by his Canaanite neighbors. His descendants followed in his footsteps. Yet God remained true to His promise.

As soon as Jacob arrived safely and bought land in Canaan, he erected an altar, thanking God for his safe passage.

But Jacob's troubles had only begun. Shechem, son of Hamor the Hivite, prince of the land, raped Dinah. He longed to marry her, seeming ashamed of his actions. His father asked Jacob for Dinah's hand in marriage for Shechem. Dinah's brothers insisted upon circumcision for all Hamor's men if the two groups were to intermarry. The Bible notes that Jacob's sons answered Shechem and Hamor with deceit.

Just at the stage when the circumcision had created the worst pain making mobility virtually impossible, Dinah's brothers fell upon the men of the city and killed them all.

One's first reaction to this story is horror. The rape appalls a thoughtful reader. Then the Bible says Shechem "spoke tenderly" to Dinah because he loved her. A little sympathy begins to surface in the mind of the reader. The author is dealing with a pagan culture. Perhaps the prince of the realm believed it his right to have any woman he wanted. But wait. Listen to Hamor and Shechem as they speak to the men of the city.

"These men are friendly with us; therefore let them live in this land and trade in it, for behold, the land is large enough for them. Let us take their daughters in marriage, and give our daughters to them. Only on this condition will the men consent to us to live with us, to become one people: that every male among us be circumcised as they are circumcised. *Will not their livestock and all their animals be ours?* Only let us consent to them and they will live with us" (Gen. 34:21-23).

What did Shechem and Hamor really want to do, right the wrong done Dinah or acquire Jacob's wealth by peaceful means? Finding decency on either side eludes the reader.

When Jacob remonstrated with them, the young men replied, "Should he treat our sister as a harlot?" What had happened to Jacob's sons to turn them into vicious bandits at a time of crisis? They even sacked the city, destroying everything in their path. They had spent a lifetime watching adults of their family practice deception. This may account for their decision to get their revenge through this means. Perhaps their father's lack of understanding of the emotional suffering their mother endured created a fierce defense in her sons for their mother and sister. At any rate, they ignored their father's protests.

Jacob's family was forced to flee from that part of the country. Listen to Jacob's own words: "You have made me odious among the inhabitants of the land, among the Canaanites and the Perizzites; and my men being few in number, they will gather together against me and attack me and I shall be destroyed and my household" (Gen. 34:30).

No doubt Jacob had tried to teach his sons a sense of morality. His moral judgments had improved since his youth. But example teaches more than words. His sons had been schooled in the university of parental observation.

God came to Jacob and said, "Arise, go up to Bethel, and live there; and make an altar there to God, who appeared to you when you fled from your brother Esau" (Gen. 35:1). God was offering another opportunity to repent and reverse their destiny.

When Jacob talked to his family, he ordered them to give up their foreign gods, purify themselves and change their clothing in preparation for travel. For once they obeyed. Jacob got rid of the idols by hiding them under an oak tree near Shechem. Their trip proved uneventful. All the cities feared them. News of massacres traveled fast even in a day of poor communication.

Jacob had already been renamed "Israel," meaning "he who strives with God," in a night of wrestling before he met Esau. At this point, God confirmed the renaming and the family became "Children of Israel."

Rachel went into labor at Bethel, delivering a son. She died. Knowing she was dying, she named the baby, "Ben-oni," meaning "the son of my sorrow." Jacob renamed him, "Benjamin," meaning "the son of my right hand."

Jacob buried Rachel on the way to Bethlehem. The family journeyed to a site beyond the tower of Eder. At this point, Reuben offered the greatest possible insult to his father. He "lay with Bilhah his father's concubine; and Israel heard of it" (Gen. 35:22). Was Reuben, his eldest son, paying Israel for the years of unhappiness Leah had endured at Jacob's hand? He certainly showed utter lack of respect for his father. Who knows the exact motivation? However, Jacob's problems with his wayward family certainly were not over!

There's an old southern expression indicating that rearing one's own family is a way of "payin' for our raisin's." We see this in Jacob's sorrow over his sons. Or as one grieving father said, "How long must I pay through my children for the wrongs of my youth?"

"Now Israel loved Joseph more than all his sons because he was the son of his old age; and he made him a varicolored tunic. And his brothers saw that their father loved him more than all his brothers; and so they hated him and could not speak to him on friendly terms" (Gen. 37:3, 4).

Joseph didn't help matters. When Jacob sent him to check on the others, he "brought back a bad report." When he dreamed all his family bowed down to him, he told his brothers. The Bible says, ". . . they hated him even more" (Gen. 37:5).

Finally, when Jacob sent Joseph to the spot where they were pasturing the flock, his brothers sold him to Midianite slave traders. Then they reported his death to their father, practicing methods of deception they had learned well through observing him and their grandfather.

Space forbids going into further detail about Israel's sons and their problems. In order to gain real insight into this family, read Genesis 29-50. For our purpose of understanding the mistakes of Jacob's family with a view to building better modern families, however, we need to look at the character of Joseph and assess it. It also becomes mandatory to see the change and development in his brothers.

Joseph stands out in Scripture as a moral giant. He accepted demotion from favorite son to slave with no apparent whimpering self-pity. Each time his lifestyle changed, he adapted, rising to the top through trust in God, superior intelligence, dependability and hard work.

When Potiphar's wife tried to seduce Joseph, he refused to be tempted saying,

> Behold, with me around, my master does not concern himself with anything in the house, and he has put all that he owns in my charge. There is no greater in this house than I, and he has withheld nothing from me except you, because you are his wife. How then could I do this great evil, and sin against God? (Gen. 39:8, 9).

Joseph's loyalty, first to God and then to Potiphar, forbade a sexual liaison with his master's wife. One might speculate that Joseph's consideration for Potiphar even prevented explanation of his own actions in order to save Potiphar the embarrassment of a faithless wife. The Bible records no defense on Joseph's part. Surely one so powerful in a household was given an opportunity to speak on his own behalf. The fact that Joseph was thrown into prison rather than executed might indicate Potiphar had been through this before.

Again Joseph faced readjustment of his hopes through no fault of his own. From second in power in Potiphar's house, Joseph descended to prison life. Soon he had charge of all the other prisoners. The Bible states, "The chief jailer did not supervise anything under Joseph's charge because the Lord was with him; and whatever he did, the Lord made to prosper" (Gen. 39:23). From his God-given talent for interpreting dreams, Joseph arose to second place in the realm just under Pharoah.

When Joseph's brothers came to buy grain, his golden opportunity arrived with them. He could send them home to starve. He could force them to do degrading labor in order to obtain food. He could berate them for their actions toward him. Instead, listen to the Bible as Joseph's revelation of his kinship to them appears:

> . . . And he said, "I am your brother Joseph, whom you sold into Egypt. And now do not be grieved or angry with yourselves, because you sold me here; for God sent me before you to preserve life. . . . And God sent me before you to preserve for you a remnant in the earth, and to keep you alive by a great deliverance. Now, therefore, it was not you who sent me here, but God; . . ." (Gen. 45:4, 5, 7, 8).

Joseph comes to us as one of the greatest men of Holy Writ, one who refused to stoop to revenge, one who lived his entire life as nearly as he could within the will of God.

For purposes of study of the family, we must raise some questions. Why was Joseph so superior to his brothers? What kept him from becoming a bitter, disillusioned man? Most of our answers must rely on conclusions drawn from the story, for the Bible makes no effort to explain this superiority but only declares it.

Joseph is spoken of as the child of Jacob's old age. Older parents tend to realize the brevity of childhood, devoting more patient attention to little ones with greater appreciation and less criticism.

Joseph also came from a true love relationship. He could not have doubted his father's devotion to his mother. A good marriage relationship leads to greater security for children.

Joseph never had any reason to doubt parental love for him. Jacob favored him at every turn. Sometimes this creates monsters, but Jacob had achieved a close personal relationship with God before Joseph's birth. In sharing himself with his favored son, he must have shared his faith also. Faith tempered the ego and provided stability in the face of adversity.

Joseph's brothers might be characterized as rascals in their youth. One could forgive their anger over the rape of their sister. However, the sin was Shechem's. The other men had nothing to do with it and didn't deserve to die. The action of Jacob's sons in taking revenge against the women and children and looting the houses degraded the entire family.

Reuben's behavior with his father's concubine was inexcusable. Their treatment of Joseph demeaned all the brothers. The reader finds himself asking, "Is there any good in these men? What kind of degenerate family produced these scoundrels?"

Reuben forms an interesting study. A sensitive young Reuben brought his mother a love potion. Granted, he showed contempt for his father by seduction of his father's concubine, but no violence is recorded for Reuben. He tried to save Joseph, intending to return him to Jacob. One sees some empathy in the personality of Reuben.

Even Judah wasn't willing to kill Joseph. He suggested selling the boy, not hurting him physically. However, all the sons participated in deceiving Jacob. Deception for this family was a way of life.

The Biblical account allows us to view the growth and development of Israel's sons judged by their reactions at the time of the famine. Several years had passed. They had families of their own. Understanding the suffering they had caused their aged father had mellowed them. When Joseph appeared harsh with them, they considered it just punishment for their sin. Joseph forced Simeon to remain in prison in Egypt until the others could return with Benjamin.

Why Simeon? Had he wanted to kill Joseph? He certainly was bloodthirsty in Shechem! Was Joseph trying to discern whether or not Simeon had changed?

They passed all Joseph's tests with flying colors. Judah even offered himself in exchange for Benjamin's safety. What had created the change?

Maturity probably helped. Few people understand parental emotion before experiencing parental responsibility.

Israel's closer relationship with God must have rubbed off on the brothers, too, as it had on Joseph. They spoke not only of their respect for their father but also of their God.

One thing that occurred to us is pure conjecture. After Rachel's death, had Jacob turned to Leah in his loneliness? Did he finally see her devotion and loyalty? Had the importance of physical beauty been replaced in the older man's heart by respect for genuine character? Was Leah happier, thereby removing the necessity for her sons to defend her? The Bible doesn't say, so we can only wonder. But it is a rational assumption. When Jacob lay dying, he asked to be buried in the cave of Machpelah, for, "There they buried Abraham and his wife, Sarah, there they buried Isaac and his wife Rebekah, and there I buried Leah . . ." (Gen. 49:31). He did not request burial with Rachel.

Even after Israel's death, his family remained in Egypt under Joseph's sponsorship. We will not pursue the families of any of Israel's sons, not even Joseph, for no particular greatness emerges in Biblical history. Instead we skip four hundred years to the family of two obscure slaves in Egypt, Amram and Jochebed.

Before leaving Jacob or Israel's family, however, we must sum up our findings. Favoritism is destructive of the peace of family life. So is polygamy. All one needs to do is pursue these ancient families to see how both sins foster discord, deception and enmity. We have also found definite proof from all the families studied thus far of the importance of moral and spiritual living on the part of parents. Few children rise above the example with which they live daily.

8

BETWEEN PROMINENT FAMILIES

The Bible tells us seventy people from the loins of Jacob entered the land of Egypt during Joseph's prominence. The sacred scribe names Reuben, Simeon, Levi, Judah, Issachar, Zebulun, Gad, Asher, Joseph, Benjamin, Dan and Naphtali as the sons of Jacob. From their listing we have compiled some information concerning their families that might be relevant to our study.

Reuben fathered four sons: Hanoch, Pallu, Hezron and Carmi (Gen. 46:8, 9; Exod. 6:14; I Chron. 5:3). He forfeited his birthright as the eldest son because he had sex relations with his father's concubine, Bilhah (Gen. 35:22; 49:3, 4). The tribe of Reuben was never prominent in Israel's history although they did receive their request to settle east of the Jordan because they helped capture the promised land.

Simeon, second son of Jacob, fathered six sons: Jemuel, Janim, Jachen, Zohar, Shaul and Ohad. Each one of them founded a tribal family except for Ohad (Gen. 46:10; Num. 26:12-14; I Chron. 4:24). This tribe settled in the extreme south of the land and was eventually absorbed by the tribe of Judah.

Levi was Jacob's third son. He sired three sons: Gershon or Gershom, Kohath and Merari (Gen. 46:11). Each founded a tribal family. Our next prominent family comes from Levi's descendants through Kohath. The Levites of Sinai remained true to God and He chose them for sanctuary service (Exod. 32:26-29; Num. 3:9, 11-13, 40, 41; 8:16-18). At thirty years of age, they became eligible for full service in the sanctuary, (Num. 4:3; I Chron. 23:3-5) although they assisted from the age of twenty (I Chron. 23:24, 28-31).

Shua, the Canaanite wife of Judah, Jacob's fourth son, bore him two sons, Er and Onan. They displeased God and forfeited their lives. Shelah, Judah's third son by Shua, founded a tribal family. Through Er's widow, Tamar, Judah fathered twin sons, Perez and Zerah (Gen. 38:11-30; 46:12; Num. 26:19). From the line of Judah through Perez came David and, eventually, Jesus. Judah was selected as the Messianic tribe in Jacob's dying prophetic vision. This was called the "Shiloh Prophecy" (Gen. 49:10). Five families formed the tribe of Judah (Num. 26:19-21; I Chron. 2:3-6). When Moses sent a spy from each tribe to observe the lay of the land in Canaan and the defenses of its people, Caleb, son of Jephunneh, from the tribe of Judah was one of the two who believed the Israelites could overcome the residents with God's assistance.

Issachar was Jacob's ninth son, the fifth born to him through Leah. Four sons are named in Genesis 46:13; Tola, Puvvah,

Iob and Shimron. The tribe of Issachar consisted of four families, descendants of these sons. Little prominence appears in Scripture referring to any of them.

Zebulun was youngest son of Jacob by Leah. He fathered three sons: Sered, Elon and Jahleel (Num. 26:23). Each headed a family in the tribe of Zebulun. This tribe occupied land in the camp of Judah.

Benjamin, Jacob's youngest, was born to Rachel, who died at his birth (Gen. 35:16-20). He became Jacob's favorite son following Joseph's disappearance, as evidenced by Jacob's distress at the thought of Benjamin's departure for Egypt with the brothers (Gen. 43:1-17). Joseph's great love for Benjamin is cited in Genesis 43:29-34. Genesis 46:21 lists ten sons for Benjamin: Bela, Becher, Ashbel, Gera, Naaman, Ehi, Rosh, Muppim, Huppim and Ard. Numbers 26:38-41 makes some of these sons grandsons. Since Biblical custom often called grandsons sons, we cannot be sure where they came in the line, but we know they were Benjamin's descendants. *Hastings Dictionary of the Bible* lists ten sons for Benjamin, accepting the Genesis figure. The tribe of Benjamin was small, but it produced Saul, the first king, and the great apostle Paul was a Benjamite. Some of the nation's greatest cities were located in the territory allotted to the tribe of Benjamin, including at least part of Jerusalem. When the nation split due to Jeroboam's revolt, part of the Benjamites remained with Judah.

Dan was Jacob's fifth son, the first by Bilhah, Rachel's maid (Gen. 30:5, 6). Genesis 46:23 lists only one son for Dan, Hushim. In Numbers 26:42, he is called Shuham and his descendants Shuhamites. Samson came from the tribe of Dan. They have been described as fierce and war-like. Samson's character bears that out.

Naphtali, sixth son of Jacob, and the second by Rachel's maid, Bilhah, fathered four sons: Jahzeel, Guni, Jezer and Shillem (Gen. 46:24). Barak was the only person apparently from the tribe of Naphtali who enters our story in a prominent role in Israel's history. The tribe occupied some of Canaan's richest land. Their border position developed a fearless, war-like spirit exemplified by Barak as he fought in cooperation with Deborah (Judg. 5:18).

Gad, son of Jacob and Zilpah, Leah's maid, fathered seven sons: Zephon, Haggai, Shuni, Ozni, Eri, Arod and Areli (Num. 26:15-18). The tribe was composed of descendants of these seven sons. Perhaps some of the most noteworthy facts from the tribe's history occur in their support of and loyalty to King David.

Asher, the eighth son of Jacob and second by Zilpah, fathered four sons and a daughter. The sons were Imnah, Ishvah, Ishvi, and Beriah; the daughter, Sarah. Little noteworthy history appears about the tribe.

Because of his great prominence, we should mention Joseph, Jacob's elder son by Rachel. Joseph married Asenath, daughter of Potiphera, priest of On. From their union came two sons, Manasseh and Ephraim. When Jacob lay dying, he made provisions for Ephraim and Manasseh to head tribes instead of their father, also offering ascendancy to Ephraim as the greater in spite of his being younger. So, no tribe of Joseph is listed, only Ephraim and Manasseh, although the two tribes are often mentioned as the "children of Joseph." See Numbers 1:10; Judges 1:22, 23; II Samuel 19:20; I Kings 11:28. (In the last reference we notice that Jeroboam, the one who split the kingdom after Rehoboam ascended the throne, was a descendant of Joseph.) There are numerous other references beyond these, but one may deduce from these verses that Joseph remained an important figure long after his death.

Joseph was a remarkable Old Testament character. Hastings describes him as "the true son, the true brother, the true servant." Characteristics listed are: "loyal and faithful, disinterested and sincere, modest and considerate" (*Hastings Dictionary of the Bible, Volume 2*, page 770). Joseph was all these things and more. We discover only one black mark on his career, his filling the coffers of Pharaoh by taking advantage of people impoverished by famine.

Perhaps this is why his sons are not part of the most prominent families of Holy Writ. They might have noted this discrimination more than the virtues of their father. Children often do, especially when they reach the age to declare their own personal freedom from the family of their childhood.

At one period in Israel's history, Ephraim was the most powerful and important tribe in the north, distinguished by wealth, influence, political and military power. Joshua, the great leader who followed Moses, was the son of Nun, of the tribe of Ephraim. He was one of the two spies who believed Canaan could be taken with God's help. Samuel, the kingmaker, also came from this tribe.

The tribe of Manasseh appears never to have gained great prominence. They are mentioned numerous times in conquests, but never as outstanding people. However, Gideon, the judge who conquered the Midianites, came from this tribe.

For our study of families, it might be well to note that at one period in Israel's early history, the tribes of Manasseh, Ephraim and Benjamin considered themselves a unit. So we observe the close ties of Rachel's sons even into later tribal history.

Perhaps it would be well to mention here, as we shall later in the study also, that sons of great men often fail to reach the level of prominence achieved by their fathers. Why?

We have no "Thus saith the Lord," to prove our thoughts, only speculation as a result of observation and reason. Fathers who gain fame through their exploits are often very poor fathers. They spend no time with their families because of their driving ambition. Without strong mothers, the children often fail, sometimes through rebellion, sometimes through neglect. Old Testament emphasis upon the dominant male role in society produced, with some exceptions, very few strong women. We might distinguish between strong and domineering here for the sake of understanding. Domineering mothers are not strong, just willfully determined to rule. Strong mothers, according to our personal definition, are those who have faith in God, faith in themselves and their ability to do the right thing with their children, and enough unselfishness to give up what they might like to do for the better good of producing stable, well-informed and spiritually vital families. The patriarchal system where only males were educated and deeply valued produced few such women. Thus the children suffered for moral and spiritual values just as they do in a system where no one is tending to their needs.

9

THE FAMILY OF AMRAM AND JOCHEBED

Amram and Jochebed remain somewhat obscure in the recorded history of Israel. All we know of them is their membership in the tribe of Levi—Amram was Levi's grandson—and their parentage of Moses, Aaron and Miriam.

Since the Bible is a very frank record, carefully delineating both good and evil in the lives of its heroes, we must assume Amram and Jochebed simply did nothing outstanding except for being good parents. That they were.

We are all familiar with the story of the little homemade, waterproofed basket floating in the Nile River with a three-month-old baby inside (Exod. 2:1ff.). How carefully Jochebed had planned! If only the princess were attracted to her baby, his life would be saved!

So we note the first characteristic of this couple, intelligence. The plan was carefully orchestrated by Miriam's presence to watch its results.

We observe two more characteristics of this family in the Biblical scene. Hiding the baby for three months and placing him at the princess' habitual bathing spot demanded courage. Miriam showed unusual bravery also. She stepped forward, appearing brazen to the princess and her companions no doubt, when she suggested a nurse for the child.

At this point, let us stray a bit to Moses' adoptive mother. She, too, possessed outstanding qualities. She surely knew Miriam was the baby's sister and the suggested nurse his mother. What other reason might the little girl have had for being there, for speaking up so promptly? Oh yes, she knew. But her loving and compassionate heart caused her to allow the Hebrew mother, Jochebed, to keep the baby for the early period of his life. One must admire Pharaoh's daughter. She, too, had courage, the courage to defy her father's monstrous decree bringing death to the Hebrew babies.

We might yearn to know in our study of families exactly how long Amram and Jochebed kept Moses in their home before returning him to Pharaoh's daughter. Surely he was a fairly young child when he moved into the palace. Yet his father and mother had trained him so well in their religious faith and family history that he maintained his allegiance to the Hebrew people even after years of Egyptian education under the most noted of their teachers (Acts 7:22). Most children, elevated from slavery to royalty at such an early age, would tend to blot out their roots, but not Moses.

Moses, admittedly, had a remarkable mind. But we need to see in this story the importance of pre-school moral and spiritual training in the life of a child. Competently done, such training is not easily erased. Another interesting aspect should make us aware of parental involvement in molding the child. Amram and Jochebed were not highly educated, outstanding people. They were humble slaves. All they had to work with was total commitment to their family and love for the endangered baby plus their faith in the eternal plan of God. What a success story!

God's plan for His people can be followed in the lives of this relatively unknown couple and their famous children. However, had they failed in their courage and commitment, God would have used a different family. Throughout the entire Bible we must deal with God's gift of free will to mankind. No one, not even God, forced Amram and Jochebed and their children to toe the mark. Only willing service counts with God.

After Moses killed the Egyptian taskmaster and fled to the wilderness, he spent forty years learning how to exist in a hostile environment. Such training made him a competent wilderness leader. His Egyptian education provided knowledge for his confrontation with Pharaoh. His deep faith, planted by his Hebrew family, made him God's chosen man and gave him the stability to endure.

Moses stood head and shoulders above the other men of his day in almost every aspect of personality. His education in the Egyptian palace put him in an idol-worshiping environment during the period most of us consider to be the most formative stage of development in a child. Yet he never compromised with idol worship and repeatedly warned against it as a leader of the Israelites. His depth far surpassed that of Miriam and Aaron. But, they, too, were outstanding leaders with only a few serious mistakes on their record.

Miriam was probably the oldest of Amram and Jochebed's children. She is described as a prophetess, a dancer, a singer and a leader in Exodus 15:20.

The Biblical account deals quite frankly with family discord in this story. Aaron and Miriam sought popularity with the people. The golden calf resulted. They also feared God. Thus the concoction of the myth of a golden calf that leaped out of the fire.

In their rebellion against Moses over his marriage to the Cushite woman, Miriam and Aaron declared, "Has the Lord spoken only through Moses? Has He not spoken through us as well?" (Num. 12:2). God heard the jealous tirade and struck Miriam with leprosy. No doubt she made more of a fuss than Aaron to have been so severely punished.

In spite of their attacks upon him, Moses prayed for his brother and sister. Miriam was healed through his pleas. No further rebellion or jealousy from them is recorded.

It is interesting to assess talents of this family. According to the Biblical writer, Moses may have been less gifted with obvious talent. Aaron was eloquent. Moses was slow of speech. Aaron and Miriam both sang and danced well. Little mention is made of this gift for Moses. He did some singing but the author indicates that the other two took more leadership in this area. All of them were gifted people, but one verse in Numbers reveals the basic difference. "Now the man Moses was very humble, more than any man who was on the face of the earth" (Num. 12:3). God respects and rewards humility.

One troublesome point in a discussion of families is Moses' relationship with his wife, Zipporah, and their sons, Gershom and Eliezer. After his marriage to Zipporah, daughter of Jethro, priest of Midian and Moses' benefactor, he lived as a shepherd for a number of years. Then God called Moses to lead his people out of bondage in Egypt.

Very little reference to Zipporah and Moses' sons appears after Moses assumed his leadership stance. Exodus 18:2-27 reveals the visit of Jethro to Moses' encampment, bringing Zipporah and the sons. Verse 2 states, "And Jethro, Moses' father-in-law, took Moses' wife Zipporah, after he had sent her away." A serious discussion about methods of government ensues between Jethro and Moses. However, we read nothing about whether or not Moses greeted his wife happily. She disappears from the account.

Did Zipporah die? Was she unable to adjust to the change of lifestyle? Had they been apart so long and Moses' duties become so pressing they couldn't make it any longer? Or did Zipporah simply fade into the background of a busy man's life? The 4th chapter of Exodus records Zipporah's rebellion against circumcision for her son. This occurred following Moses' call to lead the people. It may be that Zipporah objected to the whole thing and never adjusted to the new way of life, resulting in Moses' sending her and the boys home to her father. Eliezer and Gershom appear in later accounts, but never in an outstanding role.

Reading this story, one is forced to wonder about Moses' personal life. Due to our greater knowledge of the human personality today, we must contemplate the possibility Moses was unable to handle intimate relationships well because of the insecurity of his childhood, when he was torn between two ways of life and two beliefs. Perhaps his single-minded leadership of a complaining, rebellious people ruled out any time for personal relationships. At any rate, we read no record of success for Moses as a husband and father. Both roles appear unimportant in his life.

Josephus states that Miriam was the wife of Hur and grand-mother of Bezalel. The Biblical scribe makes no mention of this.

Aaron married Elisheba and fathered Nadab, Abihu, Eleazar and Ithamar. They became prominent in the tabernacle worship when the family of Aaron assumed responsibility there in accordance with God's command.

Leviticus 10 tells the story of the death of Nadab and Abihu because they failed to follow God's orders for their priestly office. Eleazar, Aaron's third son, and Ithamar, the fourth son, became the chief assistants to Aaron. When Aaron died, Eleazar succeeded him in all his priestly duties, helping Moses number the people. He also aided Joshua after the death of Moses.

All the high priests of Israel were descendants of Eleazer until the Maccabeean period except for the high priests between Eli and Solomon. During that time, it appears descendants of Ithamar occupied the office. According to Exodus 38:21, Numbers 4:28, and Numbers 7:8, Ithamar took charge of the tabernacle and all its equipment during the nation's wanderings in the wilderness. So Aaron did produce a line of servants to God even though his first and second sons failed.

In assessment of this family several important evidences appear. Amram and Jochebed taught their children well, creating leadership for a suffering people in a very humble home. The genes had to be good. This family enters history as superbly talented people.

The spiritual life of the family must have been superior. Except for a couple of lapses, all of the children of Amram and Jochebed remained true to their faith, often under very trying circumstances. Moses, particularly, had a unique personal relationship with God. Amram and Jochebed must have inspired their children to strive for success, both spiritually and materially. Their accomplishments indicate amazing drive.

Now comes the sad part. A pair of humble slaves produced outstanding leaders. Three outstanding leaders produced few offspring who carried on that ambitious tradition.

Why?

10

OLD TESTAMENT LAW AND FAMILIES

When we read of Moses' deliverance of Israel from bond-age in Egypt, one aspect that appears right at the beginning is the emphasis upon family units. The tenth plague visited upon the Egyptians was a family plague, the death of the first born in each family. The onset of deliverance through God came first through the family. Application of the blood of the passover lamb to the doorpost spared the first born of each Israelite family from death. Here again we observe God's special emphasis upon the family unit as the basic structure of civilization. In Exodus 12, when the Passover is instituted, instructions are given for individual families, not a great gathering together for feasting.

Exodus 13 sets apart the first born of each family as dedicated to God, a way of perpetuating religious life from generation to generation. Animals were to be sacrificed. Human beings were to be redeemed. In fact, Leviticus 20:2 expressly forbids human sacrifices as some had done to the god Molech.

Exodus 20 brings us to the ten commandments. When Jehovah commanded the people to worship only Him, a frightening statement is recorded. ". . . for I, the Lord your God, am a jealous God, visiting the iniquity of the fathers on the children, on the third and fourth generations of those who hate Me, but showing lovingkindness to thousands, to those who love Me and keep My commandments" (Exod. 20:5, 6). For those of us who have lived a long time, no explanation of that Scripture is necessary. We have all seen the results of Godless parenting upon generations of children.

Even the commands for Sabbath observance come on a family basis. ". . . you shall not do any work, you or your son or your daughter, your male servant or your female servant or your cattle or your sojourner who stays with you" (Exod. 20:10).

Basic structure of the family relies upon kindly discipline instigated by parents whom children respect. "Honor your father and your mother that your days may be prolonged in the land which the Lord your God gives you" (Exod. 20:12). God again places His benediction upon the family and parental responsibility as He promises rewards to obedient children.

The rest of the commandments might be classed as individual until the final one on coveting. Again the family assumes supreme importance. Coveting one's neighbor's possessions, particularly his wife, might result in utter destruction of that neighbor's family. Our age needs greater emphasis upon this teaching. We need to advise our young people to look over available life partners very carefully. But, after a decision is made, QUIT LOOKING!

Obedience to God forms the foundation of the ten commandments. Respect for those with whom we share the world arises on the rock of faith in Him. Strong moral fiber constructs lasting homes on the basic principles found here.

One of the difficult laws with which we deal may be found in Exodus 21.

> If you buy a Hebrew slave, he shall serve for six years; but on the seventh he shall go out as a free man without payment. If he comes alone, he shall go out alone; if he is the husband of a wife, then his wife shall go out with him. If his master gives him a wife, and she bears him sons or daughters, the wife and her children shall belong to her master, and he shall go out alone (Exod. 21:2-4).

In the next two verses provision is made for the man to remain a slave permanently to preserve his family. However, no provision appears for the owner to free the wife and children to avoid separation of the family unit. Everything is slanted for the owner. This Scripture was used in the years preceding the Civil War in the southern United States to justify the practice of selling members of slave families separately.

Fathers could legally sell daughters and female slaves were not to be freed. However, if they didn't please their masters when sold as wives or concubines, women could not be sold to strangers but must be returned to their own families. If men bought girls for their sons, they had to treat those girls as daughters (Exod. 21:7-9). Since women were not taught to earn a living, this law might be construed as protective of the female in a male-dominated society.

Any man who took a second wife was not permitted to deny food, clothing or conjugal rights to his first wife (Exod.

21:10). This again set the Hebrews apart from the others of their era. Women had no such protection in most cultures of that time.

Any son who struck his father or mother or cursed either of them was to be given the death penalty (Exod. 21:12, 17).

Preservation of family life is stressed by demand for gentle treatment for pregnant women (Exod. 21:22). Sanctity of the home prevails as the law declares a man who strikes a thief engaged in breaking into his home is not responsible if the thief dies as a result of the blow (Exod. 22:2).

The laws of the priesthood also were family oriented because only the family of Aaron performed the priestly duties. That family, possessing no land, was to be supported by the tithes of the other families. Since worship was at the very center of Old Testament life, it seems significant that a family was selected to be at the hub of that worship.

Leviticus 12 describes purification of mothers following childbirth. Attitudes toward the superiority of the male over the female appear here with forty days required for separation following the birth of a male and eighty days for a female. We find these rituals difficult to understand. However, the purification rites probably preserved life due to the lack of knowledge in that era of sanitation in obstetrics. Childbed fever killed mothers right up to the time of sterile techniques in delivery in the 20th century. Another interesting speculation arises here. Of course, it is nothing but speculation. Only in our lifetime has it been determined that the sperm of the father uniting with the ovum of the mother creates one sex or the other, for the sperm carries the sex factor in its makeup. During this purification period of the mother following birth of a baby, the father was denied sex relationships. Perhaps he was disgusted with a mother

108

who delivered a female, but he was denied sexual experience for the eighty days following that little girl's birth. Another very protective law for mothers may be observed here. Sex relations earlier than the forty days, at least, might have been very painful. Men with little or no knowledge of such things might have demanded it anyway. So the law preserved life and protected women from pain.

Leviticus 15 regulates cleanliness in personal relationships also. These rituals, too, probably were aimed at stamping out the spread of disease in addition to recognition of the right of God to set up rules for personal and family living.

Leviticus 18 identifies forbidden sexual practices. Here again we observe protective walls built around the family unit. Homosexuality is strictly banned. This is family protection. Were homosexuality to become normal rather than deviate behavior, there would be no families. Various forms of incest, so destructive of family life, are also prohibited in chapter 18 of Leviticus.

Warnings against harlotry in Leviticus charge fathers not to degrade their daughters by making harlots of them (Lev. 19:29). One cannot help recalling Lot and his daughters in Sodom. The stamp of God's disapproval of such attitudes is displayed here.

Respect for the aged is commanded in Leviticus 19:32 along with reverence for God. There's food for thought here. Do the two things necessarily go together?

In Leviticus 20, we again observe family protection in law. Verse 9 repeats the decree about cursing one's parents. Verse 10 demands the death penalty for adulterers and much of the chapter damns all sorts of incestuous relationships. Sodomy is punishable by death in verse 13.

Leviticus 21 again stresses the importance of family by permitting priests to handle the dead of their own immediate

109

families but no one else. The high priest may not approach any dead person, not even his father or mother.

Modern science has shown the danger of handling dead bodies in certain diseases. Ancient laws that appear arbitrary actually preserved the lives of God's people in many instances. The high priest was extremely important to the worship and instruction of the people in worship. This law probably preserved the lives of many high priests throughout the history of the Hebrew people.

This chapter sets up rules for the priestly families. Prohibition of marriage to divorcees or harlots is not mentioned for other men. For priests, it is forbidden (Lev. 21:7). Daughters of priests who engage in harlotry are to be burned, for they profane their fathers as well as themselves (Lev. 21:9).

The high priest is ordered to marry only a virgin. He must not marry even a widow (Lev. 21:13, 14). Anyone in a priestly family who had a defect could remain in the family and eat and serve in other ways but must not approach the altar.

As one pursues regulations as to religious observances, the importance attributed to the family unit arises again. All of the feasts centered in the family and were participated in by the family. The Old Testament continually urges marrying those of one's own nation and faith. A faithful Hebrew centered his personal life, his family life and his national life in God.

A very interesting incident occurs in Numbers 27. Zelophehad of the tribe of Manasseh died in the wilderness leaving five daughters and no sons. These women, Mahlah, Noah, Hoglah, Milcah and Tirzah, protested to Moses when they received no land among their tribe.

110

And Moses brought their case before the Lord. Then the Lord spoke to Moses saying, "The daughters of Zelophehad are right in their statements. You shall surely give them a hereditary possession among their father's brothers, and you shall transfer his inheritance to his daughters. And if he has no daughter, then you shall give his inheritance to his brothers. And if he has no brothers, then you shall give his inheritance to his father's brothers. And if his father has no brothers, then you shall give his inheritance to his nearest relative in his own family, and he shall possess it; and it shall be a statutory ordinance to the sons of Israel just as the Lord commanded Moses" (Num. 27:5-11).

In chapter 36, brotherless daughters are commanded to marry within their own tribes so inheritances of land and wealth would not move from one tribe to another causing discord and jealousy among the tribes.

This law did not establish equality in the family for daughters, but it did at least remove some of the stigma upon females by permitting them to inherit. This law also strengthened the family unit where there were no male heirs by removing destitution and poverty after the death of the last male member.

Another interesting law appears in Numbers 30. Men are totally responsible for the fulfillment of any vow they make. However, a father or husband may nullify any vow taken by a woman. Numbers 30:15 declares, "But if he indeed annuls them after he has heard them, then he shall bear her guilt."

Husbands and fathers were indeed the heads of families. They were required to assume all responsibility, even to the vows of their wives. This probably created strong, if sometimes domineering, men. Did it result in weak women unable to assume responsibility for their own actions?

111

In Deuteronomy 6:6-9, the people are commanded to teach God's law to their children in order to perpetuate God's way of life in the nation. The home was to form the center for religious instructions. In verses 20-28, the fathers are ordered to tell the story of their deliverance from bondage in Egypt through God's help to all generations of sons.

Deuteronomy 11 again stresses teaching the law to their children in the home. Verses 18-21 reiterate the method of teaching as given in the sixth chapter, promising rewards to those who continue to serve the Lord. Worshiping God in His sanctuary is commanded for families.

> But you shall seek the Lord at the place which the Lord your God shall choose from all your tribes, to establish His name there for His dwelling, and there you shall come. And there you shall bring your burnt offerings, your sacrifices, your tithes, the contribution of your hand, your votive offerings, your freewill offerings, and the first-born of your herd and of your flock. There also you and your households shall eat before the Lord your God, and rejoice in all your undertakings in which the Lord your God has blessed you (Deut. 12:5-7).

Deuteronomy 21:15-17 recalls to our minds Jacob's favoritism for the sons of Rachel as compared to those of Leah and the maids. In these verses, the law expressly forbids such discrimination.

The law provided for the stoning of a stubborn and rebellious son who would not obey his parents. One of the interesting items about family law is its insistence upon children's obedience and respect for their mother as well as father although most of the laws made women subservient.

Deuteronomy 22:13-30 deals with all types of immorality in its relationship to the family; men who reject their brides and lie about the women's purity, women who are impure, adultery, fornication, rape and incest.

The first five verses of Deuteronomy 24 deal with marriage, divorce and remarriage. Verse five issues permission for a year's honeymoon for a newly married couple, thus demonstrating the importance the ancients placed upon starting a marriage properly.

Chapter 25 of Deuteronomy establishes a brother's responsibility to his dead brother's widow in verses 5 through 10. This seems strange in our culture. However, in the primitive culture where a woman's livelihood depended upon a man to support her, and children to care for her in her old age, the law was probably quite protective of women.

Much of the last part of the book of Deuteronomy warns against allowing their families and descendants to stray from God.

Although we have barely touched the surface in the legal system of the Hebrews, we have been able to see that many of the laws actually were designed for the preservation of the family with a view to high moral living and dedication to God. Truly the Old Testament stresses the value of the family to society as a whole. Since our modern systems of law come from the Judeo-Christian traditions, we would do well to study some of these laws carefully for their value to us as individuals and as families. Naturally, some of them are geared to their culture and seem less valuable to ours.

11

FAMILIES IN THE BOOK OF JUDGES

A number of families make their appearance in Judges, but few of them remain prominent for any more than a brief period. In the early chapters, intermarriage with idol worshipers becomes the rule rather than the exception. We find few leaders with influence reaching beyond their own generation.

Othniel is described as bearing "the Spirit of the Lord," and rescuing his people from the Mesopotamians (Judg. 3:10). Apparently Othniel raised no dedicated son to follow in God's way. After forty years, Othniel died. The people flocked to the worship of foreign gods.

Following eighteen years of oppression under the Moabites, Ehud, son of Gera of the tribe of Benjamin, rescued them by killing Eglon, king of Moab, and defeating his army.

Shamgar, son of Anath, also helped by killing six hundred Philistines. Israel had peace for eighty years. Ehud died. No strength appears to have been passed on to his family or associates. Idol worship returned. Israel fell again to Jabin, king of Canaan and his army commander, Sisera. They were oppressed for twenty years.

Then came Deborah, wife of Lappidoth, "a mother in Israel" (Judg. 5:7). With Barak leading the armies and Deborah acting as judge, they overthrew the nation's enemies. The land was undisturbed for forty years. Perhaps Deborah was more successful at judging than parenting. No record appears to identify any of her children as leaders, ready to carry on in God's way after her death.

Again the nation pursued evil ways. Midian conquered them, and they were in submission to Midian for seven years. At this point, Gideon, from the tribe of Manasseh, arose to save them.

The Bible reveals something of Gideon's family as well as his conquests. Judges 8:22, 23 discloses the spirit of Gideon. "Then the men of Israel said to Gideon, 'Rule over us, both you and your son, also your son's son, for you have delivered us from the hand of Midian.' But Gideon said to them, 'I will not rule over you, nor shall my son rule over you; the Lord shall rule over you.'"

In the days of Gideon all went well. However, other revealing sentences appear in Judges 8:30, 31. "Now Gideon had seventy sons who were his direct descendants, for he had many wives. And his concubine who was in Shechem also bore him a son, and he named him Abimelech."

Verse 33 states, "Then it came about as soon as Gideon was dead, that the sons of Israel again played the harlot with the Baals and made Baal-berith their god." Apparently

116

Gideon's insistence that God should rule the people did not impress either them or his children.

Here again we observe the emotional impact of the polygamous family, particularly the anger that consumes the son with least status, the child of the concubine. Arousing relatives of his mother to proclaim him king, Abimelech attacked his half-brothers. Judges 9:4 says, "And they gave him seventy pieces of silver from the house of Baal-berith with which Abimelech hired worthless and reckless fellows, and they followed him." In other words, his bid for power was financed at the temple of one of the idols. Abimelech and his motley crew killed all the brothers except Jotham, the youngest, who fled after delivering a prophetic curse upon Abimelech.

Abimelech's rule lasted just three years before he was destroyed. He obviously was a great warrior, but a woman finally dropped a millstone on his head. With his last breath he begged his armor bearer to slay him so no one would know he had met his fate at the hands of a woman.

This is just one more story of a great leader, Gideon this time, whose desires for many women destroyed the family he created. In polygamous relationships we find little evidence of real love, mostly lust. His sons did not love each other because no real love had existed in their home from which they might learn. Statements become trite because they are true. What Gideon did in his personal life spoke so loud his sons couldn't hear what he said.

The scripture mentions Tola of the tribe of Issachar who judged Israel for twenty-three years. No reference to children appears. Tola was succeeded by Jair of Gilead, the father of thirty sons. He judged for twenty-two years.

Again Israel turned to the Baals, the Ashtaroth, the gods of Syria, the gods of Sidon, the gods of Moab, the gods of Ammon and the gods of the Philistines. It seems they could

117

not remain true without strong leaders and their leaders were too busy with their own lives to rear stable sons or train their successors. For eighteen years the Israelites suffered at the hands of their enemies.

At this point in the narrative of Judges, we meet Jephthah. The first item of note in our family study comes from Jephthah's illegitimacy. He was the son of a harlot. Judges 11:2, 3 states,

> And Gilead's wife bore him sons; and when his wife's sons grew up, they drove Jephthah out and said to him, "You shall not have an inheritance in our father's house for you are the son of another woman." So Jephthah fled from his brothers and lived in the land of Tob; and worthless fellows gathered themselves about Jephthah, and they went out with him.

We understand a young man's heartache as described in a few cryptic phrases in this study. Rejection of illegitimate children by families still happens in our society. Instead of denying the adult who created the situation, relatives often blame the child who results from an illicit relationship. Such rejection may push that child one of two ways; superior achievement to prove his or her worthiness, or rebellion against society because of the pain of separation.

Jephthah seemed to go both routes. He became a strong leader. The oppressed Israelites turned to him when the Ammonites attacked. Was this similar to asking a gang leader in New York City or Chicago to help the police fight crime? It looks that way. Such incidents may be identified in the annals of police history also.

Jephthah's reply was poignant when they requested him to be their battle chief.

> . . . "Did you not hate me and drive me from my father's house? So why have you come to me now when you are in trouble?" And the elders of Gilead said to Jephthah, "For

118

this reason we have now returned to you, that you may go with us and fight with the sons of Ammon and become head over all the inhabitants of Gilead." So Jephthah said to the elders of Gilead, "If you take me back to fight against the sons of Ammon, and the Lord gives them up to me, will I become your head?" And the elders of Gilead said to Jephthah, "The Lord is witness between us; surely we will do as you have said" (Judg. 11:7-10).

Jephthah tried to establish peace with their enemies by negotiations, but his messages were disregarded. Then God gave him victory in battle. But Jephthah had made a vow. He had declared he would sacrifice the first person who came out of his house upon his return from battle if only the Lord would make him victorious. When he returned home, his daughter, his only child, ran out the door to greet her father. Jephthah, although devastated by grief, kept his vow.

For our purpose of studying Biblical families, several things emerge from this story. The first is the prejudice and unkind discrimination of the people against Jephthah due to his illegitimacy. Hebrew law condemned the person who engaged in illicit sex. The people condemned the child who had nothing to do with his conception.

His relatives rejected Jephthah and drove him away until they needed him. Loving and courageous, were they not? God seems to have accepted him all the time. But Jephthah, steeped in the emotional agony of human rejection, apparently feared lack of acceptance by God. Hence the foolish vow!

Now we move into conjecture. Since Jephthah was illegitimate and rejected, was he also untaught? We have no way of knowing how old he was when driven from his home. Did they send him away before he had the opportunity to know Hebrew law?

God had forbidden human sacrifices. Yet Jephthah, after his terrible vow, sincerely believed God would punish him and the people were he to fail to keep that promise. Even his daughter believed this. Could her death be laid at the feet of senseless prejudice resulting in ignorance? Or was Jephthah part of the Hebrew group who had lost contact with covenant law? It could be either. Whatever the root cause, a lovely girl died because God's law was unknown to her people. One of the major lessons for us to learn from this story, however, is the possible far-reaching effects of senseless prejudice in family relationships.

A period of relative calm prevails in Israel as several somewhat obscure judges enter the story. Families are mentioned, but no greatness worthy of note.

Most of Judges 13 is devoted to the angelic prediction of Samson's birth to Manoah and his wife of the tribe of Dan. The last two verses, 24 and 25, record Samson's birth and the fact that the "Spirit of the Lord began to stir him." Samson turned out to be mighty as a warrior although extremely foolish about women. As with many men before and since, his lust for unfaithful women destroyed him. He left no family that is recorded for our study.

The final family story in Judges comes from a Levite who took a concubine from Bethlehem. She, after being unfaithful to him, returned to her father's house. He went to get her. After several days' delay, they began their journey home. They were spending the night with an old man who had come from the land of Ephraim but was living in Gibeah, part of the territory of Benjamin. Some immoral men approached the house, demanding the old man give them the Levite for sexual purposes. We find a repeat of the Genesis story of Lot's daughters. The old man offered his virgin daughter and the Levite's concubine.

The men wouldn't listen. The host grabbed the concubine and took her out to the mob. ". . . they raped her and abused her all night until morning, then let her go at the approach of dawn" (Judg. 19:25).

The concubine died. The Levite took her body home and dismembered it, cutting it into twelve pieces and sending one to each tribe. The result was war when the Benjamites refused to give the guilty men to the other tribes for punishment. Great slaughter resulted. The Benjamites were finally restored to the nation in Judges 21.

The book of Judges ends with a thought-provoking statement. "In those days there was no king in Israel; everyone did what was right in his own eyes" (Judg. 21:25). Without authority centered in God and discipline meted out by loving, godly parents, chaos results both in the family and in the nation.

Our study so far has caused us to develop several conclusions from these stories of families in the Bible. No family can be completely happy or stable without discipline rooted in faith in almighty God, no matter how prosperous or apparently successful materially that family may be. Permissive attitudes with children didn't work for the ancients. They won't work for us either. Parents who accomplish great deeds in their society while neglecting their children are failures in a foremost responsibility entrusted to them by God. There is no substitute for the stability provided by conscientious and happy family living.

12

RUTH, NAOMI AND BOAZ

Our knowledge of this family originates in the Book of Ruth with Elimelech and his wife Naomi to whom had been born two sons, Mahlon and Chilion. Although natives of Bethlehem, they moved to Moab due to a famine in their own land. Elimelech died. Mahlon and Chilion married Moabite women, Ruth and Orpah.

The Bible says the family lived in Moab about ten years before Mahlon and Chilion died. Naomi, learning the famine was over, decided to return to Bethlehem. For a while the daughters-in-law accompanied Naomi on her journey. However, the older woman insisted they return to Moab.

". . . 'Go, return each of you to her mother's house. May the Lord deal kindly with you as you have dealt with the dead and with me. May the Lord grant that you may find rest each in the house of her husband.' Then she kissed them, and they lifted up their voices and wept" (Ruth 1:8, 9).

Both of the younger women protested Naomi's decision, but she insisted, telling them she could produce no more sons for them to marry, so they'd have no personal life by accompanying her. Orpah kissed Naomi good-by and walked away.

> . . . but Ruth clung to her. Then she said, "Behold, your sister-in-law has gone back to her people and her gods; return after your sister-in-law."
>
> But Ruth said, "Do not urge me to leave you or turn back from following you; for where you go, I will go, and where you lodge, I will lodge. Your people shall be my people, and your God, my God. Where you die, I will die, and there I will be buried. Thus may the Lord do to me, and worse, if anything but death parts you and me" (Ruth 1:15-17).

Why did Naomi, a devout Hebrew, tell the two young women she loved to return to their homes and *to their gods?* We have no explanation for that part of the story. Naomi appears to have known Hebrew law, as proved by the remainder of the account.

When Ruth arrived in Bethlehem with Naomi, it was barley harvest time. Again covenant law enters the picture. Ruth went to the fields to glean. The law forbade denial of the rights of the poor to pick up the harvest left-overs. Ruth and Naomi depended upon this law to avoid discrimination against Ruth's gleaning. Ruth happened upon the field of Boaz, who belonged to the family of Elimelech.

While Ruth gleaned, Boaz visited the field to greet his workers. He noticed Ruth, included her in the conversation and asked a servant who she was. The servant explained Ruth's relationship to Naomi. Boaz talked with Ruth, insisting she stay in his fields and eat and drink with his people. Let us continue with the Bible itself.

> Then she fell on her face, bowing to the ground and said to him, "Why have I found favor in your sight that you should take notice of me, since I am a foreigner?"
>
> And Boaz answered and said to her, "All that you have done for your mother-in-law after the death of your husband has been fully reported to me, and how you left your father and your mother and the land of your birth, and came to a people that you did not previously know. May the Lord reward your work, and your wages be full from the Lord, the God of Israel, under whose wings you have come to seek refuge" (Ruth 2:10-12).

Boaz instructed his servants to pull grain from their bundles so Ruth might get better portions. He also served good food to her at mealtime from his own hand.

Naomi was thrilled when Ruth told her experiences of the day. Since Hebrew law decreed the nearest kinsman of her husband take a widow into his home, marry her, and raise sons for his kinsman, Naomi told Ruth to follow the custom of the day by offering herself to Boaz when he rested one night on the threshing floor. She was to lie down at his feet and uncover them.

Boaz certainly responded to Ruth's interest in him. However, he had to pass one hurdle. There was a nearer kinsman. Chapter four delineates Boaz's skillful handling of the relative. Then he married Ruth. Let us return to the Biblical narrative.

> So Boaz took Ruth, and she became his wife, and he went in to her. And the Lord enabled her to conceive, and she gave birth to a son. Then the women said to Naomi, "Blessed is the Lord who has not left you without a redeemer today, and my his name become famous in Israel. May he

125

also be to you a restorer of life and a sustainer of your old age; for your daughter-in-law, who loves you and is better to you than seven sons, has given birth to him." . . . And the neighbor women gave him a name, saying, "A son has been born to Naomi! . . ." (Ruth 4:13-15, 17).

Ruth, the Moabitess, became an ancestress of Jesus. Her son, Obed, was King David's grandfather. Through the line of David came the Savior.

For our purpose of learning from Biblical families, let us assess this story and its leading characters. Perhaps no greater problem rears its ugly head in our culture today than mother-in-law, daughter-in-law controversy. Yet the Book of Ruth narrates a love story between two women whose only relationship came as in-laws. Earlier in this manuscript, we encountered problems in the same area. Remember how Rebekah felt about the wives of Esau? Identical basic difficulties of understanding exist in both stories. Yet the outcome is totally different.

Esau's wives came from a pagan nation of idol worshipers. Their customs and beliefs differed radically from those of Isaac and Rebekah. Ruth and Orpah had been reared in Moab among idol worshipers. They had been taught a totally different set of values from the Hebrew family into which they married.

Rebekah protested that Jacob must marry from his own people or she would want to die. Esau's wives had kept her life from being worth living. Naomi had known nothing but kindness from both daughters-in-law, coupled with absolute loyalty from Ruth.

What was the difference?

Let's look at Naomi. When Mahlon and Chilion brought Ruth and Orpah home, Naomi's authority might have been absolute had she chosen to exercise it. Customs of the ancients decreed this. What sort of woman was Naomi?

After the death of her husband and her sons, when Naomi decided to return to her own land, she could have demanded that her daughters-in-law accompany her and care for her on the journey. She didn't. Instead, she thought of them and their future, insisting they return to their parents.

What a lonely trek she faced across the wilderness to her own land! How devastated she must have felt after losing those dearest to her! But, instead of wallowing in self-pity, she placed the welfare of her daughters-in-law above her own. Whatever our reaction to Naomi's suggestion that the two younger women return to their families and gods, we observe a woman with an open mind, an honest respect for those with differing opinions, a totally unselfish and thoughtful lady. Somehow we are sure no slurs as to their ancestry ever upset her in-laws while they lived with her. Naomi was a rare woman indeed, quite different from Rebekah who was willing even to deceive her husband in achieving her own and her favored son's aims.

We know almost no details concerning the wives of Esau but we discover a number of personality factors about Ruth. When Naomi insisted Ruth return to her own family, we think we may assume comfort and hope awaited her there. At least, Naomi's conversation would so indicate. Ruth refused security and comfort, opting for a long, tiring journey with an unknown quantity as its destination. She gave completely unselfish devotion to an old lady who could offer her nothing in return except companionship. Ruth, loving her so dearly, refused to allow Naomi to attempt the trip alone.

So, we are dealing with two remarkable women; selfless and loving, courageous and loyal, devoted and venturesome.

127

No wonder they got along well as in-laws. Neither was determined to rule.

One would like to have more information about the ten years spent in Moab. What enabled Naomi to keep a God-fearing household in a pagan land with two daughters-in-law who had been reared believing in other gods? What type of extended family relationship created such outstanding loyalty in Ruth? What sort of spiritual emphasis in the home caused Ruth to declare, "Your God shall be my God"?

The Bible answers none of these questions. All we are given is vignettes of personality, two loving and responsible women. One thing we may be sure of. Naomi sincerely lived what she professed.

The Book of Ruth, if intelligently studied, will help with in-law problems. In most areas of family strife, proper attention to the needs of other members of the family and less concentration upon one's own demands will accomplish miracles in the establishment of rewarding relationships. Ruth and Naomi got along well because both were exemplary and worked at it.

A third very strong character emerges from this love story, Boaz. He immediately noticed Ruth when she gleaned in his field. In many Biblical accounts involving women, the sacred scribe describes them as beautiful or pleasing to the eye or some other accolade of personal appearance. Nothing of that type appears in regard to Ruth. She may have been beautiful. Perhaps that is why Boaz noticed her. Yet the more we read about Boaz, the more inclined we are to think he simply was a man who was aware of others, especially those in need.

Boaz was probably older than Ruth. We note that when he talks.

And it happened in the middle of the night that the man was startled and bent forward; and behold, a woman was lying at his feet. And he said, "Who are you?" And she answered, "I am Ruth your maid. So spread your covering over your maid, for you are a close relative."

Then he said, "May you be blessed of the Lord, my daughter. You have shown your last kindness to be better than the first by not going after *young men,* whether poor or rich. And now, my daughter, do not fear. I will do for you whatever you ask, for all my people in the city know that you are a woman of excellence" (Ruth 3:8-11).

Not one word of superiority due to his prosperity and her destitute state!

His careful notice of her kindness to Naomi when she first gleaned in his field, then his acceptance of her offer of herself to him, not on the basis of physical attraction, but because of her excellent character, draw a clear picture of the depth of the man. We see even further evidence of this in his acceptance of Naomi to the degree that all the neighbor women spoke of Obed as her child.

Another remarkable tribute to Ruth appears in the story. In a time when women were considered less than valuable, Naomi's friends spoke of Ruth as being worth more than seven sons! No greater compliment could have been given in that culture.

What a beautiful family story! Would that all mothers-in-law and daughters-in-law might profit from it!

13

THE FAMILY OF ELI

The first few chapters of I Samuel introduce us to two families. One is the family of Eli, high priest of Israel, descendant of Ithamar, Aaron's fourth son, and apparently the first high priest of that line.

Eli had two sons, Hophni and Phinehas. Both men were evil. "Now the sons of Eli were worthless men; they did not know the Lord" (I Sam. 2:12). They refused to observe the sacrifices according to the law, pilfering portions for themselves that should have been offered to God. The Bible presents a blunt description of their actions. "Thus the sin of the young men was very great before the Lord, for the men despised the offering of the Lord" (I Sam. 2:17).

The two young priests did not stop there. "Now Eli was very old; and he heard all that his sons were doing to all

Israel, and how they lay with the women who served at the doorway of the tent of meeting" (I Sam. 2:22).

Eli's sons sound like Old Testament Elmer Gantry's, don't they? It is impossible to avoid the emphasis Biblical commands place upon purity in the lives of those set apart as servants of God to minister to His people. When we read the Gospel record of the life of Christ, we note His tolerant help to common sinners. But He lashed out in anger at religious leaders who profaned God's teachings by word or action. God was equally condemning of Hophni and Phinehas. They paid for their sins with their lives. Israel also suffered for permitting such corruption. They met defeat at the hands of the Philistines. "And the ark of God was taken; and the two sons of Eli, Hophni and Phinehas, died" (I Sam. 4:11).

Eli, ninety-eight years of age and blind, heard the terrible news from a man of the tribe of Benjamin who escaped the slaughter.

> And the man said to Eli, "I am the one who came from the battle line. Indeed, I escaped from the battle line today." And he said, "How did things go, my son?" Then the one who brought the news answered and said, "Israel has fled before the Philistines and there has also been a great slaughter among the people, and your two sons also, Hophni and Phinehas, are dead, and the ark of God has been taken" (I Sam. 4:16, 17).

When he learned of the loss of the ark, "Eli fell off the seat backward beside the gate, and his neck was broken and he died for he was old and heavy . . ." (I Sam. 4:18).

Phinehas' pregnant wife gave birth when she heard the news of all the deaths. She died, but not before naming her son Ichabod, saying, "The glory has departed from Israel,

132

for the ark of God was taken" (I Sam. 4:22). We read nothing of note concerning Ichabod. However, Ahitub, Ichabod's brother, acted as priest under Saul (I Sam. 14:3).

Because we need to learn as much as possible in regard to Eli's failure as a father, let us study his personality for a while. Obviously, Eli was a kind man, sincere and morally upright in his priesthood. His belief in the power of Jehovah may be seen in his submission to God's pronouncement of doom for his house.

We may observe Eli's kindness as he deals patiently with the young Samuel. Many old men would have resented time spent with the boy, especially the effort exerted in teaching him. Eli's lovingkindness is shown even more acutely when God reveals the fact that his pupil will be his successor, not his sons. A lesser man might have taken his grief out on Samuel. Instead, when Samuel told Eli of his vision, Eli said, ". . . It is the Lord; let Him do what seems good to Him" (I Sam. 3:18).

So, how could such a good man fail? He apparently lived an exemplary life before his sons. Such a gentle man would be easy to love and respect. What happened?

The Scripture presents few cut and dried answers to problems. However, we may deduce certain facts from the story. Eli knew his sons were profaning their sacred calling, engaging in greedy demands as well as illicit sex. All he did was rebuke them in a mild-mannered way. Why didn't he remove them from their priestly duties and take over himself? He was the high priest. The authority was his.

Age changes most of us. We may become cantankerous, or we may mellow. Eli was an old man in our story. But, we must deal with the fact that his sons took a long time and a lot of practice to become so degenerate. They respected neither God nor their father.

Quite often these two aspects of personality go together. A child whose father and mother are wishy-washy in the discipline of the home generally believes God didn't mean what He said either! Hophni and Phinehas might even have misread their father. When he refused to take a firm stand on discipline, they might have interpreted his attitudes as lack of faith in God who made the rules. What would that have done to their respect for him? Consistent discipline prepares children for faith. Consistent love combined with that discipline establishes that faith. Holy Writ carefully teaches these principles.

A man who fails with his family fails with his foremost responsibility in the sight of God, for the Bible asserts over and over that God gives children to their parents.

14

THE FAMILY OF ELKANAH

We meet Elkanah and his family at the very beginning of I Samuel. "Now there was a certain man from Ramathaim-zophim from the hill country of Ephraim, and his name was Elkanah the son of Jeroham, the son of Elihu, the son of Tohu, the son of Zuph, an Ephraimite" (I Sam. 1:1).

The account informs us of Elkanah's two wives, Hannah and Peninnah. Peninnah had children, but Hannah longed for a family and had none.

This was a devout family. In accordance with the law, they traveled to Shiloh annually to worship and offer sacrifices to the Lord. We discover Elkanah's preference for Hannah in I Samuel 1:4, 5. "And when the day came that Elkanah sacrificed, he would give portions to Peninnah his wife and to all her sons and her daughters; but to Hannah he would give a double portion for he loved Hannah but the Lord had closed her womb."

In this story, as in so many others, we see favoritism and jealousy aroused by polygamy. We read nothing of any love from Elkanah for Peninnah, only moral obligation. What an onus in the lives of both of them! Peninnah had no recourse with her husband. One cannot demand or force love. So Peninnah took her jealous wrath out on the childless Hannah. Shades of Jacob, Leah and Rachel!

Reading these stories, one is forced to contemplation of reasons. Jacob did not want Leah in the first place. No detailed reports appear concerning Elkanah's marriage to Peninnah. If Hannah were the first wife, her childlessness may have created the second marriage. Children to carry on the family name and traditions assumed monumental importance in the ancient world.

It is interesting to note that husbands of that era often preferred the childless wife. Since the burden of child-rearing fell almost completely upon the mother, could it be the childless wife became less harried, more ready and open for love-making, more physically attractive because of extra time for herself?

Children in any culture make the husband-wife relationship different. Some couples have great difficulty handling those differences, especially if one or the other of them is immature or used to occupying front stage center. Men in a polygamous society were certainly accustomed to being kingpins. Men of Old Testament times wanted children, but child-bearing and child-rearing under primitive circumstances aged women early. Could this explain the preference for the childless wife?

However, out of fairness to Hannah, we should note her refusal to strike back at Peninnah. Her gentle disposition comes across clearly in the account. Rather than reminding Peninnah she remained unloved in spite of her motherhood, as many women might have done, Hannah wept and took her problem to the Lord in prayer. Hannah deserved the love she received.

When Hannah prayed for a son, she accompanied the prayer with a vow.

> . . . "O Lord of hosts, if Thou wilt indeed look on the affliction of Thy maidservant and remember me, and not forget Thy maidservant, but wilt give Thy maidservant a son, then I will give him to the Lord for all the days of his life, and a razor shall never come on his head" (I Sam. 1:11).

Hannah's distress was so marked that Eli, the old priest, thought her drunk. He reprimanded her for her drunkenness.

> But Hannah answered and said, "No, my lord, I am a woman oppressed in spirit; I have drunk neither wine nor strong drink, but I have poured out my soul before the Lord. Do not consider your maidservant as a worthless woman; for I have spoken until now out of my great concern and provocation." Then Eli answered and said, "Go in peace; and may the God of Israel grant your petition that you have asked of Him" (I Sam. 1:15-17).

The Bible tells us Hannah's face no longer reflected sadness. Even the high priest had been recruited in favor of her plea. She departed for home convinced her prayer would be answered. Eli recognized and rewarded Hannah's sincerity. So did God. Hannah gave birth to Samuel within the year.

Most Hebrew women nursed their babies for approximately three years. As soon as Hannah weaned Samuel, she took him to Eli at Shiloh.

Two important attitudes must be noted here. One is the faith of Hannah and Elkanah. How difficult it must have been to release their hold upon this longed-for, prayed-for son! But Hannah had made a vow. They kept it.

Elkanah enters this picture at the point of the vow very forcibly. Remember the Jewish law saying a wife's vow could be nullified if a husband chose to do so with the responsibility falling upon the husband? (Num. 30:15). Not only did Elkanah follow the requirement for worship, but he honored Hannah's vow to God. Elkanah was a man of deep faith. God respected their commitment by giving them three more sons and two daughters.

The second item worthy of note is Samuel's relationship with Eli. The old priest had failed miserably with his own sons. He succeeded admirably with Samuel, both in his love for the boy and his teaching. Had Eli changed? Or was Samuel a different type of child, one who responded to gentle leading and needed little stern discipline? We all know children are very different in personality and response. At any rate, Samuel grew to be all the things Eli might have wished for his own sons.

Samuel had an outstanding career. He is recognized as the last of the judges and the first of the prophets after Moses. His entire life mirrored the faith of his parents and of his tutor, Eli. However, Samuel's sons, like Eli's, lived wicked lives. Also, like Eli, Samuel tried to appoint his sons to succeed him in spite of their utter lack of qualifications for the job.

> And it came about when Samuel was old that he appointed his sons judges over Israel. Now the name of his first-born was Joel, and the name of his second, Abijah; they were judging in Beersheba. His sons, however, did not walk in

138

his ways, but turned aside after dishonest gain and took bribes and perverted justice (I Sam. 8:1-3).

When Samuel died, the influence of his family died with him. His sons had been so corrupt the nation demanded a monarchy. Samuel lived long enough to anoint the first two kings, Saul and David.

Before we leave Elkanah's family, perhaps we should raise some questions. In ancient Israel, as we have already mentioned, the primary responsibility for child-rearing fell upon mothers. Is it significant that Hannah is depicted as a dedicated, God-fearing woman while we know nothing of Eli's wife or Samuel's wife? What influence did these women exert in the downfall of their sons? Eli and Samuel were outstanding leaders with demanding careers. Were their wives discontented or weak women? During the formative years, what were they teaching their sons about God and His service? The Bible does not say, but the question needs reflection.

In a long career of Christian service, we have seen many morally upright, dedicated Christian children whose mothers radiated faith while married to less committed, or completely uncommitted men. When that situation is reversed, the outcome appears less sure. Remember the old quote, "The hand that rocks the cradle rules the world"? Mothers possess an amazing power over the destiny of the children they bear. This is not to blame mothers for every problem of their children. Too much of that has happened already. But women readers might do well to ponder the point of influence, especially in view of Biblical evidence to support it.

15

THE FAMILY OF SAUL

Saul was the son of Kish, the son of Abiel, the son of Zeror, the son of Becorath, the son of Aphiah, the son of a Benjamite. The tribe of Benjamin, renowned for being fierce and war-like, provided the first king of Israel.

Many positive observations could be made in regard to Saul. He stood head and shoulders above all the other men, a splendid kingly figure. In the beginning of his reign, Saul wore humility like a badge of valor. Perhaps, however, he was not equal to the job thrust upon him. Fears and stresses racked his body, mind and soul, resulting in his deterioration. However, our purpose is family study. What do we know about Saul's family?

"Now the sons of Saul were Jonathan and Ishvi and Malchishua; and the names of his two daughters were these:

141

the name of the first-born Merab and the name of the younger Michal. And the name of Saul's wife was Ahinoam the daughter of Ahimoaz . . . (I Sam. 14:49, 50). The Scripture also identifies Abner, the captain of Saul's army, as his cousin, son of Kish's brother, Ner.

The story of Saul's family inextricably entangles with the life of David. Jonathan became David's best friend and David married Michal. The Bible never says David loved Michal, but only that Michal loved him. Both Jonathan and Michal saved David's life when their father ordered him killed because of paranoid fears of David's usurping his kingdom. That same paranoia caused Saul to give Michal to another man. Anything he could do to David was done because of his intense hatred and jealousy.

In I Samuel 31:2, we read, "And the Philistines overtook Saul and his sons; and the Philistines killed Jonathan and Abinadab and Malchishua the sons of Saul." Abinadab was not listed in I Samuel 14, but this story of their death in battle names Abinadab as one of the sons. I Chronicles 8:33 and 9:39 list the sons of Saul as Jonathan, Malchishua, Abinadab and Eshbaal. Eshbaal and Ishbosheth are different names for the same person. Ishvi is only listed in I Samuel 14:49. No other mention of that name appears, leading some scholars to believe he may be the same person as Eshbaal and Ishbosheth.

Little is known of Merab, Saul's older daughter. She had been promised to Goliath's slayer. However, Saul reneged on his promise and gave her to Adriel, the Meholathite as his wife.

As mentioned earlier, Michal had loved David so much that she actually instigated their relationship. She saved his life. But, during all his troubles with her father, David

142

appears to have exerted no effort to get Michal and take her with him. Saul, no doubt in an attempt to insult David, gave Michal to a man named Palti as his wife.

When David ascended the throne, he demanded Michal be brought to him. Her brother, Ishbosheth, dragged her from her husband's house and delivered her to David to save his own skin. Pathos leaps out at us from the story. "But her husband went with her, weeping as he went, and followed her as far as Bahurim . . . " (II Sam. 3:16). We meet Michal for a final time in II Samuel 6:16-23. In this narrative, we are informed that she despised David and lashed out at him for behaving foolishly in her opinion.

We discover three strong children in Saul's family: Jonathan, Ishbosheth and Michal. Their strengths lay in different realms.

No other Old Testament personality supersedes Jonathan in uprightness of character. Jonathan and David were close friends; Jonathan loved David. Nothing destroyed his loyalty, no matter what the cost might be. Their friendship proved very costly to Jonathan indeed.

As Saul's eldest son, Jonathan was in direct line for the throne; and, with it, the wealth and adulation accompanying his elevation in status. His only outstanding rival for that position was his friend, David. How Saul played up the potential divisiveness of the situation! But Jonathan refused to be tempted to assassinate his friend, even saying to David at one point, "If it please my father to do you harm, may the Lord do so to Jonathan and more also, if I do not make it known to you and send you away, that you may go in safety. And may the Lord be with you as He has been with my father" (I Sam. 20:13).

When Saul accused Jonathan of disloyalty to him, of uniting with David to do his father harm, Jonathan remained at his father's side. He even died while fighting beside the man who had denigrated him so severely. Jonathan presents a profile of an unswerving sense of right and wrong plus an ability to face any tragedy, protected by his loyalty to duty. Jonathan was exemplary.

Ishbosheth, too, had a well developed sense of morality. He risked offending Abner, the captain of Saul's army, by confronting him with Abner's illicit relationship with Saul's concubine, Rizpah (II Samuel 3). In so doing, he lost the support of the one strong man determined to keep Saul's line on the throne. When Abner exploded, Ishbosheth feared him as well he might, for Abner was a dangerous, unpredictable man.

Reflecting the customs of the time, Ishbosheth allowed Abner to push him into mistreatment of his sister, Michael. It was Ishbosheth, as we have mentioned before, who dragged Michal from Palti's house, from a love relationship to a power ploy, in David's determination to cement his hold on the throne by the presence of Saul's daughter as his lawful wife (II Samuel 3).

Finally two men killed Ishbosheth, thinking they were doing David a favor. Let us read the account.

> And David answered Rechab and Baanah his brother, sons of Rimmon the Beerothite, and said to them, "As the Lord lives, who has redeemed my life from all distress, when one told me, saying, 'Behold, Saul is dead,' and thought he was bringing good news, I seized him and killed him in Ziklag, which was the reward I gave him for his news. How much more, when wicked men have killed a righteous man in his own house on his bed, shall I not now require his blood from your hand, and destroy you from the earth?" (II Sam. 4:11).

David ordered Ishbosheth's assassins executed.

Ishbosheth, a somewhat obscure character, lost his throne and his life because he dared to challenge another man's behavior. His moral rectitude, according to the light of his time, made Abner desert him. That desertion left him with no defense.

We have already said a good bit about Michal. Some assessment of her and her life seems appropriate. When Michal defied the conventions of her time by declaring her desire to marry David, she showed great strength. This tough quality reasserted itself when she helped David escape from her father's guards and covered the escape by a ruse (I Sam. 19). Considering the low value placed on women in those days, one can hardly question the fact that she risked her life in so doing.

One wonders about the intervening years between David's flight from Saul and Michal's return to David's household. Did she wait in agonizing hope for him to come to claim her, only to learn of his marriages to Ahinoam and Abigail? Did she know they traveled with him while she sat and waited? Was Michal happy with Palti who genuinely loved her? Had she come to the conclusion David only married her to help his career and endear himself to Saul?

When she derided David in our last Biblical reference to her, she again evidenced strength (II Sam. 6). David obviously did not cherish her or find her company rewarding. She might have been put to death for her sarcasm. She was the daughter of his old enemy. Perhaps Michal's life meant little to her at this point. Maybe she simply did not care what happened to her.

To any thoughtful reader, Michal's life forms a study in tragedy. We see a bubbly, enthusiastic girl changed into a sarcastic, bitter woman. Most of the events triggering this change occurred at the hands of the men she loved most: Saul, David and Ishbosheth. All three men used her for their own ends. Her only apparent positive relationship with a male figure existed with Palti, who pursued her, weeping, when she was forcibly removed form his home.

Studying Saul's children opens the door to at least one positive reaction to Saul as a father. He had done something right to arouse so much loyalty in the stable Jonathan. Ishbosheth appeared more interested in preserving Saul's line than in personal recognition. Michal seemed secure in her father's love for she dared to oppose him and did not seem to fear the consequences. Saul was a failure as a king because of his taking God's prerogatives into his own hands and developing all his paranoid fears. In many ways, he was a successful father.

16

THE FAMILY OF DAVID

David came from the tribe of Judah. Jesse was his father, Obed his grandfather, and Ruth and Boaz were his great-grandparents. He spent his youth shepherding his father's flocks.

As part of the account in I Samuel 16 of David's anointing by Samuel, we find a description of the lad. ". . . Now he was ruddy, with beautiful eyes and a handsome appearance . . . (I Sam. 16:12). A more detailed picture of the young man appears later in the same chapter. "Then one of the young men answered and said, 'Behold, I have seen a son of Jesse the Bethlehemite who is a skilled musician, a mighty man of valor, a warrior, one prudent in speech, and a handsome man; and the Lord is with him'" (I Sam. 16:18).

147

Joab, captain of David's army, was his nephew, son of David's sister, Zeruiah. Reading stories of the Davidic wars, one is forced to note that many of the positions of great authority were occupied by men who appear related to David in some way. This fact coincides with information about the influence of the clans and tribes in the beginning history of the monarchy. It also applies to our family study. A man could trust his own clan best in most crises.

David accumulated quite a large harem. The culture of that era judged a man's power and wealth by the number of wives and children he possessed. "Possessed" is a good word. They were considered his personal property.

Some of David's marriages represented political alliances rather than love matches. Michal and Maacah probably fit this description. He hoped to cement a friendship with Saul through Michal. Maacah was the daughter of the king of Geshur. With her as David's wife, he avoided trouble with that nation. Abigail, the beautiful and wise widow of Nabal, created a powerful family connection with southern Judah. David's marriage to Ahinoam increased his influence in Jezreel, for she was native to that area. He also married Haggith, Abital and Eglah along with Maacah during the seven years he reigned at Hebron. Very little is known of any of these women except their motherhood of David's sons.

After David moved to Jerusalem when he became king over all Israel, he increased his harem. "Meanwhile, David took more concubines and wives from Jerusalem, after he came from Hebron; and more sons and daughters were born to David" (II Sam. 5:13). Finally we read of Bathsheba, whom we shall discuss at length later.

The Bible contains several listings of David's children. We are sure no Biblical record remains of all of them. However, we do have these names from various accounts. David's first-born son was Amnon, born to Ahinoam; Chileab, called Daniel in I Chronicles 3:1, son of Abigail; Absalom, son of Maacah; Adonijah, son of Haggith; Shephatiah, son of Abital; Ithream, son of Eglah. All these were born at Hebron and are listed in II Samuel 3:2-5.

II Samuel 5:14-16 catalogs more names of David's children: Shammua, called Shimea in I Chronicles 3:5; Shobab; Nathan; Solomon; Ibhar; Elishua; Nepheg; Japhia; Elishama; Eliada; and Eliphelet. The names of their mothers are not included in the roster. However, we do know Shimea, Shobab, Solomon and Nathan were sons of Bathsheba (I Chron. 3:5). The princely family of Nathan is specifically mentioned in Zechariah 12:12 as a division of the house of David. Nathan is also noted in Luke 3:31 in the ancestry of Jesus. Except for Amnon, Absalom, Adonijah and Solomon, little of importance appears in the records of David's children but the things we have said concerning Nathan. We shall discuss the four prominent sons later.

As far as one may discover from the Scripture itself, the only wife David loved very much was Bathsheba. The others were alliances or career-enhancing. Bathsheba in no way improved David's status. In fact, his attraction to her almost destroyed him. But it was her son, Solomon, who succeeded him on the throne in spite of the fact that he was down the line in age.

Let us look at the story. It is a very modern tale, full of desire, immoral liaison, even murder. Preachers tend to characterize Bathsheba as a temptress, deliberately bathing where David could see her because she wanted to seduce him. Moviemakers have done the same thing. Have they read the account?

"Now when evening came David arose from his bed and walked around on the roof of the king's house, and from the roof he saw a woman bathing; and the woman was very beautiful in appearance" (II Sam. 11:2). A woman attempting to seduce a man by bathing in front of him would hardly have selected night on the slim chance he might be wakeful! Any such assessment of Bathsheba reveals a prejudiced mind. "If there is evil, a woman is behind it," characterizes this type of thinking.

Shall we read further?

So David sent and inquired about the woman. And one said, "Is this not Bathsheba, the daughter of Eliam, the wife of Uriah the Hittite?"

And David sent messengers and *took* her, and when she came to him, he lay with her: and when she had purified herself from her uncleanness, she returned to her house. And the woman conceived; and she sent and told David, and said, "I am pregnant." Then David sent to Joab, saying, "Send me Uriah the Hittite." So Joab sent Uriah to David (II Sam. 11:3-6).

Several things impress us from this story. First, David knew Bathsheba was married to one of his soldiers before he sent his men to her. He deliberately planned to commit adultery.

Bathsheba's part in all this needs scrutiny. Women were chattel in that society. If she had wanted to refuse the king's attentions, would she have feared to do so? David exercised the power of life or death over his subjects. Was Bathsheba motivated by fright or flattered by the king's attentions? In the light of our present knowledge of David, we feel secure in thinking rejection by Bathsheba would not have endangered her. However, Bathsheba had no lovely poetry or historical

150

analyses by which to judge her king. The language of the text certainly opens the door for the thought that Bathsheba was taken, rather than coming willingly to the palace.

Another interesting sidelight appears in the account. Ceremonial cleansing was commanded by the law following intercourse. Bathsheba had just committed adultery, expressly forbidden by the law, yet she engaged in purification rites. Did this evidence reluctance and sorrow on her part? No one knows, but the Biblical record certainly allows questions.

When we read of David's sending for Uriah, we also need to realize he could have been motivated by several things. One, of course, was a cover-up for his own sin. However, Bathsheba was in greater danger than he. His part might have been hidden. Putting a king on trial in an absolute monarchy would have been quite an undertaking. A pregnancy cannot be concealed. According to the law, Bathsheba's stoning was mandatory.

One sees another possible motive for David's actions here. The law leaves a loophole for a man who marries the woman he violates. Was David, caught in a crisis of his own making, striving to twist the law to justify his actions?

Another very important aspect of this story is Uriah's attitude. We know the reason he gave for not spending the night with Bathsheba. His excuse sounds very feeble in the light of David's sending him to her. We have known many patriotic servicemen. We have never met one who wouldn't rush to a beautiful wife if given a pass by his commander.

One cannot help wondering if this was a loveless marriage. Most marriages of the time were arranged. Uriah certainly was not a passionate lover. Perhaps he had already heard via the military grapevine that his king was entertaining his wife in Uriah's absence. A mighty good way to terminate a loveless marriage in that day would have been to prove adultery. Uriah may have been a completely innocent victim. However, his actions arouse suspicion that Bathsheba may have felt terribly unloved and unwanted before David sent for her. This would not excuse her behavior, only explain it.

The Biblical scribe attempts no cover-up when he writes, "Now it came about in the morning that David wrote a letter to Joab, and sent it by the hand of Uriah. And he had written in the letter, saying, 'Place Uriah in the front line of the fiercest battle and withdraw from him, so that he may be struck down and die'" (II Sam. 11:14, 15).

At this point, David sank as low as any person can. How ironic that Uriah should carry his own death warrant to his commander! Joab does not amass any good conduct medals either! And what of the men with Uriah? Were they also in on the plot? What happened to the fraternal support soldiers accord to each other? How revealing of the dangers of blind acquiescence to the chain of command! This seems to be the only record of David's using his power for his own personal selfish ends, at least in such a degenerate manner!

After observing the proper amenities of mourning (another irony of the story), Bathsheba entered David's house and became his wife. The baby was accorded legitimacy. Bathsheba was not stoned as an adulteress. However, it would be very strange if the gossips of Jerusalem failed to have a field day. Nothing so evil can be permanently concealed.

Nathan, the prophet, visited David, bringing the condemnation of the Lord. He declared that the child born of the adulterous relationship would die. He also predicted that the sword would never leave David's house and that sexual immorality would prevail.

Let us pause a moment here. The English of the text might lead us to believe God caused all the ensuing evil. Some of

152

the wording appears a bit obscure. If one makes the behavior of David's sons a punishment created by God rather than a natural result of sinful living, one identifies God as a force in wickedness. We prefer to believe David's sons watched their father thwart the moral code and copied his actions. The prophet predicted these results, but God did not instigate the action.

David, the oriental potentate, might have executed his accuser, Nathan. Instead, he repented, pleading with God for the life of the child. All the way through David's life, any sin was followed by abject repentance. How tragic to note in a study of families that his sons apparently failed to see and imitate this part of their father's character!

David's love for Bathsheba moved to the forefront after the baby's death. "Then David comforted his wife Bathsheba, and went in to her and lay with her, and she gave birth to a son, and he named him Solomon. Now the Lord loved him" (II Sam. 12:24).

David's sinful example soon bore fruit. Amnon, his eldest son, raped his half-sister, Tamar. Following his violation of her, the Scripture says,

> Then Amnon hated her with a very great hatred; for the hatred with which he hated her was greater than the love with which he had loved her. And Amnon said to her, "Get up, go away!"
> But she said to him, "No, because this wrong in sending me away is greater than the other that you have done to me!" Yet he would not listen to her. Then he called his young man who attended him and said, "Now throw this woman out of my presence and lock the door behind her" (II Sam. 13:15-17).

According to Hebrew law, a man who violated a virgin must keep her as his wife. So, not only did Amnon rape Tamar, but he made her plight known to everyone when he threw her out. She was damaged merchandise, not to be desired by anyone else!

David's reaction is stated this way. "Now when King David heard all these matters, he was very angry" (II Sam. 13:21). But he did nothing!

Tamar's full brother, Absalom, took her into his house and comforted her. ". . . So Tamar remained and was desolate in her brother Absalom's house" (II Sam. 13:20). Absalom plotted Amnon's death because ". . . Absalom hated Amnon because he had violated his sister Tamar" (II Sam. 13:22). It took Absalom two years to arrange Amnon's execution. Had he been waiting for his father to act? He ordered Amnon's death. Then he fled to Geshur, his grandfather's land.

One poignant note emerges from the story of Absalom. In the register of his children, we read of a daughter named Tamar (II Sam. 14:27). Did he name a child for his heart-broken sister? Did Tamar seek out Absalom because they had an especially close familial bond? It would appear so.

Can we open a window into the mind of Amnon? David sent messengers and "took" the woman who had attracted him. When Amnon tried to get Tamar to have sex with him, she pled that he ask their father to permit them to marry rather than do this evil thing. But he wouldn't wait. The Scripture says, ". . . since he was stronger than she, he violated her and lay with her" (II Sam. 13:14). Tamar obviously put up a fight. Was that why he hated her afterward? Were all women supposed to be overwhelmed by his charm? Was he reasoning, "If my father can demand the woman he lusts after, why can't I? Am I not a prince of the realm?"

David's sons probably knew he had ordered Uriah's death to achieve his aim to marry Bathsheba. Did Absalom think he could do the same thing because of his hatred for Amnon? After all, he was of royal blood on both sides! He was also the most handsome man in the kingdom and used to having his own way. Why should revenge be denied him? Obviously his grandfather in Geshur had few moral reservations about such actions. He gave Absalom sanctuary.

Again David grieved but did nothing. A pretty clear picture emerges here of a family where the father, a strong warrior, a successful king, exerted little disciplinary influence in his home. These favorite sons of his had never known the parental control essential for the development of self-control. Combine laxity of discipline with poor moral example. The result breeds contempt and rebellion.

No matter what Absalom had done, David missed him, longing for his return. So Joab took matters into his own hands and brought Absalom back. David's relationship with Joab gives another clue to the king's weakness with his family. David disliked many of Joab's tactics, but never took a strong stand about them. Even though Absalom was back in the country, it was two years before he was restored to the court. Again Joab maneuvered the situation.

Most authorities believe Chileab had also died at this time. The demise of his two older brothers made Absalom the natural heir to the throne. His estrangement from David precipitated a crisis. Absalom set out to undermine his father with the people and make himself king. Again he was patient. He worked at his underground revolt for four years before bringing it out into the open.

During those years, Absalom was able to get Ahithophel, one of David's main counselors, to join him in his efforts to usurp the throne. Again family pressure and pride enter the picture. Some authorities believe Ahithophel was Bathsheba's grandfather (II Sam. 23:34; 11:3). If so, David's use of Bathsheba, disgraced Ahithophel's family. Losing face remains a terrible burden in that area of our world. Bathsheba obviously loved David. That emotion might not have been shared by her family. When the rebellion failed, Ahithophel hanged himself. This is a situation similar to that of Judas in the New Testament, an intimate friend turned traitor to the cause.

Finally Absalom entered Hebron and declared himself king. Was it significant that Absalom chose Hebron as the site of his anarchy? It was his birthplace and the spot where David had ascended the throne.

David's people eventually came to his aid. David's forces and Absalom's battled. David was victorious. The king was persuaded not to enter the fray. But he feared for Absalom in spite of the young man's treachery. "And the king charged Joab and Abishai and Ittai, saying, 'Deal gently for my sake with the young man Absalom' . . ." (II Sam. 18:5). Joab ignored David's orders and killed Absalom.

Perhaps one of the most pathetic expressions of grief in all literature comes in this part of the narrative. "And the king was deeply moved and went up to the chamber over the gate and wept. And thus he said as he walked, 'O my son Absalom, my son, my son Absalom! Would I had died instead of you, O Absalom, my son, my son!'" (II Sam. 18:33).

David grieved so deeply that Joab protested.

> Then Joab came into the house of the king and said, "Today you have covered with shame the faces of all your servants, who today have saved your life and the lives of sons and daughters, the lives of your wives, and the lives of your concubines; by loving those who hate you, and by hating those who love you. For you have shown today that

princes and servants are nothing to you; for I know this day that if Absalom were alive and all of us were dead today, then you would be pleased. Now therefore arise, go out and speak kindly to your servants, for I swear by the Lord, if you do not go out, surely not a man will pass the night with you, and this will be worse for you than all the evil that has come upon you from your youth until now" (II Sam. 19:5-7).

Joab, the practical politician and soldier, dared to confront David, the absolute monarch, with facts he did not want to hear. David, the dreamer, then marched to the tune of Joab, the pragmatist.

Why did David weep so pitifully for the son who despised him? Was he recalling Nathan's words? Perhaps David grieved partly for himself, blaming his own conduct for his son's defection and revolt. But David, the king, superseded David, the father, and he returned to the people.

One of the most interesting facts coming from the story of Absalom's rebellion was Amasa's role in it. Amasa, son of Ithra, an Ishmaelite, and David's sister, Abigail, led Absalom's army. David not only pardoned him but placed him in command of his own troops, replacing Joab. Shortly after Absalom's rebellion, another arose led by Sheba. During the fighting, Joab murdered Amasa. Since Joab and Amasa were cousins, another family killing occurred. Joab, the determined warrior, refused to let anyone take his job!

One cannot help wondering about David's wisdom in this. Joab, in spite of his willful personality, had displayed outstanding loyalty to David, not only through these rebellions, but ever since David had ascended the throne. Absalom had tried to seize everything David held dear. Amasa had deserted David to help Absalom overthrow his government. In addition to all these facts, Amasa's prowess compared to that of Joab is certainly open to question. Joab defeated him miserably in repressing the revolt. Why was David's judgment so faulty? Was David, the father, striking out at the killer of his son while also attempting to establish a close relationship with one of that son's best friends?

When David was a very old man, Adonijah, his fourth son, decided he wouldn't wait until his father's death to become king. It was probably natural for Adonijah to expect to ascend the throne at David's death, but no law of succession existed. The patriarchal system, however, gave precedence to the eldest son.

The Scripture sheds light on the basis for Adonijah's spoiled brat attitudes. "And his father had never crossed him at any time by asking, 'Why have you done so?' And he was also a very handsome man; and he was born after Absalom" (I Kings 1:6). Again David's lack of discipline surfaces. Adonijah had never been forced to obey any authority outside his own wishes and whims. So those wishes and whims became his god and king!

In Adonijah's rebellion, we finally discover Joab and Abiathar defecting to the enemy. There might be several reasons for this. Joab despised weakness, or what he thought to be weakness. Not only had David been weak in his treatment of Absalom in Joab's opinion, but he was now an old man, grown weak and frail with age. Perhaps Joab also carried a grudge against David because of the king's rejection of him in favor of Amasa at the conclusion of Absalom's revolt. Even though this was not obvious in his recorded actions, it might have been a natural result in a man of Joab's type of personality.

It is a bit hard to defend David's attitude about Joab, especially taking into account the mind-set of a civilized animal type like Joab. Abiathar, Joab's brother, followed Joab's lead most of the time. Several references to Zeruiah's sons appear in the Scripture. Until this point in the narrative, they had exhibited unswerving loyalty to their Uncle David, risking their lives for him. Had they finally decided, "Enough is enough already"?

Adonijah set up a coronation. His guest list might be noted more for the uninvited than for the invited. "But he did not invite Nathan the prophet, Benaiah, the mighty men, and Solomon his brother" (I Kings 1:10).

Nathan moved into the story.

> Then Nathan spoke to Bathsheba the mother of Solomon, saying, "Have you not heard that Adonijah the son of Haggith has become king, and David our lord does not know it? So now come, please let me give you counsel and save your life and the life of your son Solomon. Go at once to King David and say to him, 'Have you not, my lord, O king, sworn to your maidservant, saying, "Surely Solomon your son shall be king after me, and he shall sit on my throne?" Why then has Adonijah become king?'
>
> "Behold, while you are still there speaking with the king, I will come in after you and confirm your words" (I Kings 1:11-14).

When David was informed of Adonijah's treachery, he called for Zadok the priest, Nathan the prophet and Benaiah the son of Jehoiada and one of his greatest warriors to appear before him. Then David sent them all to Gihon to crown Solomon king. Zadok and Nathan anointed Solomon accompanied by Benaiah and his mighty men, the Cherethites and the Pelethites.

When Adonijah's followers heard the celebration and learned of Solomon's coronation, they fled, leaving Adonijah to his own devices. Adonijah hurried to the house of worship, holding the horns of the altar, begging for his life. "And Solomon said, 'If he will be a worthy man, not one of his hairs will fall to the ground; but if wickedness is found in him, he will die'" (I Kings 1:52). Solomon sent Adonijah home.

However, Adonijah visited Bathsheba with a request he asked her to present to Solomon for him. "So he said, 'You know that the kingdom was mine and that all Israel expected me to be king; however, the kingdom has turned about and become my brother's, for it was his from the Lord'" (I Kings 2:15). Since we have read of little genuine piety from the arrogant Adonijah, this apparent submission sounds phony. After this prologue, he asked for the hand of Abishag in marriage.

Abishag, a concubine of David, had cared for him in his last days. The Scripture tells us they never had sex relations (see I Kings 1:4), but the general public knew about her close relationship to David as she kept him warm when he was no longer able to provide warmth for himself. Giving her to Adonijah would have been a symbol of Adonijah's rightful claim to the throne. Solomon, not so strangely in the light of the customs of the time, considered the request tantamount to treason.

"And King Solomon answered and said to his mother, 'And why are you asking Abishag the Shunammite for Adonijah? Ask for him also the kingdom—for he is my older brother—even for him, for Abiathar the priest, and for Joab the son of Zeruiah!'" (I Kings 2:22). Adonijah was executed by Benaiah that day. Abiathar was removed from the priesthood and sent home. Benaiah also killed Joab at Solomon's command.

Perhaps it would be well at this point in our account to assess the strengths and weaknesses of David.

Strengths

1. Warm, outgoing personality inspiring love and loyalty in his subjects.
2. Brave and successful warrior, freeing his people from foreign domination.
3. Just, without his justice depending upon the social status of the persons involved.
4. Generous, sparing Saul, rewarding loyal service in most instances, sparing Jonathan's son.
5. Warm and tender in personal relationships. Loved his family; if, at times, unwisely.
6. Far above his time in simple pious faith. His religious poetry was exceptional. A man after God's own heart.
7. Accepted misfortune with resignation, admitting personal guilt.
8. Sincerely repentant. Showed no anger at Nathan, no blame for Bathsheba, only disgust with himself. (Remember Adam?)
9. Splendid administrator.
10. Zealously labored for his people.

Negative Aspects

1. Very cruel in wars he waged. (Typical of his time)
2. Practiced deception and cunning to achieve what he wanted.
3. Probably never practiced idolatry, but allowed it in his home. (Michal and the household god.)
4. Wondered if Jahweh sent Saul to harass him.

5. Allowed the execution of seven innocent men, thinking to appease Jahweh. This and the former attribute fail to show the close relationship to God seen in other experiences of David's life.

6. Was impulsive in judgment at times with little evidence to back up his decisions.

7. Hot-tempered as evidenced by his setting out in vengeance to destroy Nabal before Abigail interceded.

8. Adultery, not from momentary temptation but from deliberate planning.

9. A weak, vacillating father.

Some things should be noted here about Solomon since he was David's child and his successor on the throne. Reading of Solomon's older brothers, the ones who might have been king, and aligning them with David's strengths and weaknesses, one readily sees that they showed few of their father's pluses and most of his minuses. Solomon truly was different. We might wonder why as we study families. We are forced by this evidence to zero in on Bathsheba.

Bathsheba remains a bit of an enigma. However, a few clues present themselves for our thoughtful pursuit. Her ritual purification following sex relations with David might signify deep personal faith, a symbol of repentance. Did she, of all David's wives and concubines, make an effort to teach her son the ways of the Lord?

Bathsheba appears also to have maintained her closeness to David until his death, a remarkable feat in the light of the harem system of the time. Did this create more stability in Solomon? Biblical evidence exists to portray Bathsheba as not only beautiful but wise. No woman could have kept her hold on David in that society over many years without combining beauty with brains.

162

Part of the blame for David's failure as a father may be laid at the feet of the polygamous household. Polygamy never created peace and tranquility with maximum opportunity for growth. However, Solomon, although not up to our Christian standards of morality, certainly outshone his brothers. Had any of the others succeeded David on the throne, division probably would have come before it did. Since David refused to discipline his sons and Solomon was a scholar, a fine administrator, and a warm, loving man in many personal relationships, Bathsheba may well have been the catalyst.

Some authorities believe Nathan educated Solomon. If this were true, Nathan's intervention to make Solomon king could be explained on the human as well as divine level. However, one would scarcely attribute Solomon's gentle spirit to the firebrand, Nathan. In addition to this, little evidence of prophetic influence appears in Solomon's reign, making a prophetic education a bit doubtful. Solomon's moral defects might more clearly indicate a palace education with all of its undercurrents and innuendos.

In the beginning of his reign, Solomon, overwhelmed by the awesome task facing him, made just one request of God.

> And now, O Lord my God, Thou hast made Thy servant king in place of my father David; yet I am but a little child: I do not know how to go out or come in. And Thy servant is in the midst of Thy people which Thou hast chosen, a great people who cannot be numbered or counted for multitude. So give Thy servant an understanding heart to judge Thy people to discern between good and evil. For who is able to judge this great people of Thine (I Kings 3:7-9).

Any thoughtful reader finds it impossible to imagine such a prayer on the lips of Amnon, Absalom or Adonijah. Very little is recorded for them in recognition of God, not to mention such a humble prayer. Solomon began his reign with a humility not to be found in anyone who had not experienced discipline in youth. So we must realize the influence of Bathsheba, for we know David refused to discipline any of his sons.

Solomon, like David, was an absolute monarch. He allowed no rivals, crushed all dangerous adversaries for his crown, was actually an oriental despot. Yet Solomon was by nature gentle rather than cruel. He had no taste for war, the most peace-loving of the Hebrew kings. Solomon's name means "peaceful." At the time of his birth, David was exhausted by war and had become keenly aware of the blessings of peace both for the king and his kingdom. This is probably the reason for Solomon's name. Solomon was not weak, just not warlike. Even his military fortifications evidenced ability. He was handsome, possessed a rare brilliance and strong personality.

However, in spite of his native intelligence and special blessing from God, Solomon abused his power. From absolute power inevitably proceeds corruption. The human personality appears unable to sustain moral fiber under such circumstances.

I Kings 4:32 says Solomon spoke 3000 proverbs and wrote 1005 songs. One of the greatest evidences of Solomon's depth of religious faith and concept of God far beyond his time is found in I Kings 8:27. "But will God indeed dwell on the earth? Behold, heaven and the highest heaven cannot contain Thee, how much less this house which I have built!" His entire prayer of dedication of the temple is a masterpiece of thoughtful devotion.

We may read throughout the first eleven chapters of I Kings of all the splendors of Solomon, his riches and his wisdom. Then in I Kings 11:1-3, the sacred scribe tells us,

> Now King Solomon loved many foreign women along with the daughter of Pharaoh: Moabite, Ammonite, Edomite, Sidonian, and Hittite women, from the nations concerning which the Lord had said to the sons of Israel, "You shall not associate with them, neither shall they associate with you, for they will surely turn your heart away after their gods." Solomon held fast to these in love. And he had seven hundred wives, princesses, and three hundred concubines, and his wives turned his heart away.

Politics began to supersede religion. Solomon found alliances with other nations through marriage more important than his relationship with God. So, actually, it was Solomon's concept of family that began the downfall of the kingdom of Israel, again indicating the importance of the family in the history of God's people.

For a man with so many wives and concubines, Solomon produced few children who are recorded in the Bible. Rehoboam, son of Naamah, the Ammonitess, ascended the throne at Solomon's death. No other son is mentioned for Solomon. We do have some daughters named in the account, but no one of prominence. No one could accuse Rehoboam of inheriting either his father's brains or his administrative skills. After Solomon's death, except for a few good kings whose influence was limited to their own period of time in a small area, the kingdom's pathway was consistently downhill.

Modern psychology teaches the ambivalent feelings sons often possess toward their fathers. The truth of this premise might be observed in Rehoboam's reaction to advice at the beginning of his reign. The older men, seasoned by many years in court and greater understanding of the emotions of people, advised lightening the yoke of Rehoboam's subjects, asserting, ". . . grant them their petition, and speak good words to them, then they will be your servants forever" (I Kings 12:7).

Consulting his young peers, Rehoboam received the opposite advice. They counseled him to say, "Whereas my father loaded you with a heavy yoke, I will add to your yoke; my father disciplined you with whips, but I will discipline you with scorpions" (I Kings 12:11). He liked their approach. He used their words. He lost most of his kingdom.

Not only arrogance arises from the stance of Rehoboam, but also a son's determination to assume superiority over the memory of his father. "Maybe you think Dad was tough, but you ain't seen nothin' yet!" might be a modern way of saying the same thing in slang. His inexperience, his failure to realize his own lack of wisdom, his inability from his vantage point of luxury and affluence to handle the emotional rebellion of a pained and suffering people, combined with his egotistical failure to rely upon God defeated this young king before he began. Again we see evidence of the environmental effect of a polygamous palace with all sorts of religions and very few ethics upon the weak and self-centered character of a young man who grew up there.

Rehoboam determined he would not permit Jeroboam to walk away with most of his kingdom without a fight. So he raised an army from the tribes of Judah and Benjamin. They did not fight, however. In our study of families, the reason assumes importance. Shemaiah, the man of God, received the following message:

> "Speak to Rehoboam the son of Solomon, king of Judah, and to all the house of Judah and Benjamin and to the rest of the people, saying, 'Thus says the Lord, "You must not

go up and fight against your relatives the sons of Israel; return every man to his house, for this thing has come from me"'" (I Kings 12:23, 24).

The sacred scribe records no reaction on Rehoboam's part, but does tell us all the men went home. Not even a tremendous ego can fight a war alone! The people were still heeding God's Word, at least to a degree. God placed great emphasis upon their relationship to each other. War among brothers creates even greater havoc than other types of wars. We in America learned that lesson the hard way from 1860-1865. Families are valuable. Family wounds heal slowly, sometimes not at all. God forbade their battle plan.

Both Rehoboam and Jeroboam forsook their commitment to God. Eventually constant war erupted between the two divisions of the kingdom. Rehoboam took eighteen wives and sixty concubines and fathered twenty-eight sons and sixty daughters (II Chron. 11:21). He placed his sons throughout the kingdom in the fortified cities, a plus in administrative quality.

We shall continue with the small amount of existing information about the descendants of Rehoboam, as well as a study of the lesser known kings and their families of both kingdoms.

In our study of families, we appear to be amassing a wealth of information to indicate few people were good parents in the polygamous system. Love seems to have been in short supply while jockeying for position and power reigned supreme. With such negative emotions in ascendancy, children did not receive the type of moral and spiritual teaching to produce greatness. This result of poor quality homelife may be observed throughout the entire Old Testament with a few exceptions. There were far more failures than successes noted among the ancient households.

Such motivations will ruin modern homes and families, too. We can learn much from Biblical Writ if we will only study. Cultures can and do change. People do not. Children still need love and spiritual values assuming primary importance in their rearing. When Solomon concentrated upon wealth and international prominence, he failed as a father just as David before him had failed. Rehoboam earned no awards in the parental department either.

Parents today who place success, competence on the job, personal career rewards and advancement ahead of parenting may awaken someday to a devastated homelife. In the days of the ancients whom we have studied, no one seemed to be working with the children; at least, no one who cared enough to discipline and train.

Are we, instead of learning from history, repeating it?

17

FAMILIES OF THE KINGS OF JUDAH

I Kings 15 lists Abijam, son of Rehoboam, as king of Judah following his father's death. This record names his mother Maacah, the daughter of Absalom.

II Chronicles calls him Abijah, son of Micaiah, daughter of Uriel of Gibeah. The chronological data make Abijam and Abijah the same man as both accounts say he ascended the throne of Judah in the 18th year of Jeroboam's reign in Israel.

The confusion in regard to Abijah or Abijam's mother could be the result of Micaiah's name being "Maacah" in Syriac. Some authorities believe she was actually the granddaughter of Absalom, that Uriel of Gibeah married Tamar, Absalom's daughter. Since the ancients often designated all descendants as sons and daughters, the apparent discrepancy creates no problem.

I Kings 15 delineates Abijam as an evil king while II Chronicles 13 tells of his victories over Jeroboam because he called upon the name of the Lord. His speech preceding battle with the northern kingdom delivered on Mount Zemaraim is a masterpiece of oratorical declaration of their dependence upon Jahweh. It is recorded in II Chronicles 13.

It is impossible for us to know exactly how to reconcile these two accounts. We might suggest two possible routes. I Kings 15:4 states, "But for David's sake the Lord his God gave him a lamp in Jerusalem, to raise up his son after him and to establish Jerusalem."

We all have known politicians who espouse religion to achieve their own ends. What a man says and what he truly believes may be worlds apart. Such could have been the case in Abijah's life and heart and God permitted him to retain the throne in order that Asa, a reformer, might be next in line.

One fact perhaps indicating Abijah's attitudes were superior to some of the other kings appears in the life of Asa, his son. Asa's reign returned the people to greater respect for the commands of God. In his desire to get the kingdom on the right track again, Asa even deposed the king mother because she had built an obscene image to Asherah. Her actions rule out godly maternal influence on Asa. But it came from somewhere. So Abijah may have become the catalyst in the life of his son binding him to a sincere faith in God. Sometimes children of dogma-expounding parents, even if those parents practice hypocrisy in their own lives, develop a personal belief because of truths that are uttered in their presence.

Little of Asa's family is recorded. We do know his son Jehoshaphat succeeded him on the throne. Jehoshaphat's mother was Azubah, daughter of Shilhi.

Jehoshaphat's reign was more peaceful than most. Part of that resulted from his dependence upon Jahweh. However, he was a "peace at any price" type of man, finally marrying his son Jehoram to Athaliah, daughter of Ahab and Jezebel, reigning monarchs of the kingdom of Israel, to establish an alliance between the two kingdoms. Few women of Scripture fit the role of "devil's emissary" quite so well as Jezebel. Athaliah proved to be a carbon copy of her mother. Destruction of Judah became inevitable.

Athaliah's strong personality influenced both Jehoram and their son, Ahaziah, for evil. Only God's promise to David saved Judah from complete annihilation during Jehoram's reign. Not only was Jehoram an evil king with a queen who reveled in degradation, but he killed all six of his brothers when he ascended the throne (II Chron. 21:2-4). Obviously, the household of Jehoshaphat had failed to foster love and respect among the siblings who grew up there.

The Scripture depicts Athaliah's influence when we read,

> Then a letter came to him from Elijah the prophet saying, "Thus says the Lord God of your father David, 'Because you have not walked in the ways of Jehoshaphat your father and the ways of Asa king of Judah, but *have walked in the way of the kings of Israel,* and have caused Judah and the inhabitants of Israel to play the harlot *as the house of Ahab played the harlot, and you have also killed your brothers, your own family, who were better than you,* behold, the Lord is going to strike your people, your sons, your wives, and all your possessions with a great calamity; and you will suffer severe sickness, a disease of your bowels, until your bowels come out because of the sickness, day by day'" (II Chron. 21:12-15).

All that Elijah prophesied came true. Perhaps it might be well to note here that modern medicine indicates a direct correlation many times between emotions and sickness of the digestive system. Not to detract at all from the prophecy of Elijah, but might we be dealing here with guilt? Jehoram's father had been a godly man. In other words, Jehoram had been led down the garden path into attitudes and actions in direct contradiction to the teaching of his youth. Was he personally torn between two philosophies of life? Are we observing a scientific truth here as well as a spiritual prophecy?

The last verse of chapter 21 forms an assessment of Jehoram. "He was thirty-two years old when he became king, and he reigned in Jerusalem eight years; and he departed with no one's regret, and they buried him in the city of David, but not in the tombs of the kings." Popular fellow, wasn't he? We are told "his people made no fire for him like the fire for his fathers" (II Chron. 21:19).

Perhaps we would do well to consider influence even upon the adult personality by the environment in which he lives and people frequenting that environment.

In many marriages, one personality assumes prominence. In the case of the marriage of Jehoram and Athaliah, Athaliah was evidently the stronger of the two. Jehoshaphat had reasoned that a marriage with the daughter of Ahab and Jezebel would create an alliance between the quarreling divisions of the original nation, perhaps even fostering unity. Was Jehoshaphat a dreamer? Did he know little or nothing of the lifestyle of Ahab and Jezebel? The Bible describes Jehoshaphat as a true believer. Yet he was willing to arrange a marriage for his son with the daughter of two of the most wicked rulers recorded in the history of God's people! Had peace in his time become more important to Jehoshaphat than worship of God? Or did Jehoshaphat have so much pride in his son that he considered him capable of handling

172

the wily Athaliah? No one knows. We do know Jehoram, instead of changing Athaliah, became like her.

There is food for thought in this story for modern families. In selection of a mate, character and spiritual depth should be more important than beauty, physical attraction, social standing or wealth. No one can depend upon changing a partner after marriage.

Another fact comes to light in the story of Jehoram and Athaliah. The Biblical writer makes it clear that Athaliah's influence worked predominantly in the fall of Jehoram. However, God held Jehoram accountable for his own sins. He refused to allow escape via the "Athaliah made me do it" route. Had Jehoram been a man of prayer, he might have surmounted Athaliah's decadent effect and changed the course of history.

We discover anew God's emphasis upon family as He condemns Jehoram for murdering his brothers. We see in God's adverse judgment upon King Jehoram His respect for the family as the primary unit of society.

Perhaps no greater reason for careful selection of a mate arises than in planning for children. Not only did Athaliah ruin the weak Jehoram's life, but she also destroyed all possibility of moral and spiritual influence in the life of her son Ahaziah.

Following Ahaziah's brief reign, the evil Athaliah ordered all her grandchildren killed so she might be queen of Judah herself. Only Joash escaped the massacre. His father's sister, Jehoshabeath, wife of Jehoiada the priest, rescued him and hid him. He was only one year old.

Let us consider here the power of a strong personality in effecting good in the life of a marriage partner. Jehoiada was a very strong man. He was a priest, characterized as

173

a very good priest. He married Jehoshabeath, a girl who had grown up in the same home that Ahaziah shared. Yet she risked her own life to save the life of her little nephew. One would like to know what she was like when she married Jehoiada. How much influence had his deep faith exerted in her life? We meet in this story two people who had shared the same parents. One lives in history as good, the other evil. May we discover the reason in the persons they married?

Athaliah reigned for six years, being overthrown by a *coup d' etat* led by the high priest, Jehoiada, who crowned the young Joash king. This account may be found both in I and II Kings and in II Chronicles.

Joash (Jehoash in some places) was only seven years old when his coronation took place. Jehoiada's influence upon the young king guaranteed the return of Jehovah worship to the land. Here again we observe the importance of spiritual influence in the formative years of a child's life.

As we have witnessed frequently in the stories of the kings, Joash became corrupt after Jehoiada died, leaving him to the guidance of scheming, plotting courtiers. Had Jehoiada managed the young king too completely, not offering opportunities for him to form his own judgments, thus creating weakness rather than strength? Joash abandoned his devotions to Jehovah and joined with the officials of Judah in idol worship.

> Then the spirit of God came on Zechariah the son of Jehoiada the priest; and he stood above the people and said to them, "Thus God has said, 'Why do you transgress the commandments of the Lord and do not prosper? Because you have forsaken the Lord, He has also forsaken you.'" So they conspired against him and *at the command of the king* they stoned him to death in the court of the house of the Lord (II Chron. 24:20, 21).

174

Jehoiada and Jehoshabeath had saved Joash's life! Where was his gratitude? One cannot help wondering about the theory of inborn personality defects after reading such stories. After all, Joash was the great grandson of Ahab and Jezebel, the grandson of the evil Athaliah. Are some character traits hereditary?

The Syrian army attacked Judah and was victorious. "Indeed the army of the Syrians came with a small number of men; yet the Lord delivered a very great army into their hands, because they had forsaken the Lord, the God of their fathers. Thus they executed judgment on Joash" (II Chron. 24:24). The account continues by recording the death of Joash at the hands of two of his servants, "because of the blood of the son of Jehoiada the priest." They buried him in the city of David but not in the tombs of the kings (II Chron. 24:25).

Amaziah, son of Joash by Jehoaddin of Jerusalem, ascended the throne following his father's death. "And he did right in the sight of the Lord, yet not with a whole heart" (II Chron. 25:2). Here again we discover the importance attached to family in the early Hebrew civilization. Amaziah assembled an army "according to their fathers' households" (II Chron. 25:5).

Azariah (II Kings 15:1) or Uzziah (II Chron. 26:1) followed his father Amaziah to the throne. His mother's name is given as Jecoliah of Jerusalem in II Kings, Jechiliah in II Chronicles. Uzziah was blessed by God until power went to his head. Then he was stricken with leprosy and lived separated from his family until his death. His son, Jotham, assumed control during Uzziah's illness and succeeded to the throne upon his death.

Jotham was Uzziah's son by Jerushah, daughter of Zadok. Since most Biblical genealogies read from father to son

175

rather than father to daughter, in places where a mother is listed with her father, we must assume the mother's father was prominent. Some scholars believe the Zadok mentioned here was a priest. This would fit the character of Jotham, son of a fairly good king, at least for that time, who was married to the daughter of an influential priest. II Chronicles 27:6 informs us, "So Jotham became mighty because he ordered his ways before the Lord his God."

Ahaz followed his father Jotham to the throne. The Bible fails to name his mother. Ahaz appears weak and stubborn, silly, perhaps an enthusiast for artistic things. (See II Kings 16:10.) He was also very superstitious. Ahaz pursued an alliance with Tiglath-Pileser, king of Assyria, thus making himself a vassal of the mightier king and Judah a tributary. Isaiah the prophet warned against such a move, but was ignored. Isaiah 2-5 describes the degradation of Judah under Ahaz.

Here again we find a son living in complete defiance of all his father had cherished. The Bible makes no explanations, just states the fact. Since we know nothing of Ahaz's mother, no information may be assembled from that background.

Hezekiah, son of Ahaz, ascended the throne when Ahaz died. His mother's name is given as Abi in II Kings, Abijah in II Chronicles. She was the daughter of Zechariah. Isaiah 8:2 lists Zechariah the son of Jeberechiah as a faithful witness. This man was a contemporary of Ahaz. II Chronicles 29:13 names a Zechariah as a descendant of Levi, one of those who cleansed the temple during Hezekiah's reform.

For our family study this is noteworthy. We don't know which of these men might have been Hezekiah's grandfather. But either of them would have been an influence for good. Ahaz appeared to possess little depth in his devotion to Jahweh. He worshiped God but other gods as well. His son, Hezekiah, restored proper reverence to the nation. II Chronicles 29:2 states, "And he did right in the sight of the Lord, according to all that his father David had done." What was the root of Hezekiah's piety? It almost had to come from his mother and his maternal grandfather.

Another authority in Hezekiah's life was Isaiah, the prophet. Hezekiah listened to the prophet, learned and grew. Again we must note that he had to have been prepared for this through his formative years. None of the arrogance we have observed in other kingly sons is recorded for Hezekiah.

Because of Hezekiah's faithfulness to God, he proved victorious in battle, was miraculously healed of a life-threatening disease, and the Lord gave him fifteen additional years to live. When death finally came to Hezekiah, the Bible describes it for us. "So Hezekiah slept with his fathers, and they buried him in the upper section of the tombs of the sons of David; and all Judah and the inhabitants of Jerusalem honored him at his death. . ." (II Chron. 32:33). Finally a king righteous enough to be accorded a place in the tombs of the sons of David!

Hezekiah's son Manasseh became king in his place. Manasseh espoused all the evil his father had shunned, making his son pass through the fire, practicing witchcraft and using divination, and dealing with mediums and spiritists. He even placed a carved image of Asherah in the temple of God and persecuted faithful worshipers of Jehovah. II Chronicles does record a period of repentance for Manasseh in the 33rd chapter. We see a repeat of a godly father who produced a very wicked son.

Manasseh was so corrupt they buried him in the garden of Uzza, not even in the vicinity of the tombs of the kings.

177

II Chronicles says, "So Manasseh slept with his fathers, and they buried him in his own house" (33:20).

Honor connected with death and burial rites still constitutes an important part of living in oriental culture. When one travels in the east, tombs of the kings are sites for tourists all over the area. No worse insult could be given than for a king to fail to be buried with his ancestors.

When Manasseh died, his son Amon ascended the throne of Judah. Amon proved even more wicked than his father. II Chronicles says he multiplied guilt (33:23). His mother was Meshullemeth, his grandfather Haruz of Jotbah. We know nothing about them.

We learn in II Chronicles 33:24 that Amon's own servants put him to death. They must have hoped their conspiracy would result in overthrow of the dynasty, but it did not. II Chronicles 33:25 announces, "But the people of the land killed all the conspirators against King Amon, and the people of the land made Josiah his son king in his place." One wonders why. You would think they would have been delighted to get someone like Amon off their backs.

Perhaps the people had become as evil as their king. A nation rarely rises above the spirit of its leaders. Another possibility occurred to us. Folk who have become accustomed to dictation find it hard to make decisions without it. At any rate, Josiah came to the throne at eight years of age. Josiah's mother was Jedidah, the daughter of Adaiah of Bozkath. The Bible tells us nothing but their names.

Josiah proved to be a good king, reestablishing the worship of Jehovah and commanding obedience to the law when a copy was found in the temple by Hilkiah the priest and read to Josiah by Shaphan the scribe.

An unusual character for this period of Hebrew history is introduced to us here. Josiah sent prominent envoys

178

to Huldah, the prophetess, requesting her help. Some authorities believe a college existed at the place where Huldah was approached and that she might have been a teacher there. She brought God's word to them, assuring Josiah that, although Judah would suffer for the sins the nation had committed, God would not allow Josiah to be punished because he had righted the wrongs as soon as he learned from the law. A woman of such prominence was rare in that day. She is named the wife of Shallum.

When Josiah's reforms were put into practice, we again meet special emphasis upon the family. They observed the law by worshiping as families (II Chron. 35:4, 5ff.). The Biblical scribe reports, "And there had not been celebrated a Passover like it in Israel since the days of Samuel the prophet; nor had any of the kings of Israel celebrated such a Passover as Josiah did with the priests, the Levites, all Judah and Israel who were present, and the inhabitants of Jerusalem" (II Chron. 35:18).

Josiah was mortally wounded in battle with Neco king of Egypt. "So his servants took him out of the chariot and carried him in the second chariot which he had, and brought him to Jerusalem where he died and was buried in the tombs of his fathers. And all Judah and Jerusalem mourned for Josiah" (II Chron. 35:24). Jeremiah chanted a lament at his funeral.

Jehoahaz, Josiah's son, ascended the throne following the death of his father. His mother's name was Hamutal, the daughter of Jeremiah of Libnah. It is thought that Jeremiah of Libnah was a priest leading some of the reforms instigated by Josiah. Jehoahaz only reigned three months. Neco, Pharaoh of Egypt, carried him to Egypt where he died. We are given no explanation for this, only that Jehoahaz

179

was evil, another instance where the son of a good father turned out badly.

The king of Egypt placed Eliakim, Jehoahaz's brother on the throne of Judah and changed his name to Jehoiakim. Jehoiakim's mother was Zebidah the daughter of Pedaiah of Rumah. We know little about his mother or grandfather. He was an evil king, another son of the good Josiah with, apparently, no redeeming virtues.

Nebuchadnezzar king of Babylon moved on Judah, making Jehoiakim his servant. After three years, Jehoiakim rebelled. We are told in II Chronicles 36:6 that Nebuchadnezzar carried Jehoiakim to Babylon in bronze chains. We only know Jehoiakim died, not the place or circumstances of his death nor his burial spot.

Jehoiachin, son of Jehoiakim and Nehushta the daughter of Elnathan of Jerusalem ascended the throne. The fact that the narrative in II Kings 24 mentions the king mother specifically ahead of his wives and the officials of the realm probably indicates she was a tremendous influence in the life of the young monarch. The Bible declares his actions to have been evil, so Nehushta was no force for good; at least, not a successful force for good.

Nebuchadnezzar placed Jehoiachin's uncle, Mattaniah, on the throne and changed his name to Zedekiah. Zedekiah was a full brother of Jehoahaz, with Josiah and Hamutal as parents. He, too, was wicked.

What was Josiah's record as a father? Was he, like David, too busy being king, reforming everyone else, to spend time and effort disciplining his sons? We find definite Biblical evidence to indicate career-oriented people often make poor parents unless someone devotes quality time to the children. There seems to be no substitute for loving care, discipline, and moral and spiritual teaching in the early years of a child's life. One might describe many of these sons of the palace as "poor little rich boys." May we not see a repetition of that in our society today?

Zedekiah rebelled against Nebuchadnezzar who responded by laying siege to Jerusalem. II Kings 25:3 reads, "On the ninth day of the fourth month, the famine was so severe in the city that there was no food for the people of the land."

Zedekiah fled in the middle of the night but was captured on the plains of Jericho. As was the custom in those days, the king of Babylon treated Zedekiah brutally. "And they slaughtered the sons of Zedekiah before his eyes, then put out the eyes of Zedekiah and bound him with bronze fetters and brought him to Babylon" (II Kings 25:7). How could a father live with that memory as his last sight?

This was the end of the kingdom of Judah as the people had known it. Never again in Biblical times did the kingdom assume a position of greatness among the nations of the known world. No doubt the people, distressed by their exile, wondered what had caused their downfall as they wept by the waters of Babylon. The serious student realizes the kingdom was doomed to decline when the homes failed to produce sterling leadership for that kingdom, leadership dedicated first to God and then to the political problems whose proper solutions determined survival. Most of their kings were evil, devoted to grabbing wealth and power for themselves.

Strong families build strong nations. Weak, immoral families destroy civilization. Biblical history describes it. Are we learning or repeating?

18

FAMILIES OF THE KINGS OF ISRAEL

One of the reasons for the division of the kingdom may have originated with their concept of family. When Saul became king, he was chosen both by God and by popular demand. David ascended the throne the same way. However, Solomon obtained the crown through the efforts of a small number of leaders and the determination of the aged David to anoint his successor. God appears from the text to have placed his stamp of approval upon Solomon also. However, one must be careful in accentuating this too much, for God never really approved the establishment of a kingdom in the first place and warned about the dangers involved in that type of government. The people were given no opportunity to express themselves in the selection of Solomon.

When Solomon placed his own personal glory ahead of the welfare of his people, seething anger and rumbling complaints formed an undercurrent throughout the land. All that was needed to instigate a full scale revolt was Rehoboam's foolish reply to the petition of the people to lighten their load. The division might have happened anyway. After the combination of theocracy and democracy to which they had become accustomed, the people disliked the idea of an established dynasty.

The Hebrews were an independent people, much more accustomed to thinking as tribes than as a nation. This attitude is reflected in I Kings 12:16.

> When all Israel saw that the king did not listen to them, the people answered the king, saying, "What portion have we in David?
>> We have no inheritance in the son of Jesse;
>> To your tents, O Israel!
>> Now look after your own house, David!"
> So Israel departed to their tents.

These words had been spoken in the revolt led by Sheba during David's reign many years before (II Sam. 20:1). This time they meant something! Rehoboam neither received nor merited the love of the people as David had. This time ten of the twelve tribes walked away for good. This might be stated in modern language, "Who needs David and his tyrant grandson? We can make it on our own and choose our own king!" So they did.

We find a similar type of thought in the United States at the time of the war between the states. Most have thought of that war as a conflict to end slavery. The root lay more, perhaps, in the difference of opinion concerning the type of government acceptable to the opposing parts of the nation. Southerners were strong supporters of states' rights. Northern officials believed in a strong central government. Slavery made good newspaper copy, but the division was deeper than that.

The oppression of the people under Solomon would have made good newspaper copy in ancient Israel, too. But part of the problem lay in their thinking more as clans or tribes than as a nation. They had much deeper loyalties to their own families or tribes than they felt toward the nation as a whole.

They chose Jeroboam, the leader of an earlier revolt against Solomon (I Kings 12:20). He was an Ephraimite, the son of Nebat of Zeredah and his wife, Zeruah, a widow (I Kings 11:26). Nebat must have died before Jeroboam became prominent.

Jeroboam's membership in the tribe of Ephraim is significant. Ephraim formed a much larger segment of the Israelites than Judah. Granting the strong tribal loyalties of that era, the other tribes probably chafed at being dominated by a king who represented a small tribe like Judah. Family pride may be witnessed in the designation of members of the tribes of Ephraim and Manasseh as "children of Joseph" many years after Joseph's death. No doubt they gathered around their campfires when angry over their oppression and discussed their ancestry. We can almost hear them saying, "Who was greater, Joseph or Judah? Why should we let this descendant of Judah mistreat the children of Joseph?"

So the issue of family definitely entered into the division of the kingdom. Animosities among the tribes simmering for generations finally precipitated separation. Rehoboam's stupidity and Jeroboam's ambition were only the matches that finally lit the fire that had been laid many years before.

Jeroboam recognized the danger of permitting the people to travel to Jerusalem to worship. Such pilgrimages might change their allegiance due to nostalgia for the old ways. So he set up worship centers at Bethel and Dan with golden images for the people to revere. Obviously Jeroboam did not have enough religion for the idolatry to bother his conscience. From the time of this apostasy, the die was cast. Israel was doomed but they went through several kings first.

God sent a man to warn Jeroboam. He refused to change his ways. Jeroboam had married a princess of Egypt during his exile there following the revolt against Solomon. Maybe her influence was stronger than the words of the man of God. Family again!

Abijah, Jeroboam's son, became sick. Jeroboam sent his wife in disguise to inquire of the prophet Ahijah. God told Ahijah who she was and gave him a message for her to take to Jeroboam. After condemning him for his misuse of power to lead the people in the worship of idols, Ahijah prophesied about Jeroboam's family.

> Therefore, behold, I am bringing calamity on the house of Jeroboam, and will cut off from Jeroboam every male person, both bound and free in Israel, and I will make a clean sweep of the house of Jeroboam, as one sweeps away dung until it is all gone. Anyone belonging to Jeroboam who dies in the city the dogs will eat. And he who dies in the field the birds of the heavens will eat; for the Lord has spoken it (I Kings 14:10, 11).

Ahijah told Jeroboam's wife that Abijah would die and would be the only one with proper burial "because in him something good was found toward the Lord God of Israel in the

186

house of Jeroboam" (I Kings 14:13). So God spared Abijah in whom He saw good by taking him before he could suffer as the wicked ones would. This is a very thought-provoking statement in regard to death.

II Chronicles 13 records a battle between the troops of Abijah, king of Judah, and Jeroboam's army. Israel was soundly defeated. The chronicler says, "And Jeroboam did not again recover strength in the days of Abijah; and the Lord struck him and he died" (13:20).

Nadab ascended the throne of Israel following the death of his father. He only reigned two years, but these were evil years. During a war against the Philistines at Gibbethon, Baasha, son of Ahijah of the tribe of Issachar, assassinated Nadab and claimed the throne for himself. This is another clue to conflict among the tribes. As we have mentioned earlier, the tribal fighting might be compared to Scottish clan wars for supremacy and Appalachian family feuds. After killing Nadab, Baasha wiped out Jeroboam's entire family.

Baasha was certainly no improvement over Jeroboam and Nadab. He was a very evil king, too. Jehu warned Baasha with the same prophecy Ahijah had used in regard to Jeroboam. Baasha ruled in Israel at the same time Asa occupied the throne of Judah. "And there was war between Asa and Baasha king of Israel all their days" (I Kings 15:32).

We might note in regard to this Scripture that family feuds or battles among those who once were very close seem more violent than battles between people who have always disliked each other. We may observe this in personal relationships as well as family relationships. This is one of the greatest tragedies of humanity. We often appear unable to tolerate disagreements with those whose opinions we value. This separates families into armed camps and destroys happiness.

Following Baasha's death, his son Elah became king. He was no prize either. After two years on the throne, Elah was assassinated by Zimri, commander of half his chariots. "Now he (Elah) was at Tirzah drinking himself drunk in the house of Arza, who was over the household at Tirzah. Then Zimri went in and struck him and put him to death . . . , and became king in his place" (I Kings 16:9, 10).

". . . as soon as he sat on his throne, . . . he killed all the household of Baasha; he did not leave a single male, neither of his relatives nor of his friends" (I Kings 16:11). It may have been unrewarding to be a woman in Old Testament days, but it certainly was healthier. They showed little interest in what a woman thought or felt, but they didn't kill all the women when they assassinated royal families. Some of them were carried away to fates worse than death, however.

Zimri lasted seven days. He obviously had little support from the people. They selected Omri, commander of the army as their king. They besieged the city of Tirzah. ". . . when Zimri saw that the city was taken, . . . he went into the citadel of the king's house and burned the king's house over him with fire, and died" (I Kings 16:18). The Scripture tells us half the people wanted Omri as king while the other half followed Tibni the son of Ginath. Omri triumphed and Tibni died.

Omri was quite a general, transferring the capital from Tirzah to Samaria, a much easier city to fortify. However, he was a very evil man, ". . . and acted more wickedly than all who were before him" (I Kings 16:25).

At the death of Omri, his son Ahab became king. With the reign of Ahab, Israel hit an all-time low, partly because of his marriage to Jezebel, daughter of Ethbaal, king of

188

the Sidonians. Jezebel was so totally depraved that her name has been used as a derogatory term describing wicked women for centuries. "She's a Jezebel" has become an epithet!

Jezebel might be termed a religious fanatic in the worship of Baal. She determined to wipe out all vestiges of Jehovah worship in the land by exterminating all the prophets of God. A godly servant, manager of the household, Obadiah, hid one hundred of the prophets, feeding them and saving their lives.

The confrontation between Elijah and the prophets of Baal on Mount Carmel fascinates all of us. However, for family study, we must focus on Ahab and Jezebel.

Ahab, although evil, was naive compared to Jezebel. She was the strong partner of the marriage. It was Jezebel, not Ahab, who threatened Elijah after the destruction of the prophets of Baal. Ahab used some sarcastic phrases, but Jezebel scared the prophet, as well she might. Jezebel was a terrible enemy with no ethics to inhibit her. It was Jezebel who engineered the death of Naboth when the pouting Ahab couldn't get him to sell his vineyard (I Kings 21). One cannot read the Biblical story without realizing Jezebel ran the show!

Jezebel helped destroy Israel and Ahab. She also destroyed her children because they copied her ways. We have already discussed Athaliah and her part in the downfall of Jehoram and the eventual fall of Judah. So, in one sense, Jezebel was influential in the annihilation of both kingdoms. She lives in history as one of the most evil women of all time.

After the wicked destruction of Naboth by Jezebel, Elijah pronounced the same curse upon the family of Ahab that had been uttered against the family of Jeroboam. He also declared the dogs would lick up Ahab's blood at the same spot where they had drunk the blood of Naboth (I Kings 21). I Kings 21:25 says, "Surely there was no one like Ahab who sold himself to do evil in the sight of the Lord, because Jezebel his wife incited him." Upon hearing this condemnation of himself and his family, Ahab repented in sackcloth and ashes. God accepted his change of life, but it did not last long. He soon returned to his old tricks, but not before God had helped him win a battle with Ben-hadad of Syria. Any thoughtful reader stands in awe at the many opportunities God provides for unappreciative and wicked families of men. This runs throughout the entire Bible.

In a renewed battle with Syria, Ahab was killed. They took his body back to Samaria. "And they washed the chariot by the pool of Samaria, and the dogs licked up the blood . . . according to the word of the Lord which He spoke" (I Kings 22:38).

Ahaziah, the son of Ahab, became king of Israel after Ahab's death. No wife is mentioned other than Jezebel for Ahab. He did have a harem, for seventy sons appear in the record. We know nothing of the other wives or concubines. Jezebel obviously topped the list. She would have accepted no other position!

Jezebel probably fulfilled most of the needs of the spineless, morally depraved Ahab. She did get things done, especially the things he pouted about. At any rate, Ahaziah was her son. Little is recorded for his short reign except for its evil quality. He appeared to inherit the callous character of Ahab plus the stubbornness of Jezebel. He died after approximately two years on the throne.

Ahaziah had no son to succeed him, so Jehoram, his brother, came to the throne. (At part of this period, two men of the same name reigned in the divided kingdoms: Jehoram, son of Jehoshaphat king of Judah, the husband of Athaliah, daughter of Ahab and Jezebel; and Jehoram, son of Ahab and Jezebel.) Apparently Jehoram of Israel was not quite so evil as his father, brother or sister. He even destroyed some Baal worship. (Perhaps he possessed no religion of any kind and was simply rebelling against his domineering mother!)

Due to the relationship of the two royal families, an alliance was formed between Israel and Judah with a third member of the group, the king of Edom. They battled Moab and won. Jehosphaphat was still reigning in Judah at the time of this battle. He was a godly king. The Scripture says God gave the victory to the triumvirate because of him.

II Kings 8:28 tells of the wounding of Jehoram of Israel in a war waged by Ahaziah of Judah and Jehoram of Israel against the Syrians at Ramoth-Gilead. He went to Jezreel to convalesce from his wounds. His brother-in-law, Ahaziah king of Judah, paid him a visit. In a *coup d' etat* engineered by the prophet Elisha, Jehu and his captains went to Jezreel to kill both Jehoram and Ahaziah. "And Jehu drew his bow with his full strength and shot Joram (Jehoram) between his arms; and the arrow went through his heart and he sank in his chariot" (II Kings 9:24). They carried his body and threw it in Naboth's vineyard. Ahaziah was also shot, but did not die immediately.

Jezebel heard of the assassinations. A determined woman to the end, she met Jehu with sarcasm when he arrived in Jezreel. She scoffed at him from an upstairs window of the palace. Jehu ordered the officials who were peering out of the window with the queen to throw her out. They did. The horses trampled her body. When

191

Jehu returned to bury her some time later, nothing remained but her skull, feet and the palms of her hands.

Perhaps no more bloodthirsty king than Jehu is recorded in Old Testament history. II Kings 10:1 informs us Ahab had seventy sons in Samaria. Jehu wrote letters about them, finally demanding that the officials deliver their heads in baskets to him to prove their loyalty to his regime. The text indicates some of them were small boys. It was done.

"So Jehu killed all who remained of the house of Ahab in Jezreel, and all his great men and his acquaintances and his priests, until he left him without a survivor" (II Kings 10:11). As we can see, it didn't even pay to have a nodding acquaintance with anyone from Ahab's household!

After wiping out all Ahab's descendants in Jezreel, Jehu headed for Samaria. On the road he met forty-two men who were relatives of Ahaziah. Jehu's men killed them, too. Upon arriving in Samaria, he killed all of Ahab's family remaining there. Then he pretended to plan a worship service honoring Baal. Everyone who attended was executed by Jehu and his men.

We read these accounts of massacres of whole families and shudder. In the light of Christian commitment, we cannot understand the ancient concept of the worship of God. What a far cry from the Christ who died for the sins of the world! How far removed all this is from "turning the other cheek!"

It was a different era. The one thing making these stories possible to endure is the fact that, given the opportunity, the men Jehu killed would have treated him the same way. It was a barbarous age and these Hebrews were in step with their times.

One interesting point coming from this gory story may be found in II Kings 10:28, 29. "Thus Jehu eradicated Baal

192

out of Israel. However, as for the sins of Jeroboam the son of Nebat, which he made Israel sin, from these Jehu did not depart, even the golden calves that were at Bethel and that were at Dan." The Adolph Hitlers of this world always find what they consider to be righteous reasons for their behavior. But when all is said and done, personal ambition often turns out to be their god. The reformer, Jehu, only kept up the reform until he reached his goal, a seat on the throne of Israel.

II Kings 10:35, 36 tells of Jehu's death and his long reign of twenty-eight years. No revolt occurred. He had killed everyone who might have led one!

Jehoahaz, Jehu's son, became king in his place. He was no great improvement, but he was not quite so bloodthirsty as his father. He worshiped the golden calves, too. Piece by piece, Syria began taking over the country.

Jehoahaz died and Jehoash his son ascended the throne. His reign appears marked by nothing of great import except his evil ways. He did defeat Amaziah of Judah in battle and took the gold and silver of the temple as battle spoils.

Upon the death of Jehoahaz, his son Jeroboam II came into power. He seems to have been a practical man although an evil one. He restored the border of Israel. Little else is given of his reign.

When Jeroboam II died, his son Zechariah became king in his place. He lasted six months. Shallum the son of Jabesh led a revolt against Zechariah and killed him, assuming the throne himself.

Shallum managed to hang onto the throne for one month. Then Menahem son of Gadi assassinated him and usurped power. He reigned for ten years, but was evil. Menahem and King Pul of Assyria made a treaty by which Menahem and his people became vassals of Assyria, paying tremendous tribute. The Bible carefully states that Menahem paid none of this himself but took it from the citizens of the realm.

When Menahem died, his son Pekahiah became king. He, too, was evil and was struck down in the second year of his reign in a conspiracy instigated by Pekah, son of Remaliah, his officer.

Pekah, according to II Kings 15, held the throne for twenty years. During his reign, Tiglath-pileser of Assyria overran much of the land taking many captives to Assyria.

Hoshea, son of Elah, conjured up a plot to rid the country of Pekah. He killed the king and took the throne himself. Apparently he was not quite so evil as the others, but no one was pinning any blue ribbons on him either for wisdom or righteousness. During his reign, Shalmaneser king of Assyria attacked Israel and Hoshea had to pay him tribute. It seems Hoshea quit paying and tried to form an alliance with the king of Egypt. So the king of Assyria invaded the entire land.

Israel fell. The people were carried away into captivity. In summing up the kings of Israel after the division of the kingdom, there is little anyone can say.

Different men attempted to establish dynasties, nine in all. The first dynasty consisted of Jeroboam and his son Nadab; the second, Baasha and his son, Elah; the third, Zimri; the fourth, Omri, Ahab, Ahaziah, and Jehoram; the fifth, Jehu, Jehoahaz, Jehoash, Jeroboam II, and Zechariah; the sixth, Shallum; the seventh, Menahem and Pekahiah; the eighth, Pekah; the ninth, Hoshea.

They all lacked moral and spiritual devotion and strength. One keeps thinking while reading that they certainly deserved each other! From generation to generation their evil ways were inherited. Throughout the entire period, prophets issued frightening warnings. Yet not one good king emerges to stem the tide of decadence!

Among the kings of Judah, there were some redemptive periods. Several times a godly mother or grandfather, priest or prophet intervened to establish a young king's proper values. Prophets tried in Israel. They were always ignored or persecuted.

Perhaps the strongest character to emerge from this period of Israel following the division of the kingdom was Jezebel. Strong she was! Good she was not! So her children, her grandchildren, her nation and her world suffered. Women of that period were seldom supposed to know anything or do anything that would be of special note. Yet here was one lone woman who changed the course of history for evil.

It is amazing how influential either for good or evil a mother and grandmother can be!

19

FAMILIES IN THE BOOKS OF EZRA AND NEHEMIAH

After they had served for seventy years in captivity in Babylon, Cyrus king of Persia, offered an opportunity for all Jews who desired to return to make their way back to Palestine. The Book of Ezra occupies itself primarily with the restoration of Jehovah worship and the laws controlling that worship. Nehemiah concentrates on political restoration of the nation and its defenses. Neither book contains large amounts of family reference.

One thing noted in these books may also be observed in most ancient civilizations and continues to apply in many modern nations. Families tended to pursue the same occupations for generations. Fathers taught their sons trades and few broke away from the family mold.

Priestly and Levitical duties passed from father to son by divine command. However, we see numerous other positions that appear to be hereditary. "The singers: the sons of Asaph" are mentioned in Ezra 2:41. That chapter also names the sons of the gatekeepers, the temple servants and the sons of Solomon's servants, still denoted that way many generations after Solomon's death.

It is interesting to observe that several who claimed to be sons of priests before the exile had to prove the fact. "These searched among their ancestral registration, but they could not be located; therefore they were considered unclean and were excluded from the priesthood" (Ezra 2:62). Were they trying to get up in the world?

The priests and Levites and their sons acted as overseers in the restoration of the temple. Ezra himself could trace his lineage many generations back to Aaron. It is interesting to note that such careful records of genealogy were kept, seeming a bit strange in that era. But it does show the emphasis they placed upon family. Ezra is described as "a scribe skilled in the law of Moses, which the Lord God of Israel had given; and the king granted him all he requested because the hand of the Lord his God was upon him" (Ezra 7:6).

Chapter 8 of Ezra gives genealogical listings. Then chapter 9 reveals the grief of Ezra over intermarriage with idol worshipers combined with his beautiful prayer of praise to God who delivered the remnant in spite of their sins.

Shecaniah the son of Jehiel suggested legal divorces for all such marriages. In a huge assembly, they voted to conduct a court session with elders and judges of each city presiding. Two men objected strongly, Jonathan son of Asahel, and Jahzeiah the son of Tikvah. They were supported in their opposition by Meshullam and Shabbethai, the Levite.

After Ezra selected heads of families to conduct investigations, they learned several priests had married foreign women, as had numerous other men. The book of Ezra closes by saying, "All these had married foreign wives, and some of them had wives by whom they had children" (Ezra 10:44). All the wives and children were sent away. Shades of Hagar and Ishmael!

To those of us who have grown up under the American system of separation of church and state with complete liberty for all religions, this decision appears harsh. However, let us note a few things.

The first of these is the change of attitude in regard to the action taken with these women and children. Remember how Jehu disposed of those considered impure and a menace to the nation? No one was killed in this reform of Ezra's. They had grown in their understanding.

An interesting sidelight came to our attention. None of the men who objected to the hardline settlement of the problem are on the roster of those who had married idol worshipers. Were they motivated by compassion? Meshullam's daughter, however, had married Johanan, the son of Tobiah the Ammonite. He might have been trying to protect his daughter and grandchildren.

Another observation seems apropos. Throughout the section of the Old Testament already covered in our study, we have noted the tremendous influence of mothers upon the destiny of children. We have seen the effect of godly mothers upon the lives of great men of God. We also noted the role Jezebel played in the decline of two kingdoms. The decision to put away idol worshiping women and their children rubs most of us the wrong way, particularly for the children. But was that judgment for the greater good of a large number of people over a long period of time?

As we have mentioned earlier in the book, Naomi gave complete acceptance and unqualified love to her pagan daughter-in-law, Ruth. Through this approach, Ruth learned to cherish both Naomi and her God. Were there some "Ruths" among these women and children? Did anyone try to convert them to worship of Jehovah? We may be sure God did not disapprove of Naomi's method or Ruth would not have been part of the lineage of the Savior.

Perhaps all these things had been tried first with no result. The Bible never includes everything that happened in any given situation. Or maybe Ezra knew that the men, like many Christians today, would be more liable to become pagan than to persuade anyone else to be godly.

We also thought of many divorces we have seen because one person was a believer and the other totally pagan. Tragedy may be averted in any culture by careful decisions in the selection of a mate.

We also wondered what they did about Jewish girls who had married foreign men. Did they remove their daughters or leave them to pursue other gods? Ezra does not mention this side of the problem.

An interesting fact about families arises as we get into Nehemiah. Families worked together on the restoration of the gates and walls. A curious statement appears in Nehemiah 3:12. "And next to him Shallum the son of Hallohesh, the official of half the district of Jerusalem, made repairs, he and his daughters." So everyone got into the act; officials as well as laborers, women as well as men.

When the surrounding people decided to destroy them and their work, we read, "then I stationed men in the lowest parts of the space behind the wall, the exposed places, and I stationed the people in *families* with their swords, spears and bows" (Neh. 4:13).

Another emphasis upon families comes in Nehemiah's statement to the people in verse 14. ". . . Do not be afraid of them; remember the Lord who is great and awesome, and fight for your brothers, your sons, your daughters, your wives, and your houses." Note the levels of importance. Wives made it just before houses. However, this is a great improvement over Lot and his daughters and the incident of the Levite's concubine!

The people continued to work, all the families, with tools in one hand and weapons in the other. They had been exiled long enough! They craved homes and settled situations in the land of their fathers. They were not so different from us, were they?

In the record of the reading of the law to the returned exiles, emphasis upon the family appears again. "Then on the second day the heads of fathers' households of all the people, the priests and the Levites were gathered to Ezra the scribe that they might gain insight into the words of the law" (Neh. 8:13).

The books of Ezra and Nehemiah place a threefold stress upon family relationships. The first one is, "Don't marry outside your faith." The second is, "Observe the laws of God." The third is, "When a project is worth doing, work at it, you and all your family!" This advice seems practical in the modern world as well.

20

FAMILIES FROM THE BOOK OF ESTHER

The Book of Esther begins with the story of a very brave woman, Vashti, queen of Persia.

King Ahasuerus gave a banquet lasting for seven days. All the princes and nobles had been drinking. "Drinks were served in golden vessels of various kinds, and the royal wine was plentiful according to the king's bounty" (Esth. 1:7). In other words, it was a drunken brawl.

King Ahasuerus had busied himself showing off his wealth. Not one thing had been spared in his determination to impress the visitors with his importance. "On the seventh day, when the heart of the king was merry with wine, he commanded . . . the seven eunuchs . . . to bring Queen Vashti before the king with her royal crown in order to display her beauty to the people and the princes, for she was beautiful" (Esth. 1:10, 11). In our time we might say, "The old boy got bombed out of his skull and tried to force his wife to display all her charms at a drunken orgy with all his plastered playmates!"

Vashti refused the order. The Bible never says why. We might mention several good reasons. Ashasuerus or Xerxes was notoriously explosive. Once out of the harem and into that room full of drunks, she might have faced almost anything.

When her refusal was delivered to the king, he was furious. The alcohol didn't help any with his self-control! Not only was the king angry, but his companions joined him in a council of war against uppity wives. In their inebriated state, they probably considered themselves fountains of wisdom.

> "If it pleases the king, let a royal edict be issued by him and let it be written in the laws of Persia and Media so that it cannot be repealed, that Vashti should come no more into the presence of King Ahasuerus, and let the king give her royal position to another who is more worthy than she. And when the king's edict which he shall make is heard throughout all his kingdom, great as it is, then all women will give honor to their husbands, great and small,"

said Memucan, one of the princes (Esth. 1:19, 20).

Ahasuerus acted immediately. "So he sent letters to all the king's provinces, to each province according to its script and to every people according to their language, that every man should be the master in his own house and the one who speaks in the language of his own people" (Esth. 1:22).

He must have awakened the next day with a terrible hangover. What appeared such a great idea in the presence of his cronies just might have seemed stupid when he sobered up. The Scripture says, "After these things when the anger of King Ahasuerus had subsided, he remembered Vashti and what she had done and what had been decreed against her" (Esth. 2:1).

What did he remember about Vashti? Was it her beauty, her sense of propriety, her determination not to be lowered to the indignity of being paraded before a room full of drunks like a prize horse or a handful of jewels? What did he think of himself and his behavior in the sober thrust of daylight? Did he miss her? If so, he had created an impossible situation for himself because decrees once sent could not be changed. With such immutable laws, it would appear wise to write no decrees at drunken brawls. But alcohol helps no one with wisdom.

This refers to family. Ahasuerus and Vashti were family. He and the other nobles and princes with their inflated sense of the superiority of males over females broke up a family because a wife dared to take a stand she deemed important. She was never permitted to explain her reasons to the king. Do you suppose she was glad to be rid of him?

Heavy drinking still destroys families and underwrites stupid decisions. Many, many homes have been ruined because of judgments fogged by alcohol. Any notion of the superiority of one sex over another is destructive in our day also. Different we are. Superior we are not. That goes both ways.

We see one plus for Ahasuerus. He did not have Vashti killed. He could have. Except for that one positive part of the story, Ahasuerus comes across here as a classic boor!

Vashti's fate, however, had nothing to do with Esther except to explain her opportunity to save her people.

Obviously, King Ahasuerus was depressed when he no longer had the charms of Queen Vashti to rely upon. So the king's attendants rushed around to find him another beautiful young woman. Did they fear his recall of their part in the dismissal of Vashti? Had his memories of Vashti resulted in his condemnation of them for any suggestions of discipline, heads might have rolled! So they needed to occupy him immediately with beautiful young virgins!

Perhaps we should examine the way so many must have hurried to have their daughters replace Vashti. Why? Ahasuerus' track record was pretty poor. He did represent power and affluence, but even that was short-lived in a day when conspiracies created "here today, gone tomorrow" kings. Their families were usually assassinated with them.

We still behave this way. Magazines describe various men as "the world's most eligible bachelors." Often these men leave a trail of broken hearts and smashed lives. Still mothers push their pretty young daughters their way because they have money and social position. These men would fit right into Ahasuerus' crowd!

Esther, a beautiful young Jewess from the tribe of Benjamin, lived in the home of her cousin Mordecai. He had made her his daughter ever since the death of her father, his uncle. Whether Mordecai offered Esther or she was seized in the round-up of beautiful virgins is not explained. We do know she arrived at the palace harem. Mordecai instructed her to tell no one she was a Jew.

For family study, we should establish the fact that Esther remained loyal to her people and to Mordecai after being taken from poverty and anonymity to wealth and prestige. Esther was wise and stable as well as beautiful. The sense of family responsibility Mordecai exhibited also impressed us. Even before Esther was selected as queen, the Bible tells us, "And every day Mordecai walked back and forth in front of the court of the harem to learn how Esther was and how she fared" (Esth. 2:11). An admirable family relationship existed between Mordecai and Esther. Esther might be termed an adopted child. Mordecai loved her as a daughter and truly cared what happened to her.

After months of coaching and preparation, Esther finally received her summons to spend the night with Ahasuerus. (Do moderns believe sleeping together before marriage is a new wrinkle? This *pagan* society tested women for the king that way about 2500 years ago!) "And the king loved Esther more than all the women, and she found favor and kindness with him more than all the virgins, so that he set the royal crown on her head and made her queen instead of Vashti" (Esth. 2:17).

Mordecai continued to watch over her. She followed his advice "as she had done when under his care" (2:20). Each day Mordecai sat at the king's gate to keep in touch with Esther. While resting there one day, he overheard a plot to assassinate the king. "He told Queen Esther, and Esther informed the king in Mordecai's name" (2:22). The king's men investigated, learned the validity of the accusations and hanged the offenders.

The king appointed a man named Haman as second in authority to him. We might designate him as prime minister. With the promotion came a type of prestige demanding obeisance of the citizenry when Haman passed by. Everyone obeyed but Mordecai. Apparently Mordecai's concept of Jewish law forbade his bowing down to an officer such as Haman.

Why do small-souled people have such gigantic egos? If everyone else bowed down to him, what difference did one little Jew make? Why did it fill Haman with such rage because Mordecai did not think he was so great? A genuine leader would have ignored the little Jew at the side of the road. But not Haman.

Haman considered it beneath his dignity to strike out at Mordecai. He resolved to stamp out every Jew in the kingdom. So he laid his careful plan. He would get that independent Jew by killing not only him but everything he held dear. Just the type of leader for the establishment of justice in a nation!

Haman approached the king with his plot. Ahasuerus had no way of knowing Haman had a personal grudge against one Jew. So, Haman tried to couch his suggestion in language that would make him appear the model servant of the king.

> . . . "There is a certain people scattered and dispersed among the peoples in all the provinces of your kingdom; their laws are different from those of all other people, and they do not observe the king's laws, so it is not in the king's interest to let them remain. If it is pleasing to the king, let it be decreed that they be destroyed, and I will pay ten thousand talents of silver into the hands of those who carry on the king's business, to put into the king's treasury" (Esth. 3:8, 9).

Reading this story makes one wonder about Ahasuerus' I.Q.! Any idiot could have figured out that Haman was engaged in a personal vendetta when he offered to give that much money to the king's treasury for getting to annihilate a particular people! Ahasuerus' respect for human life, admittedly, was not one of his strong points. So he gave Haman the go-ahead signal and the decree was issued. Even a time was set when all the Jews were to be put to death.

208

After their little excursion into murder plans, Ahasuerus and Haman sat down to have a drink together. ". . . while the king and Haman sat down to drink, the city of Susa was in confusion" (Esth. 3:15).

Mordecai assumed his regular position at the palace gate, only this time he wore sackcloth and ashes. Esther learned of his plight and sent him some good clothing but he refused to don it. Finally, Esther dispatched a eunuch to the old Jew to learn the reason for his mourning. The eunuch returned to the queen with a copy of the decree. Mordecai asked her to plead with the king for her people.

> Esther replied, "All the king's servants and the people of the king's provinces know that for any man or woman who comes to the king to the inner court who is not summoned, he has but one law, that he be put to death; unless the king holds out to him the golden scepter so that he may live. And I have not been summoned to the king for these thirty days" (Esth. 4:11).

Mordecai warned her that her position in the palace would not save her if the conditions of the edict were carried out. "For if you remain silent at this time, relief and deliverance will arise for the Jews from another place and you and your father's house will perish. And who knows whether you have not attained royalty for such a time as this?" (Esth. 4:14).

Esther asked Mordecai to request all the Jews to fast along with her for three days. At the end of that time, she would approach the king. "And if I perish, I perish" (Esth. 4:16).

At this point Esther turned to feminine wiles. One would think she had been reading some of the modern books applauding the femininity of women who use tricks to manipulate men. That is another approach considered modern although it is as old as Eve. Manipulation of another human

209

being always turns us off. But if two persons ever richly deserved it, those two were Ahasuerus and Haman.

Esther adorned herself to be at her ravishing best and stepped into the edge of the throne room. The king asked her to come to him and held out the golden scepter. One must admit, knowing Ahasuerus, that he would never have held out that scepter to a hag! Then he asked what she wanted, declaring, "Even to half of the kingdom it will be given to you" (5:3). She really must have looked good!

Then Esther used the second of a woman's arsenal of weapons. She invited those two scoundrels to a banquet. After the banquet, the king again asked her petition. She invited them to another banquet the next evening.

Haman was walking three feet off the ground! Everything was working out just as he had planned. He was not only the king's favorite but the queen's as well. But as he left the palace, there was Mordecai refusing to grovel again!

Haman went home and bragged about himself to his family and friends, declaring his happiness would be complete were it not for Mordecai. They suggested he build a gallows and get the king's permission to hang Mordecai from it the next morning. "Then go joyfully with the king to the banquet" (5:14). What strong stomachs those people had!

The king was wakeful during the night. He asked his servants to bring him the book of records and read to him. They read the part about Mordecai's uncovering the plot upon the king's life.

"And the king said, 'What honor or dignity has been bestowed on Mordecai for this?' Then the king's servants who attended him said, 'Nothing has been done for him'" (6:3). Suddenly one begins to like Ahasuerus a little better.

Haman entered the court at this auspicious moment intent upon asking permission to hang Mordecai on his newly constructed gallows. The king asked his advice. ". . . 'What is to be done for the man whom the king desires to honor?' . . ." (6:6).

A naturally modest man and brilliant thinker like Haman immediately added two and two and got sixteen, deciding he was the man to be honored. Of course! Who else was there in the kingdom who could possibly be worthy of honor but the mighty Haman! So Haman tried to think of something outstanding. He suggested the king place royal robes and a royal crown on the man and have one of the king's most noble princes lead that man on horseback, crying out, "Thus it shall be done to the man whom the king desires to honor" (6:9).

It is a miracle Haman did not die of apoplexy when informed the honoree was Mordecai! Then the king ordered Haman to lead the Jew through the city. Haman obeyed the king. Then he hurried home in a state of mourning with his head covered. His wife, Zeresh, and his wise men warned him he would fall before Mordecai.

Time for the second banquet arrived. After eating, Ahasuerus asked Esther for her petition, promising to grant it before even hearing it. Queen Esther pled for her life and the lives of her people. Obviously, the king had never connected her with the decree he had issued for the slaughter of the Jews. He was very angry, asking who would do such a thing. Esther named Haman. The king's anger was probably multiplied because he felt like such a fool. If he didn't, he should have! He stalked into the palace garden, perhaps to come to grips with his own stupidity.

Haman, begging for his life, fell upon the couch where Esther was reclining just as the king returned from the garden. "Will he even assault the queen with me in the

211

house?" the angry king asked. Anger is always twice as intense when one feels used. The king knew he had been.

Ahasuerus ordered Haman to be hanged on the gallows built for Mordecai. Haman's house was given to Esther. Mordecai became prime minister in Haman's place.

However, something still had to be done about that decree. Since the original decree could not be revoked, a second was sent giving the Jews of the realm the right to defend themselves against anyone trying to kill them. They were granted permission to destroy their enemies. In the fighting that ensued, the Jews went much further than self-defense demanded. They were victorious, annihilating their opponents including all of the ten sons of Haman.

This battle is the source for the Feast of Purim. Esther's loyalty and courage combined with the wisdom of Mordecai saved all her people from extinction.

From the standpoint of family, the main thrust of this book appears twofold. 1) Bad situations can be used for good of the family if opportunities are seized. Our opportunities probably will never be so dramatic. However, wringing one's hands in holy horror will not solve them. We must look at every bad situation for the gateway to opportunity provided by God. 2) Outstanding people remain loyal to their families even if elevated to positions above them in the human caste system. Great souls do not allow prominence to separate them from those who brought them into the world and protected them during the years when they needed that protection.

One very strange fact comes from this book making its inclusion in the canon unusual. God's name or any reference to Him never appears.

PART V: WISDOM IN POETRY

21

THE FAMILY OF JOB

We meet a wealthy man, Job, in the first verse of the book that bears his name. He lived in the land of Uz, "was blameless, upright, fearing God, and turning away from evil" (Job 1:1).

Job was a loving father with seven sons and three daughters. This was a closely knit family. "And his sons used to go and hold a feast in the house of each one on his day, and they would send and invite their three sisters to eat and drink with them" (1:4). After each feast, Job offered burnt offerings for his children. ". . . for Job said, 'Perhaps my sons have sinned and cursed God in their hearts.' Thus did Job continually" (1:5).

Both God and Satan had observed this model family. When they met, Satan asserted he had been roaming the earth. So God asked, "Have you seen My servant Job? He is blameless and upright, fearing God and turning away from evil."

"Why shouldn't he?" Satan retorted. "He has everything he wants and needs. If You take all he has, he will curse You." (How often we play the devil's role, exclaiming about some prosperous person, "Well, I could be like that, too, if I had all the things he has!") God allowed Satan to take everything Job possessed, stipulating that he not touch Job himself.

Satan struck. All Job's children were killed and all his wealth disappeared overnight.

Then Job arose and tore his robe and shaved his head, and he fell to the ground and worshiped. And he said,

"Naked I came from my mother's womb,
And naked I shall return there.
The Lord gave and the Lord has taken away.
Blessed be the name of the Lord."

Through all this Job did not sin nor did he blame God (1:20-22).

God and Satan met a second time. Again God pointed out Job's sterling character even through testing. Satan protested. "But you didn't let me hurt him personally. If you make him sick and in pain, he will curse you!"

God permitted Satan to afflict Job with illness, commanding him not to take Job's life. "Then Satan went out from the presence of the Lord, and smote Job with sore boils from the sole of his foot to the crown of his head" (2:7).

An aged doctor we once knew who had practiced medicine during smallpox epidemics, told us the designation of Job's illness throughout the book might form a classic description of smallpox.

At this point we deal with family response to illness and grief. Job's wife had lost all her children and been reduced to poverty. In addition to that, she was watching her husband suffer with a terrible, nauseating type of sickness. She could not handle the stress.

> Then his wife said to him, "Do you still hold fast to your integrity? Curse God and die!"
> But Job said to her, "You speak as one of the foolish women speaks. Shall we indeed accept good from God and not accept adversity?" In all this Job did not sin with his lips (2:9, 10).

We read no reply from Job's wife. Perhaps she was sobbing so hard she couldn't talk. We may not admire her reaction to all their troubles, but we can certainly understand it. She added to Job's distress with her inability to accept and adjust to their problems. But we notice Job's rebuke was soft. No statement appears in Holy Writ condemning her. She was not ill like Job, but her illness might have been more intense though not so obvious. Severe emotional damage accompanies a mother's loss of her entire family. The Bible accords the suffering woman that sympathy.

Job's three friends, Eliphaz the Temanite, Bildad the Shuhite, and Zophar the Naamathite came to call on the sick man. They sat with him for seven days without uttering a word, "For they saw that his pain was very great" (2:13).

Job finally spoke, not cursing God but the day he was born.

> "Why is light given to him who suffers,
> And life to the bitter of soul;
> Who long for death, but there is none,
> And dig for it more than for hidden treasures;
> Who rejoice greatly,
> They exult when they find the grave?" (3:20-22).

215

Eliphaz reminds Job of all the things Job has said to suffering people.

> "But now it has come to you, and you are impatient;
> It touches you, and you are dismayed.
> Is not your fear of God your confidence,
> And the integrity of your ways your hope?" (4:5, 6).

Eliphaz expounds upon his belief that no one is truly righteous, that God does not afflict the pure. Then, trying to console his suffering friend, he asserts,

> "You will know also that your descendants will be many,
> And your offspring as the grass of the earth" (5:25).

The suffering Job refuses to be comforted by the awkward consolation offered by Eliphaz. Instead he protests he has done nothing to deserve this and a "despairing man" should receive kindness from his friend.

> "Therefore, I will not restrain my mouth;
> I will speak in the anguish of my spirit,
> I will complain in the bitterness of my soul" (7:11).

Then Job speaks to God in his pain.

> "Have I sinned? What have I done to Thee,
> O watcher of men?
> Why hast Thou set me as Thy target,
> So that I am a burden to myself?" (7:20).

Job's friend, Bildad, suggested his sons might have sinned and reiterated the thoughts of Eliphaz. He contended that only the sinful suffer, that Job needed to confess his sins so God would heal him.

Job agrees somewhat with Bildad. However, he protests, no one has strength enough to deal with the omnipotence of God. Job's cry is filled with bitterness as he again defies his friends and longs for death.

Zophar the Naamathite enters the conversation by accusing Job of boasting about himself. He, too, assumes Job's guilt.

Job's bitterness appears to be replaced by anger when he answers Zophar.

> "Truly then you are the people.
> And with you wisdom will die.
> But I have intelligence as well as you;
> I am not inferior to you." (12:2, 3)

Job asserts that it is easy to judge when you are not the one experiencing calamity. Then he argues that wicked people prosper and appear secure, even come into power in the world. He accuses his friends of being "worthless physicians" (13:4), suggesting they keep still and let him talk to God about it.

From the depths of Job's bitterness and anger, we hear him say,

> "Though He slay me,
> I will hope in Him.
> Nevertheless I will argue my ways before Him.
> This also will be my salvation,
> For a Godless man may not come before His presence"
> (13:15, 16).

He follows this by crying out,

> "Why dost Thou hide Thy face,
> And consider me Thine enemy?" (13:24).

In his pain, Job really believes God is not listening, has completely deserted him. He asks the eternal question, "Why?"

217

Eliphaz accuses Job again of pretending to wisdom he cannot possess. Obviously, Eliphaz also is angry. He points out to Job that the wise men of the ages have always believed suffering is the result of wickedness. In essence, he asserts, "Who do you think you are to set your small knowledge against the wisdom of centuries?"

Job replies in despair, "It would be easy for me to come up with platitudes if you were the one who was suffering. Since I am the one in pain, it is not quite so simple." By this time, Job is weeping profusely. His depth of depression appears in Job 17:13-16.

> "If I look for Sheol as my home,
> I make my bed in the darkness;
> If I call to the pit, 'You are my father';
> To the worm, my mother and my sister;
> Where now is my Hope? And who regards my hope?
> Shall we together go down into the dust?"

In a fit of anger, Bildad replies to Job. He protests Job's attitude toward them in the midst of his speech.

> "Why are we regarded as beasts.
> As stupid in your eyes?" (18:2)

Then he describes the destiny of the wicked, asserting Job should fear speaking as he had.

Job pleads for understanding, insisting no one respects him or cares for him since all these afflictions have come upon him.

> "He has removed my brothers far from me,
> And my acquaintances are completely estranged
> from me.
> My relatives have failed,
> And my intimate friends have forgotten me.

218

My breath is offensive to my wife,
And I am loathsome to my own brothers.

. . .

And those I love have turned against me."
(19:13, 14, 17, 19)

He pleads again for pity and understanding while pronouncing these beautiful words of faith.

"For I know that my redeemer liveth,
And that he shall stand at the latter day upon the earth;
And though after my skin worms destroy this body,
Yet in my flesh shall I see God" (19:25, 26, KJV).

Zophar replies by carefully outlining the terrible destiny of the wicked.

Job remains unimpressed. Agreeing that in the end, the wicked suffer, he insists they often prosper. "Why are their children untouched?" he asks. Then Job demands of his friends.

"How then will you vainly comfort me,
For your answers remain full of falsehood?" (21:34).

Eliphaz accuses Job of injuring the poor, the widows and the orphans. Then he urges Job to make his peace with God.

Job denies all the charges. He says he has struggled in his suffering to find God but feels that God is avoiding him. He returns to his premise that evil people do not experience the grief he has born.

Bildad answers that no man can be just and pure, calling men and their sons "worms" and "maggots."

Job rebels again at the unsympathetic and critical attitudes of Bildad. He questions sarcastically, ". . . whose spirit was expressed through you?" (26:4). He repeats his denial of the accusations they have made, contending he will enter his grave with his integrity intact.

Then Job becomes nostalgic, longing for the days when life was simple and filled with family, good health, good friends and understanding. Again he bewails his fate. He protests anew that he had done nothing to merit such severe punishment.

Eliphaz, Bildad and Zophar stop talking with Job, "because he was righteous in his own eyes" (32:1).

Now we hear from the young man of the group, Elihu, son of Barachel the Buzite of the family of Ram. One might describe him as a know-it-all. The Scripture says his anger burned; "against Job his anger burned because he justified himself before God. And his anger burned against his three friends because they had found no answer, and yet had condemned Job" (32:2, 3). Elihu had lived just long enough to make him think he knew all the answers. His speech displayed his inexperience, many words with little depth. The gist of his many words is that suffering is the result of sin and is intended by God to be corrective rather than punitive.

Elihu continues speaking telling the others God cannot be accused by human reason and will not answer pride and vanity. He avers that Job considers himself more righteous than God. He insists that, if God afflicts the righteous, it is for their instruction.

One would like to know Elihu's age. Anyone who has reared a family knows teen-agers often reach the stage of knowing all the answers for questions they have never dealt with in life. They also love to point out the stupidity of their elders. Thousands of years seem to make little difference in human behavior.

As we read Job again we thought of what would happen to these visitors in a modern hospital. Any self-respecting physician would throw them out on their ears.

Finally God enters the conversation. He never condemns Job, but questions him instead.

"Where were you when I laid the foundation of the earth!
Tell Me, if you have understanding,
Who set its measurements, since you know?" (38:4, 5)

God points out the many fallacies in the reasoning of men due to their lack of true information. God suggests several times that Job instruct Him since Job knows so much. Job humbly admits his lack of understanding of eternal truth, asking that God instruct him.

God speaks to Job's friends. He tells them they had not spoken truth about Him as Job had done. He commands them to go to Job to make sacrifice for their sins. Job prays for them and they receive forgiveness.

The story closes with the restoration of Job's wealth and status, and God's gift of seven sons and three daughters to Job and his wife. "And he named the first Jemimah, and the second Keziah, and the third Keren-happuch. And in all the land no women were found so fair as Job's daughters: and their father gave them inheritance among their brothers" (40:14, 15).

Job lived following his period of suffering for one hundred and forty more years, seeing his sons and grandsons, four generations.

The language of the poetry of Job surpasses the beauty of most other books, even in the Bible. The lovely imagery expressed as God describes creation and the natural beauty of his world is awe inspiring. But the book is also practical for families.

221

All families at some point in their lives are devastated by the apparently unfair tragedies of this world. Every family goes through periods of suffering. We believe Job is included in the Bible for that very reason.

For many years, Bible students have extolled the patience of Job. The fact of the matter as recorded in the text is just the opposite. The meaning of the word patience is "endurance without complaint." Job endured. He endured with his faith intact. But he screamed at the top of his lungs about the pain and heartache forced upon him through no fault of his own. Yet when God finally spoke to the group of men, He praised Job for his truthfulness. God rebuked the others for insisting suffering and tragedy always result from sin. He scolded Job also for daring to criticize Him, pointing to Job's inability to judge competently due to his lack of knowledge.

The reader is fascinated by God's speaking of Job as "My servant Job" even after Job had complained so angrily of the treatment he had received, arguing that God had deserted him and would not even listen to him. The reactions of Job were natural. God understood this even if his friends did not.

In reading this, one wonders if the phrase, "With friends like them, who needs enemies?" originated with Job. His friends certainly offered no comfort to the aching heart of Job. However, they presented arguments one still hears in regard to suffering. A renewal of these age-old lies has swept down upon our miracle-seeking society of today.

Job tells us we shall never understand suffering. Our knowledge remains too limited. But we may be assured that tragedies our families experience do not always reflect personal sin and neglect. Sometimes they do, but certainly not always.

Another fundamental truth emerges from this story for us to remember when our families face trouble. There is a cycle of grief. We pass through all sorts of emotional turmoil, questions, anger and blame before our lives assume a happier, more nearly normal course.

Thank God for books like Job to help us understand ourselves and our families.

22

THE PSALMS

Most of us learn to appreciate the Book of Psalms as we age. It is a very beautiful book of poetry with lovely imagery and glorious language. This book also contains valuable insights for family living.

In the first psalm, the writer extols the importance of righteous living as compared with wickedness. We like this aspect of many parts of the psalms. We do not believe righteous living will free one of trouble. However, we do think an ingrained set of ethics plus a close relationship with God guarantee more happiness in this life. It is not all "pie in the sky by and by" as indicated by some who consider religion an opiate. We are convinced the family that makes morality, righteousness and a walk with God an integral part of family living will be happier. The first and fifteenth psalms describe a righteous man. In order to insure a stable family, the head of that family needs to copy the righteous man of these psalms.

One of the most vital lessons to be gained from Psalms is the ability to drop one's problems and troubles in the loving arms of God and get on with life. We read this throughout the book. When we achieve this depth of spiritual trust, we develop a consummate strength to undergird the substance of family living.

Another important teaching of Psalms is to meet God in the morning in prayer.

> In the morning, O Lord, Thou wilt hear my voice;
> In the morning I will order my prayer to Thee and
> eagerly watch (5:3).

We found that failure to meet God in the morning fouled up our whole day when we were busy rearing a family. No one can meet the physical, emotional, mental and spiritual needs of children adequately without help. The psalmist teaches us God gives that help.

The Psalms accent the importance of the individual, a concept desperately needed in abundant family living.

> What is man, that Thou dost take thought of him?
> And the son of man, that Thou dost care for him?
> Yet Thou hast made him a little lower than God,
> And dost crown him with glory and majesty (8:5).

This totally removes the idea of being "only human." The psalmist visits humanity with grace and beauty beyond our scope of understanding. Such concepts of the value of each human being raise our sights as we train children, especially those who march to a different drummer.

Often the psalmist cries out with grief and fear, sometimes with an accusing tone. But he closes these psalms with thanks to God for His help. The validity of this approach may be observed all around us in stable families. It's important to discuss our problems honestly and freely with our heavenly Father. It is all right to fuss in anger and frustration. Only then do we find the peace of faith enabling us to continue even through strife and grief. Very few seem able to accept deep trouble without some emotional reaction. Many of us have been taught we must never become angry at the forces of life that make us put our faith under a microscope. The Bible does not teach this. Rather it comes from the Victorian Period when any exhibition of emotion or pain was considered beneath us and wicked. Job complained. The psalmist complained. Complaint should not occupy front stage center in family living, but it is normal and the Bible does not condemn it.

> Let the words of my mouth and the meditation of my heart
> Be acceptable in Thy sight,
> O Lord, my rock and my redeemer (19:14).

This portion of the 19th Psalm does not contradict what we have just said. If the great saints of God were acceptable even while frustrated with their lot in life, will He not also accept us? Job complained and lost patience. He never lost faith! David's enemies almost destroyed him. His faith in God survived the stress. We need similar strength. Could Proverbs 19:14 be our prayer in times of grief and disappointment? We build upon the Lord, our "rock and redeemer."

When the family faces death of a beloved member, where may we find greater comfort than in the 23rd Psalm? But it is sustaining for life as well. We are even reminded that God's discipline protects us.

The poet recalls to our consciousness the fact that periods of grief and heartache do pass, allowing us to revive our spirits through communion with God.

> Weeping may last for the night,
> But a shout of joy comes in the morning (30:5).

The psalmist brings out a truth we, too, have felt in daily living. Things seem so much worse in the middle of the night. Who has not been awake with a sick child or perhaps some family crisis, feeling that all is blackness just like the night? Suddenly dawn breaks. The same situation exists. But crises appear less devastating in bright sunlight. Perhaps we should accept some implied advice from the psalmist as expressed in this verse. We should postpone decision making until the light of day whenever possible. Midnight anxiety makes for poor decisions.

Another implied precept may be found in this verse. Crisis should mean prayer time, especially in the middle of the night. We need to practice the presence of God, turning our problems and heartaches over to Him. Morning will bring relief from the tensions if we have formed the habit of giving our burdens to the Lord. There is an old song we need to revive. "Take your burdens to the Lord and leave them there," it advises us. Dawn brings hope.

The 46th Psalm helps us when death strikes our families by describing heaven and assuring us of God's presence.

The psalms provide comfort when we have sinned either individually or as a family. One of the foremost of these soothing passages is the 51st Psalm, but there are many others.

Psalm 68 points out ways in which God helps us. One verse applies specifically to sources of depression in the human personality, especially family loss.

A father of the fatherless and a judge for the widows,
Is God in His holy habitation.
God makes a home for the lonely (68:5, 6).

When the psalmist calls upon God for vengeance upon his enemies, he reveals the importance attached to family in the early civilization in which the psalms were written. Often he asks that the adversary's sins be visited upon his family because that would hurt him most. No Christian can advocate such feelings of revenge, but it is evidence of the stress they placed upon family.

The same emphasis appears when the psalmist asks for blessing. Often he requests these things for himself and for his children.

The 119th Psalm is one of the most beautiful. It is also filled with prayer for proper attitudes toward living, all applicable to families.

Teach me, O Lord, the way of Thy statutes,
And I shall observe it to the end.
Give me understanding that I may observe Thy law,
And keep it with all my heart.
Make me walk in the path of Thy commandments,
For I delight in it.
Incline my heart to Thy testimonies,
And not to dishonest gain.
Turn away my eyes from looking at vanity,
And revive me in Thy ways.
Establish Thy word to Thy servant,
As that which produces reverence for Thee.
Turn away my reproach which I dread,
For Thine ordinances are good.
Behold, I long for Thy precepts;
Revive me through Thy righteousness (119:33-40).

229

Thy word is a lamp to my feet,
And a light to my path.
I have sworn, and I will confirm it,
That I will keep Thy righteous ordinances (119:105, 106).

Psalm 128 declares blessedness for the family that fears the Lord and lives in His way.

How blessed is everyone who fears the Lord,
Who walks in His ways.
When you shall eat of the fruit of your hands,
You will be happy and it will be well with you.
Your wife shall be like a fruitful vine,
Within your house,
Your children like olive plants
Around your table.
Behold, for thus shall the man be blessed
Who fears the Lord.

The Lord bless you from Zion,
And may you see the prosperity of Jerusalem all the days
    of your life.
Indeed, may you see your children's children.
Peace be upon Israel! (128:1-6).

Those of us who have grandchildren know the joys they bring. The psalmist echoes our thoughts as he includes in the blessing the happiness of seeing "your children's children." The relationship of grandparents and grandchildren can scarcely be described because of the blessings it provides. Obviously it was one of the delights of old age in an earlier time also.

Psalm 133 is wholly devoted to the gratification experienced when brothers know the meaning of peaceful unity. This, of course, applied at the time of its writing to the nation of Israel. However, it is a wonderful thing for the extended family today. Nothing else plays havoc with the human spirit quite like family disunity.

Behold, how good and how pleasant it is
For brothers to dwell together in unity!
It is like precious oil upon the head,
Coming down upon the beard,
Even Aaron's beard,
Coming down upon the edge of his robes.
It is like the dew of Hermon,
Coming down upon the mountains of Zion;
For there the Lord commanded the blessing—life forever.

The imagery of the precious oil upon one's head, even running down upon the beard and to the edge of the robe indicates the healing power of family unity. The ancients considered oil to have healing properties at time of illness. So, the psalmist is actually telling us that family cooperation and love heal the spirit of mankind.

In the 144th Psalm, the poet utters the prayer that may be found upon the lips of all godly parents.

Let our sons in their youth be as grown-up plants,
And our daughters as corner pillars fashioned as for a
    palace (144:12).

Grown-up plants produce good fruit. So the psalmist is praying for mature sons who will live up to the demands of life. Asking that the daughters be as pillars indicates the stability and security provided by the love of a genuinely mature woman. What a beautiful prayer! Our words might be less poetic, but have we not also prayed that our children might meet the demands of life in a mature and stable way?

Training children to reverence God is mentioned in Psalm 145.

> One generation shall praise Thy works to another,
> And shall declare Thy mighty acts (145:4).

Do children learn a spirit of thanksgiving and prayer at the knees of unpraying parents?

In a summation of the values of Psalms upon family living, perhaps it might be well to assess the main emphases of the book.

"Trust" forms the cornerstone for the teaching of the book, trust in God and in the wisdom and justice of His love for us. This should also form the cornerstone of the family.

"Praise" arises like an eternal song to God throughout the entire poetry of the book; praise that is spoken, praise that is sung. A family that centers its existence on praise to God for blessings and praise of each other rather than criticism will be happier and more content than a highly critical family.

"Rejoice" is another favorite word of the psalmist. Sometimes in the course of anyone's life, that rejoicing comes through tears. Families who can learn to rejoice in their blessings even while enduring suffering and hardship will rear stronger children, those who can accept adversity along with prosperity. Even in the deepest hour of grief, one may rejoice through memories.

"Mercy" may be found hundreds of times in the Psalms. If we meditate carefully upon the mercies of God, we ourselves can learn to be merciful. Those least deserving of it often need mercy most. This is true of family members as well as those of whom the psalmist wrote.

The book of Psalms is a book of consolation. Family members need to be consoled during periods of trial. Turn to the poetry of the psalmists. You may replace heartache with beauty, faith and peace.

23

THE PROVERBS

Proverbs is a book of wise sayings, attributed primarily to the pen of Solomon. We might define its central theme as "practical ethics." As such, it certainly applies to the family. The family home forms the child's first school room. If ethics are ever to be learned, the need must be sown in pre-school years. Thomas Campbell, one of the great leaders in the reformation of the 19th century here in America, ordered his son, Alexander, to memorize the entire book. Many of our great leaders of the past found the ethics of this book challenging, among them Abraham Lincoln.

The Mosaic Law uses the "Thus saith the Lord" terminology. Proverbs states many of the same precepts. However, this time they come to us as experiential. The author appears to have tried about everything. He arrived at the conclusion, via the trial and error method, that truths learned at his mother's knee could be trusted.

I Kings 4:29-34 states,

> Now God gave Solomon wisdom and very great discernment and breadth of mind, like the sand that is on the seashore. And Solomon's wisdom surpassed the wisdom of all the sons of the east and all the wisdom of Egypt. For he was wiser than all men, than Ethan the Ezrahite, Heman, Calcol and Darda, the sons of Mahol; and his fame was known in all the surrounding nations. He also spoke 3000 proverbs, and his songs were 1005. And he spoke of trees, from the cedar that is in Lebanon even to the hyssop that grows on the wall; and he spoke also of animals and birds and creeping things and fish. And men came from all people to hear the wisdom of Solomon, from all the kings of the earth who had heard of his wisdom.

So, many of the proverbs were written by a man who was recognized in his day as an authority in several fields of learning. These sayings are pithy, thought-provoking and brief. They are not connected by a procession of ideas. They often make their point by the use of antithesis.

The economic condition of Solomon's time formed a background for the imperative of moral teachings. Throughout all history of mankind, morals seem to sink lower in time of affluence. We have observed that in our own nation. When prosperity prevails, people begin to consider themselves self-sufficient masters of their own fate. Morals go down the drain in a search for material wealth and personal recognition. So it was when these proverbs first appeared. The Psalms teach us God is near at time of trouble. The book of Proverbs declares that same God demands certain standards of behavior both in prosperity and adversity.

The entire book of Proverbs deserves our sincere study. Most chapters begin, "My son," making it applicable to a book on family study. We have selected some verses aimed specifically at families.

Much of the theme of the book of Proverbs centers around wisdom. That wisdom is tied up in sayings that make sense even in our time.

> The fear of the Lord is the beginning of knowledge;
> Fools despise wisdom and instruction (1:7).

This thought runs throughout the book. The author obviously agrees with the psalmist who declares that only a fool believes there is no God.

> Hear, my son, your father's instruction,
> And do not forsake your mother's teaching;
> Indeed, they are a graceful wreath to your head,
> And ornaments about your neck (1:8, 9).

This is another recurring theme, but nowhere more beautifully stated than in this quotation.

> Trust in the Lord with all your heart,
> And do not lean on your own understanding.
> In all your ways acknowledge Him,
> And He will make your paths straight (3:5, 6).

Would that all families included this verse as a motto in their homes!

> My son, do not reject the discipline of the Lord;
> Or loathe His reproof.
> For whom the Lord loves He reproves,
> Even as a father the son in whom he delights (3:11, 12)

Family discipline is recommended all the way through Proverbs.

235

Did Solomon see the failure of his father to discipline his brothers? The proverbs are great, but one wonders about Solomon's handling of Rehoboam. Wisdom was not one of Rehoboam's strong points!

> Hear, O sons, the instruction of a father,
> And give attention that you may gain understanding,
> For I give you sound teaching;
> Do not abandon my instruction.
> When I was a son to my father,
> Tender and the only son in the sight of my mother,
> Then he taught me and said to me,
> "Let your heart hold fast my words;
> Keep my commandments and live;
> Acquire wisdom! Acquire understanding!
> Do not forget nor turn away from the words of my
>   mouth.
> Do not forsake her, and she will guard you;
> Love her, and she will watch over you" (4:1-6).

Here we see the wisdom of the multi-generation family as it is passed down to the children.

Proverbs contains repetitive warnings against sexual immorality. The author does not vilify sex, only its misuse in adulterous relationships and with harlots. In the fifth chapter some beautiful descriptive phrases are used in regard to love-making between husband and wife.

> Let your fountain be blessed,
> And rejoice in the wife of your youth.
> As a loving hind and a graceful doe,
> Let her breasts satisfy you at all times;
> Be exhilarated always with her love.
> For why should you, my son, be exhilarated with an
>   adulteress,

236

And embrace the bosom of a foreigner?
For the ways of a man are before the eyes of the Lord,
And He watches all his paths (5:18-21).

In the sixth chapter we again find exhortations to respect the commands of parents.

My son, observe the commandment of your father,
And do not forsake the teaching of your mother;
Bind them continually on your heart;
Tie them around your neck (6:20, 21).

One cannot help noticing the reference here similar to that in earlier Old Testament passages about binding the law around one's forehead as a constant reminder of its force in one's life.

Again speaking of the dangers of adulterous relationships, the writer urges,

Can a man take fire in his bosom,
And his clothes not be burned?
Or can a man walk on hot coals,
And his feet not be scorched?
So is the one who goes in to his neighbor's wife;
Whoever touches her will not go unpunished (6:27-29).

This book ties a son's behavior to his father's pride and happiness continually, thus showing the period's emphasis upon family.

A wise son makes a father glad,
But a foolish son is a grief to his mother (10:1).

Continuing some of the same theme, the author declares,

Whoever loves discipline loves knowledge,
But he who hates reproof is stupid (12:1).

A glorious marriage relationship edifies. A bad one may be destructive of both partners.

237

An excellent wife is the crown of her husband,
But she who shames him is as rottenness in his bones
(12:4).

The theme of accepting discipline occurs again in the 13th chapter of the book.

A wise son accepts his father's discipline,
But a scoffer does not listen to rebuke (13:1).

The multi-generational family appears again in this chapter.

A good man leaves an inheritance to his children's children (13:22).

We very often think of inheritance solely as some sort of material wealth. The writer may not have had this in mind when he wrote. Descendants benefit more from a heritage of faith and fine attitudes toward life than they ever derive from money alone. A heritage of spiritual values cannot be taken away by economic upheaval.

Was King Solomon thinking of the tragedies created by his brothers and David's weakness in dealing with them when he penned the following words?

He who spares the rod hates his son,
But he who loves him disciplines him diligently (13:24).

What was a man with 700 wives and 300 concubines thinking when he wrote,

The wise woman builds her house,
But the foolish tears it down with her own hands (14:1)?

We didn't develop visions of a wife who flew into a fit of rage and started wielding a crowbar when we read these words. No, it is obviously figurative language. In a polygamous system, men had ample opportunity to observe contrasting styles of behavior of women in family relationships. The statement is still true today. We quite often destroy what we want to preserve by unwise handling of crises, or just daily living, perhaps, in our homes.

The home no longer occupies the sacred position in our society that it did in former years. Women's liberation has kept women from putting up with many rude forms of behavior they once considered their lot in life. In the same way, men refuse to remain true to a nag or a shrew. The acceptance of divorce on a large scale in our culture, even among Christians, has changed our reactions. So, both partners in marriage must work at being the kind of person whose company creates joy rather than anger or disgust if the marriage is to survive. This development is not all bad. Should marriage not provide a cornerstone for creativity in the human personality? We owe it to our Creator to give our best possible performance in life. He gave us great depths of spirit to plumb. Most of us just scratch the surface, so the seeds of spiritual growth cannot find root, mature and bear fruit in our lives. The key to family happiness is a climate of loving joy. Many of us reserve this approach for outsiders.

Proverbs places the burden for pleasant home life exclusively on the wife. This no longer works in our society the way it did even fifty years ago. The Scripture is still valid, however. A couple certainly can tear down a house with their own hands. In fact, in most divorces, that is exactly what happens.

One of the most vital teachings for peaceful home life may be found in the 15th chapter of Proverbs.

A gentle answer turns away wrath,
But a harsh word stirs up anger (15:1).

One family member who gets up on the wrong side of the bed, angry and frustrated in dealing with all the others, can ruin the day for an entire family. Or one person coming home from work or school with a chip on his or her shoulder can destroy all camaraderie around a dinner table. How does one handle someone like that? What about, "I am so sorry you had such a bad day. Why don't you rest a bit before dinner?" Or should we respond, "So things were tough for you today? Well, my life was no bed of roses either"? Being a peacemaker takes a great deal of selflessness and brains! But it works, just the way Proverbs says it will. And it takes far less energy than a knock-down, drag-out verbal battle!

> Much wealth is in the house of the righteous,
> But trouble is in the income of the wicked (15:6).

We, with our penchant for materialistic thinking in our affluent society, believe the word "wealth" indicates monetary returns. We cannot see into the mind of the writer. But there are all types of wealth. The least valuable for happiness is the kind you can jingle in your pocket!

Some of the wealthiest homes we have known in our ministry had difficulty making it from pay check to pay check. The writer knew what he was talking about when he penned these words from Proverbs. Who is happier in life, the "Scrooges," or the "Cratchits"? Who reaps more emotional and spiritual trouble, the righteous or the wicked? Money is not the only form of wealth! We don't mean to rail against money. It can be a force for good. That, however, depends upon whether we have it or it has us!

The next quotation from Proverbs says what we have just mentioned in a different way.

> Better is a dish of vegetables where love is,
> Than a fattened ox and hatred with it (15:17).

Again the relationship of a son's way of life to the happiness and pride of his parents recurs.

> A wise son makes a father glad,
> But a foolish man despises his mother (15:20).

The double meaning of wealth leaps out at us again, also social consciousness, from the pages of the book as we read,

> Better is a little with righteousness
> Than great income with injustice (16:8).

Respect for the aged comes to the forefront in the 16th chapter of the book.

> A gray head is a crown of glory;
> It is found in the way of righteousness (16:31).

Is the writer implying one lives long enough to achieve gray hair if the way of righteousness is one's lifestyle? Or does he intend to indicate a steady growth in righteous living achieving a pinnacle only in the later years? Perhaps a little bit of both?

One of the most important proverbs for family living may be found in this same chapter. It might accompany the one about the gentle answer that turns away wrath.

> He who is slow to anger is better than the mighty,
> And he who rules his spirit, than he who captures a city
> (16:32).

Solomon's reign was mostly peaceful. He admired the quiet times of peace much more than conquests.

Any completely honest soul will admit having more trouble controlling his or her own personality than dealing with anyone else. Is it not our own reaction to others that makes us blow situations? Suppose we were to rule those reactions. Would life not be more bearable for everyone concerned? And how are we defeated in our lives and in our homes? Do others cause our failures or we ourselves?

The same issue of peaceful homes is found in our next quotation from the book. It is interesting, is it not, that the same heart-wrenching problems were found in the homes of the Old Testament era? They hated the little stresses that sapped their energies just as we do and they needed help to recognize their source just as modern people do.

> Better is a dry morsel and quietness with it
> Than a house full of feasting with strife (17:1).

A man with 700 wives and 300 concubines probably qualified as an expert on strife in the home!

The next quotation involves the multi-generational family.

> Grandchildren are the crown of old men,
> And the glory of sons is their fathers (17:6).

We all know how grandparents feel about grandchildren. Many of us carry SOGWPIP books. (Translation: Silly old grandmother with pictures in purse. Or, Silly old grandfather with pictures in pocket!) A friend with her first grandchild said not long ago, "I was prepared to love her, but I was not prepared for the depth of my love!" Obviously, grandparents felt the same way at the time of Solomon.

The second part of this proverb receives scant notice in our society. A child of divorce confided to us the other day, "I want to be proud of my Dad. That is as important to me as being proud of myself. But he lives a life that makes me ashamed instead of proud. It seems silly to say, but I'm not as proud of myself because I can't be proud of him."

242

We sympathized with the truth of the statement. Children long to glory in the reputation and accomplishments of their fathers and mothers. Even when we stand by the side of a casket holding the form of a loved parent, what comfort comes from that sense of glory, especially in the spiritual achievements of that parent! Such realizations can turn grief into rejoicing. Death becomes a graduation ceremony. We may feel lonely, but the eternal destiny of that loved soul is not in dispute. What a challenge to parents!

Both friendship and brotherhood are extolled in our next verse.

> A friend loves at all times,
> And a brother is born for adversity (17:17).

Is this not a command for faithfulness to our friends and family even under stress? One of the tragic things about the book of Job was the desertion of the suffering Job by those most dear to him. At the time he needed them most, both his brothers and his wife found him repulsive. His wife even suggested he curse God and die. Adversity brings out the best in some relationships and destroys others. Where should the Christian friend or brother be at such times?

A son's effect upon his father is mentioned in this chapter again.

> He who begets a fool does so to his sorrow,
> And the father of a fool has no joy (17:21).

Have we not seen this time after time in modern society?

In the last generation, great strides have been made in what we have called psychosomatic medicine. This is just a big word that indicates the connection between mind and body in the cause or prevention of illness. The book of Proverbs taught the concept long ago.

A joyful heart is good medicine,
But a broken spirit dries up the bones (17:22).

Most of us have seen the chart giving certain point values to stresses. We are told we may expect to be sick if we have experienced various forms of stress or grief in the past year. This has been considered a new concept of physical health. Since our subject is families, we might mention happy homes are usually healthier ones.

Again the foolish son.

A foolish son is a grief to his father,
And bitterness to her who bore him (17:25).

One of the unhappy truths of family living is exemplified by our next quotation.

A brother offended is harder to be won than a strong
city,
And contentions are like the bars of a castle (18:19).

We have mentioned before in the manuscript the difficulty of healing family breaches once they occur. Because of the emotional involvement we feel with each other, family quarrels tend to be more bitter than any other kind. Bars of castles are usually installed to keep enemies out, not to hold family members in. So it is with contentions in families. They bar the way to understanding. A personal drive to be right all the time can make one very lonely.

Wives are praised in our next Scripture.

He who finds a wife finds a good thing,
And obtains favor from the Lord (18:22).

Family discord makes headlines again.

A foolish son is destruction to his father,
And the contentions of a wife are a constant dripping.

244

House and wealth are an inheritance from fathers,
But a prudent wife is from the Lord (19:13, 14).
He who assaults his father and drives his mother away
Is a shameful and disgraceful son (19:26).

If you will recall, the law ordered stoning of sons who assaulted their parents.

One cannot help wondering about the prudent wife who comes from God. Is the inference here that prudence or wisdom originates only with God?

Again the author calls attention to the reputation of the father as it affects the son.

A righteous man walks in his integrity—
How blessed are his sons after him (20:7).

Respect for parents occupies the mind of the author again.

He who curses his father or his mother,
His lamp will go out in time of darkness (20:20).

We wondered about the symbolism involved in this statement. Is it literal? Or does the author mean that one gets the light of understanding through discipline of godly parents?

An unhappy home gets front stage center again in the thinking of the writer.

It is better to live in a corner of a roof,
Than in a house shared with a contentious woman
(21:9).

What about a contentious man?

God's emphasis upon another type of wealth rather than money appears in the 22nd chapter.

A good name is to be more desired than great riches
(22:1).

Discipline in the family is recommended in this chapter again.

Train up a child in the way he should go,
Even when he is old, he will not depart from it (22:6).

It might be comforting for suffering parents to realize some children do not find themselves until those later years and can cause much heartache before they recognize the wisdom of parental instruction.

Another thought on discipline; in fact, a series of thoughts.

Foolishness is bound up in the heart of a child;
The rod of discipline will remove it far from him (22:15).
Do not hold back discipline from the child,
Although you beat him with the rod, he will not die.
You shall beat him with the rod,
And deliver his soul from Sheol (23:13, 14).
The rod and reproof give wisdom,
But a child who gets his own way brings shame to his
mother (29:15).
Correct your son, and he will give you comfort;
He will also delight your soul (29:17).

We purposely grouped a number of the verses concerned with the discipline of children by use of the rod together. The Hebrew people had a background as shepherds. Even Solomon's father had been a shepherd before becoming a warrior. Thus the rod came to be symbolic of numerous things in their teaching.

The shepherd's rod had many functions. A recalcitrant sheep might be struck with it or pulled back by its crook from dangerous situations. Those who would lead the sheep astray or kill them, the enemies of the flock,

246

were beaten off with that rod. Difficult terrains became simpler by using the rod as a help in climbing or finding places where the sheep might stumble. It was a multi-purpose tool.

So is the rod of discipline. Mentioning the rod in Proverbs is not just a license to use corporal punishment for every slight infraction of the rules as has been suggested by some. The writer did not use the imperative form in the sentence. So it is probably not a command but a permission.

Since the remark is made that foolishness is bound up in the heart of a child and the rod will remove it, one must realize the teaching involved in that rod of discipline. Foolishness may be removed only through learning better. Indiscriminate use of the rod for whipping children only makes it appear wiser to refrain from actions someone bigger than you forbids. Corporal punishment without explanation does not provide the self-discipline that eventually must rule the heart of any person. So we believe the rod that changes foolishness to wisdom often removes the child from the source of that foolishness as the shepherd uses the crook of his rod to remove the ignorant sheep from danger.

The second part of this section on discipline of the child definitely teaches corporal punishment. The phrase, "Although you beat him with the rod, he will not die," seems aimed at the faint-hearted who fear any form of corporal punishment. As we said before, this is not a command. It is simply permission from God to use the rod and assurance that corporal punishment, if properly administered, will not seriously injure the child. Solomon had been reared by a father who used no form of discipline in his household. The Bible tells us David never made his children behave. Solomon saw the error in this and taught against it.

We must avoid overly accenting this form of discipline in a society riddled by child abuse. Corporal punishment, although permitted, must be lovingly done. No devils will be driven out with rods. In fact, some might be implanted.

We considered the verse pairing the rod and reproof as further evidence true discipline teaches as well as punishes. Reproof explains where the error lies, therefore giving opportunity for understanding proper courses of action. A rod used without explanation is of little value when it comes to learning. In fact, children who are brought up this way are in as deep a fog about behavioral guidelines as those who experience no discipline at all. They become meat for theorists practicing any form of immorality if not versed in "whys" as well as denials. Discipline is stabilizing to the personality, but it must be intelligent discipline.

How often we have observed the child who never knows the comfort of discipline! Such children become laws unto themselves. They wallow in instability and chaos. Most of them do bring shame to their mothers.

The final statement concerning comfort provided by the son who is corrected declares another truth pervading our social structure today as well as that early one. Spoiled children are notoriously unable to comfort anyone else. They have lived too many years in a vacuum of emotion regulated only by their own personal wants and lusts. Another reason they cannot comfort parents is because they don't want to. Children know they need authority. They recognize, even if parents do not, that they are incapable of handling their world. When parents fail to provide authority figures, respect goes out the window along with self-discipline needed for maturity. Such children often form the ranks in adult life of the perpetual adolescents who think others should favor them and the world owes them a living.

> Listen to your father who begot you,
> And do not despise your mother when she is old (23:22).

This is the first time an aged mother is mentioned in the book. We need this admonition in our society. It is very difficult to watch parents succumb to old age with its disabilities and pressures. Our nursing homes are full of people who have few if any visitors. Nursing homes were not prevalent in Solomon's day. Obviously neglect was!

> The father of the righteous will greatly rejoice,
> And he who begets a wise son will be glad in him,
> Let your father and your mother be glad,
> And let her rejoice who gave birth to you (23:24, 25).

The writer throws out a gauntlet of sorts here to sons. The challenge this time is not to parents to discipline but to sons to be worthy of parental love and pride.

> By wisdom a house is built,
> And by understanding it is established;
> And by knowledge the rooms are filled
> With all precious and pleasant riches (24:3, 4).

Is this like the wise man who built his house upon a rock? A play on words here makes us wonder if the riches filling those rooms are much more liable to be riches of love and kindness rather than the things money can buy. Wisdom, understanding and knowledge make us value the unseen more than things one can purchase.

One of the passages that impressed us because of its descriptive quality is Proverbs 27:15, 16.

249

A constant dripping on a day of steady rain
And a contentious woman are alike;
He who would restrain her restrains the wind,
And grasps oil with his right hand.

Who could say it better?

During the time of Jesus, Pharisees gave money to the synagogue when they should have supported their parents with it. Such attitudes met with wholesale condemnation. Were they already doing a similar type of thing in the name of religion in Solomon's era?

He who robs his father or his mother,
And says, "It is not a transgression,"
Is the companion of a man who destroys (28:24).

Of course, the statement could refer to simple robbery. Much of that goes on today also. In 1983, an elderly woman in northwest England was robbed and beaten by a gang of young thugs who got the equivalent of $7.50 in American money. She died. The leader of the gang was her grandson.

How about sons and daughters who talk aged parents out of their money, then refuse to care for them? An age-old social problem!

Our final Scripture comes from the 31st chapter of Proverbs.

An excellent wife, who can find?
For her worth is far above jewels (31:10).

People are more valuable than things, especially the excellent wives of this world.

The heart of her husband trusts in her,
And he will have no lack of gain (31:11).

Trust, the bulwark of family relationships, must be earned. An excellent wife adds to the family treasures, both material and spiritual, and will not detract from her husband's wealth.

> She does him good and not evil
> All the days of her life (31:12).

How many, many ways we may do good instead of evil: morally, spiritually, physically and economically! A doctor once told us one of the functions of a good wife is to nag her husband into taking proper care of his body. Marriage is for stable, thoughtful adults.

> She looks for wool and flax,
> And works with her hands in delight.
> She is like merchant ships;
> She brings her food from afar.
> She rises also while it is still night,
> And gives food to her household,
> And portions to her maidens (31:13-15).

This is a classic description of a good housekeeper for the day in which it was written. But it is more than that. She works "with delight." This woman did not sit and bemoan the fate that made her a housewife! She was happy to be providing such comfort for her family, the beloved ones of her life.

> She considers a field and buys it;
> From her earnings she plants a vineyard.
> She girds herself with strength,
> And makes her arms strong.
> She senses that her gain is good;
> Her lamp does not go out at night (31:16-18).

That is quite a gal! She is not only a homemaker but a business woman as well. An early efficiency expert, if you please!

> She stretches out her hands to the distaff,
> And her hands grasp the spindle (31:19).

Homemaking again! This time she is making cloth for her family.

> She extends her hand to the poor;
> And she stretches out her hands to the needy (31:20).

An early collector for the United Way? No, in those days, each household took care of benevolence in its own way. But this woman certainly was community-minded!

> She is not afraid of the snow for her household,
> For all her household are clothed with scarlet (31:21).

This goes back to the spinning and weaving. Busy, wasn't she?

> She makes coverings for herself;
> Her clothing is fine linen and purple (31:22).

This is the only statement in the entire description that has any selfish overtones. In this one, she does do something for herself. The fact that it is included indicates that this admirable woman had a right to be considered a person, too, and not just the family provider.

> Her husband is known in the gates,
> When he sits among the elders of the land (31:23).

This surprised us very little. There was nothing left for him to do except to act in any advisory capacity in the gates of the city!

> She makes linen garments and sells them,
> And supplies belts to the tradesmen (31:24).

Business woman again!

> Strength and dignity are her clothing,
> And she smiles at the future.
> She opens her mouth in wisdom,
> And the teaching of kindness is on her tongue.
> She looks well to the ways of her household,
> And does not eat the bread of idleness (31:25-27).

One does not doubt the connotation of strength in reference to this woman! The amazing accomplishments attributed to her would demand strength, both physical and spiritual! We are glad the author mentioned wisdom and teaching, as well as kindness, as part of the lady's talents. We also appreciated the description of dignity. Mothers receive some plaudits in Proverbs, but this is the main spot where a woman is applauded as erudite.

We had one unholy thought in regard to this passage. Might the revered lady have smiled at the future partly in anticipation of a slight possibilty of rest in her old age? The thought also occurred to us that her family was doubly blessed by her kind spirit. Otherwise, anyone who worked that hard might have become downright witchy! In the light of 20th century thought, the reader would not be too surprised if women who labored this way turned into the contentious women described other places in the book. Some wives with less sweetness of spirit probably suggested it was time for their husbands to do something besides sit in the gates!

Many mothers in our present day economy could give this woman a run for her money as far as work is concerned. Many of today's mothers help earn the living. Statistics tell us the same women must take most of the responsibility for home and family work as well. If they become witchy and contentious, is it because everyone, husbands and children, expect them to carry a double load?

Her children rise up and bless her;
Her husband also, and he praises her, saying:
"Many daughters have done nobly,
But you excel them all" (31:28, 29).

This statement hits pay dirt! In counseling for many years in pastorates, we learned that a few words of blessing and praise might have averted disaster in homes and marriages. We tend to take those we love most for granted. We fail to see the tired look, the strained behavior signifying needs we don't even notice, important requirements of the human spirit. We are quick with words of criticism, slow with words of praise. We frequently reserve our compliments for those we are trying to impress and let those close to us die of love starvation. The husband in this Scripture may have sat in the gates, but he at least told her he appreciated her and thought she was wonderful!

Charm is deceitful and beauty is vain,
But a woman who fears the Lord, she shall be praised.
Give her the product of her hands,
And let her works praise her in the gates (31:30, 31).

Might we call this the punch line for women in the book? Not only is physical beauty vain, but it tends to disappear with the years. Spiritual beauty grows greater if one cultivates it. Apparently this woman did, for she delighted in caring for her home and was wise and kind. If we are not beautiful at sixteen, we can't help it. Lack of spiritual beauty at sixty is our own fault. Faith, accomplishment and reputation live on when vanity dies.

All of Proverbs is worth our study. The Scriptures we have quoted have special bearing for families.

24

ECCLESIASTES

Most people attribute Ecclesiastes to Solomon. He was an old man when he penned this manuscript. All his life had been spent in the lap of luxury. He could buy anything he wanted. He had lived in splendor such as his people had never known before. When he entered a room, its occupants bowed and scraped. He was obviously brilliant, respected and powerful. So why is Ecclesiastes filled with unhappiness? Its pages echo phrases of unspeakable pathos and irritation. Yet they were written by a man who apparently had the world by the tail!

Solomon had asked God for wisdom and understanding. He had received them in abundance. Yet, after all the years he had spent in study and experience, he came down to his closing days with unfulfilled yearnings. He cried out for understanding of life, for wisdom beyond himself.

At the close of a life that had included satisfaction of every whim, tremendous polygamous sexuality, all the things so deified by a humanistic society, Solomon found himself in a state of deep depression. In spite of his mental condition, however, he never stooped to embrace atheism, materialism, or even pessimism in his analysis of life. In fact, his final conclusion rests upon a doctrine of mankind's hopelessness apart from faith in the eternal purposes of God.

Although this book, quite different in its purpose from the practical Proverbs, is not specifically a family book, there are teachings in it providing the type of understanding one requires for abundant family living.

One of the major points to be understood by families is the age of the author. As we grow old, most of us tend to assess the scope of our lives; what was, and what might have been. As the infirmities of age creep up on us, a tendency arises for us to wonder if we have wasted days that appeared countless at the beginning and quite sparse in retrospect. Philosophizing may afflict or uplift the elderly, depending upon the path it pursues.

Dwelling upon the past often creates depression. In family living, we must try to keep a hopeful, futuristic approach in our thinking. Solomon's assessments would help us all. Frequently we learn in old age the shallowness of youthful values. Solomon did. When it was too late to change his ways, when he had to rely upon others for help, he saw the vanity of most pursuits except for a personal walk with God. In more elegant language, Solomon stated what the Pennyslvania Dutch put in few words. "We grow too soon old, too late shmart!"

There are some important statements in this book for our reflection.

"And I set my mind to know wisdom and to know madness and folly; I realized that this also is striving after the wind. Because in much wisdom, there is much grief, and increasing knowledge results in increasing pain" (1:17, 18).

We cannot deny the truth of these words. Modern platitudes agree with them. Most trite statements result from a certain amount of truth inherent within them. "Ignorance is bliss" is one of these. Sometimes understanding and knowledge do bring intense pain.

However, pain provides opportunity. Solomon was too depressed to comprehend this fact at the moment he was expressing that sense of depression so eloquently. Only when we have suffered personally can we comfort others.

For instance, parents who have felt awkward, unattractive, and unpopular know how to sympathize with teenagers passing through adolescence. One in the throes of rejected first love may receive comfort from an older person who has survived that phase and recovered to live more abundantly later. These are simple examples, but illustrate the way parents may actually help children because they, too, have experienced pain in personal relationships.

Adults who have loved and lost that beloved can empathize with those going through "the valley of the shadow of death" with a family member. Knowledge, even painful knowledge, possesses value in the family. It does not remove the pain, only softens its impact a bit.

> Thus I hated all the fruit of my labor for which I had labored under the sun, for I must leave it to the man who will come after me. And who knows whether he will be a wise man or a fool? Yet he will have control over all the fruit of my labor

257

for which I have labored by acting wisely under the sun. This too is vanity (2:18, 19).

Was the aged Solomon despairing of relinquishing the kingdom to his foolish son, Rehoboam? If so, he was right. His son completely lacked wisdom for dealing with humanity and lost all his father's work!

This certainly applies to families today. How many fathers have struggled to provide wealth as family inheritance only to have it squandered by sons who had never learned to work or manage finances? Anyone engaged in a family study must deal with this situation time after time. Great careers or tremendous wealth are usually the result of single-minded ambition. This type of drive often allows no time for quality personal relationships. Fathers whose sons misuse their inheritance often neglect to foster a filial bond that will develop the qualities of character and leadership they want those boys to have. Families need to be cherished. Great men, revered by their civilization, frequently produce worthless children. We have seen that all through the Old Testament.

We also observe this in our modern culture. Now the problem has been multiplied by single-minded career women whose thoughts are on promotions and achievements at work while no one tends to the home and children. Often parents of this type are consumed by guilt and heap upon their children all the luxuries money can buy. Responsibility for personal development bites the dust. Rewards no one earns are the order of the day. So, they go through the wealth it took a lifetime for the parents to amass in a few short years. Is that so strange?

Our present day economy forces many women to help earn a living. Children need not suffer neglect from this.

In fact, they can be taught responsibility for their share of household duties. After all, they live there, too! But parents must make time spent in that home quality time. Office duties must give way to single-minded attention to children's needs and happiness as well as their personal relationship with each other during home time. Otherwise, personal development will be sacrificed to career advancement. If that happens, one comes to the end of life crying, "Vanity of vanities! All is vanity" (1:2). To lose one's children is to lose the most important gift of God.

Chapter 3 begins with a typical acceptance acquired in old age of appointed times for most of life's functions. However, the old king's thoughts appear to wander a bit in this part of the book. He speaks of gifts of God to men, that work is even a gift. Then depression takes over again. He declares men and beasts have the same end. ". . . All came from dust and all return to the dust" (3:20).

Like Job, Solomon declares death to be better than life; the one never born, the most blessed of all.

Then the old man returns nostalgically to his youth and the value systems one needs to build. "Remember also your Creator in the days of your youth, before the evil days come and the years draw near when you will say, 'I have no delight in them'" (12:1). The old man had lost his taste for living. He wished there were some way he could go back and make some of his choices differently. The new choices would be made with his Lord in mind.

There is a lesson here for the family. Children only remember their Creator and concentrate upon His will for their lives if that Creator is a constant guest in their homes.

Finally, the old king reaches some important conclusions as a result of his philosophizing. Much of his life has been wasted in pursuits he no longer considers important. Only a righteous, godly life fills the bill.

"The conclusion, when all has been heard, is: fear God and keep His commandments, because this applies to every person. Because God will bring every act to judgment, everything which is hidden, whether it is good or evil" (12:13-14).

One wonders what might have happened with Solomon and his family as well as his kingdom had he reached these conclusions earlier in his career. Do we make our families conscious of the eternal presence of God? Such concepts alter not only behavior but destiny!

25

THE SONG OF SOLOMON

Scholars have argued for generations about the meaning of this book. Some consider it a collection of love poems with no special plot. Others assess it an allegory with the bridegroom representing Jehovah or Christ and the bride symbolic of Israel or the church. No one knows for certain.

However, literal meaning makes it applicable to the family. The poetry is lovely, filled with oriental imagery, expressive of the beauty of marital love. We are told in I Kings of Solomon's fondness for nature and his knowledge of gardens, meadows, vineyards, orchards, even flocks of sheep. He employs all his learning to draw word pictures of the beauty of the marriage relationship in this group of poems.

The collection is entitled, "Song of Songs" in the first verse. Did Solomon, the lover, prefer these poems to all the rest of his writing? That connotation might so indicate. Hebrew scholars say the book is a superb example of Hebrew poetry.

We might name the book, "A Eulogy to Love," for joys of wedded life are extolled throughout its pages. The author leaves little to the imagination as he describes the delights of intimacy experienced by the bride and bridegroom. The depth of expression amazes the reader. Solomon already had sixty wives and eighty concubines. Yet he waxed lyrical about this new wife, considered by many scholars his favorite.

What meaning may we find for families from this book?

A deep love relationship lays the foundation for a happy home. Sex is not a dirty word, nor is it ugly and sinful unless we misuse it. On the contrary, it is blessed of God, given to humanity to bind us together in marriage in a relationship that meets physical, emotional and spiritual needs of the individual. Married couples who delight in each other will build better homes and give children greater stability. It helps little tots to see that Mama and Daddy are deeply in love, completely committed. A beautiful marriage relationship displayed for them to see makes teenagers less likely to form sexual liaisons because the crowd pressures them to do so. When children observe true love between their parents, they want that type of relationship, not a fly-by-night affair.

Sex is not hush-hush, a bit shameful! The Bible considers it openly and describes it beautifully in lyrical language not often used. Even if the book is allegorical and means only the relationship of Jehovah with Israel or Christ with the church, what made the inspired writer select marital love as the symbol? The Song of Solomon recommends the intimacy of the sex relationship in marriage.

26

FAMILIES IN THE MAJOR PROPHETS

Since very little is known of the personal lives of the prophets, scant information can be accumulated to show what types of families they produced. One insight emerges from this. God considered the message more important than detailed data about the men who presented that message. Does this fact contain guidelines for us?

In preparation of this book, we often longed for more intimate detail. However, the faithful reader must accept the premise that God gave us all the information we really need to come to a close relationship with Him. If every nuance of thought were carefully delineated logically point by point, who would need to have faith? Our response to God involves acceptance of the data given and trust in the gaps.

The Book of Isaiah

The Book of Isaiah gives us a few facts about Isaiah and his family. The prophet was the son of Amoz. Rabbinic tradition among the Jews makes Amoz the brother of King Amaziah of Judah. If this is true, Isaiah was a member of the royal family, a cousin of King Uzziah and grandson of King Joash. Thus Isaiah's acceptance in the palace was assured. He prophesied in the reigns of Uzziah, Jotham, Ahaz and Hezekiah in Judah. One might assess Isaiah's work as successful, since three of these four kings are described in Holy Writ as good. Ahaz was the lone reprobate.

Isaiah was married to a prophetess who remains nameless in the Scripture (8:3). We know of two sons for the prophet: Shearjashub, named in Isaiah 7:3, and Maher-shalal-hash-baz, mentioned in Isaiah 8:3. The Bible reveals little of the family relationships. The seventh chapter of Isaiah divulges the fact that Shearjashub accompanied his father in his confrontation with King Ahaz. We must assume Isaiah was close to his son if Shearjashub attended such an important meeting with the prophet. We also may take for granted Isaiah was training the boy in the faith of his fathers.

The only thing we know of Maher-shalal-hash-baz is his birth. We never meet either boy in the Scriptures again. However, we like what we see of Isaiah as a father. So many Old Testament characters completely separated their careers from their families; at least, the prominent ones from the royal families did. A son likes to feel important enough to accompany his father on significant ventures. Often this companionship makes a tremendous difference. We might recall the companionship of Saul and Jonathan, the lack of camaraderie of David and his sons, plus the overall effect of the two attitudes.

264

Isaiah comes down to us as the Messianic Prophet because of his dedication to the concept of his nation as the one through whom the Messiah would come. His language is beautiful, his imagery superb, his descriptions of the coming Savior amazingly accurate. II Chronicles 26:22 reveals the fact that Isaiah wrote a book about Uzziah that we do not have. II Chronicles 32:32 mentions a manuscript concerning the kings of Judah and Israel that has been lost. Isaiah was an outstanding man.

In the very beginning of his book, Isaiah uses the analogy of the famiy to describe the apostasy of Israel when he speaks of "Sons I have reared and brought up, but they have revolted against me" (1:2). We find a double thrust here, that of the disciplined family and the dedicated nation.

Importance of family appears again when the prophet lashes out at unfaithful and immoral officialdom.

> They do not defend the orphan,
> Nor does the widow's plea come before them (1:23).

In the song of thanksgiving attributed to Hezekiah in Isaiah 38:19, we read,

> "It is the living who give thanks to Thee, as I do today;
> A father tells his sons about Thy faithfulness."

The stamp of approval appears here for religious instruction from father to son.

In Isaiah 54:5, 6, the prophet speaks to widows and forsaken wives, referring to Israel but also apropos as a comfort in our time.

> "For your husband is your Maker.
> Whose name is the Lord of hosts;
> And your Redeemer is the Holy One of Israel,

Who is called the God of all the earth.
For the Lord has called you.
Like a wife forsaken and grieved in spirit,
Even like a wife of one's youth when she is rejected,"
Says your God.

What a beautiful promise to the widows and deserted wives of our day! God will be their Husband, their Comforter!

Much of the Book of Isaiah, although scathingly denunciatory of the sins of the people, offers hope to our families. The prophet, after describing some great wickedness, says,

For all this His anger is not spent,
But His hand is still stretched out (5:25).

We noted these same words more than once. His stretched out hand provides optimism in a troubled world.

Let us quote two favorite Scriptures from the pen of Isaiah that help in times of family stress.

But they that wait upon the Lord shall renew their strength; they shall mount up with wings as eagles; they shall run, and not be weary; and they shall walk, and not faint (40:31, KJV).

Fear thou not; for I am with thee; be not dismayed; for I am thy God: I will strengthen thee; yea, I will help thee; yea, I will uphold thee with the right hand of my righteousness (41:10, KJV).

Most of us who have brought up families have experienced a "Give me strength" stage apt to be followed by a clobbering stage. We have found these two Scriptures helpful when patience is exhausted.

Read Isaiah. You will learn more about your Savior. You will find help in time of trouble.

266

The Book of Jeremiah

The second major prophet is Jeremiah. He was born of a priestly family in the village of Anathoth, northeast of Jerusalem. His father was Hilkiah, probably a descendant of Abiathar, a priest whom Solomon had banished to Anathoth when he first ascended the throne. Abiathar had supported Adonijah's rebellion against David. Solomon refused to order his execution because of his priestly status.

Jeremiah began his prophecy during the 13th year of the reign of the godly Josiah in Judah. He continued to prophesy through the remaining kings until the nation was carried into captivity in Babylon. This made his prophecy extend through five monarchs: Josiah, Jehoahaz, Jehoiakim, Jehoiachin and Zedekiah.

Since Hilkiah, Jeremiah's father, was intimately involved in the reforms accomplished during Josiah's monarchy, we know the depth of his religious convictions. Jeremiah, steeped in the tenets of the law, remained faithful throughout his entire lifetime. He challenged the people to godly living even though his preaching finally resulted in imprisonment. Jeremiah offers us a picture of stalwart courage, buffeted by life but unshaken to the end. His father, Hilkiah, trained the prophet well.

So far as we know, Jeremiah never married. In fact, chapter 16:1, 2 says, "The word of the Lord also came to me saying, 'You shall not take a wife for yourself nor have sons or daughters in this place.'" He describes the fate of children in such a decadent society as the reason.

Jeremiah, as Isaiah one hundred years before him, compared the nation to faithless family relationships. In chapter 3, he speaks of a husband who divorces his wife and she

267

goes from him to another lover. Then the prophet accuses the nation.

> "But you are a harlot with many lovers;
> Yet you turn to me," declares the Lord (3:1).

The prophet constantly uses the analogy of family divorce for the way God is divorcing His people. This is no particular message to individual families today, but does exemplify the important role played by the family in Old Testament culture and the emphasis God placed upon faithfulness to our marriage vows.

Some passages from Jeremiah deal directly with families.

> Pour out Thy wrath on the nations that do not know
>   Thee,
> And on the families that do not call Thy name (10:25).

> "Woe to him who builds his house without righteous-
>   ness
> And his upper rooms without justice,
> Who uses his neighbor's services without pay
> And does not give him his wages.
> Who says, 'I will build myself a roomy house
> With spacious upper rooms.
> And cut out its windows,
> Paneling it with cedar and painting it bright red.'
> Do you become a king because you are competing in
>   cedar?
> Did not your father eat and drink,
> And do justice and righteousness?
> Then it was well with him.
> He pled the cause of the afflicted and needy;
> Then it was well.
> Is not that what it means to know Me?"
> Declares the Lord (22:13-16).

How modern the prophet sounds! How many of us concentrate upon building houses that might be featured in magazines rather than emphasizing the spiritual and benevolent sides of life?

The primary message of the book of Jeremiah as well as Lamentations is the devastation that overcomes a sinful, degraded society. Everything Jeremiah predicted happened. The prophet declares this to be the fate of any person, family or nation that deserts the worship of God.

The Book of Ezekiel

Ezekiel is the third major prophet, with his period of prophecy occurring during the last years of Jeremiah's prophetic service and extending beyond it. He was about thirty years of age when he began his ministry. Ezekiel was the son of Buzi and belonged to the priestly order. He was carried into captivity in the first onslaught of the Kingdom of Judah in approximately 597 B.C. So, he acted as a pastor among the exiles, explaining their plight on the basis of their sin, especially their idol worship. He must have impressed them. No record exists of their worship of idols after their return from captivity.

We know Ezekiel was married, for the Bible records the death of his wife in the 24th chapter of the book that bears his name. No mention is made of any children.

Ezekiel, as Isaiah and Jeremiah prior to his preaching career, uses the allegory of profligate, adulterous wives as a description of the nation's relationship to God. Again, this places emphasis upon the marriage vows and the absolute revulsion God feels toward adulterous relationships.

Another emphasis in Ezekiel, this time more prominent than in either Isaiah or Jeremiah, is the stress upon individual responsibility for sin. We have alluded to this concept in earlier parts of this manuscript. We find it accented here. In chapter 18, very strong assertions appear as to the sins of fathers and sons. The prophet plainly states that sons are not punished for their fathers' sins, nor fathers for the wickedness of their sons. This is further evidence of what we said earlier in this book. The visitation of the sins of fathers upon their children lies in natural environmental and physiological results of those sins and has nothing to do with the eternal destiny of the soul unless personally embraced by the child as he grows to adult life. In other words, we do not believe the Bible teaches a doctrine of original sin visited upon a helpless infant at birth.

In this same chapter, Ezekiel asserts we are not victims of our past or anyone else's. By turning to God, we may wipe the slate clean.

Ezekiel sounds a note of hope not only for his generation of families, but also for ours. We need not be hopeless victims. We can rise far above our hereditary problems through hard work and trust in Almighty God.

The Book of Daniel

Daniel is the last of the major prophets. He was a youth of noble descent and high physical and intellectual promise, who was carried into captivity by Nebuchadnezzar in the third year of the reign of Jehoiakim in Judah.

We know nothing of Daniel's family, except that he came from the nobility of the land. We also find no information as to his descendants.

Daniel's stalwart faith and outstanding stability become even more remarkable in the light of his membership in one of the families surrounding the throne of Jehoiakim. King Jehoiakim was a monster, persecuting prophets of

God and living a very evil life. We may only speculate, but we wondered if some of the nobles still believed as the godly Josiah's reforms had dictated and Daniel came from one of these families.

Another possibility emerges. Sometimes we only understand the meaning of faith when it costs something. These young men had been removed from home and family to a foreign land. In spite of being well-treated and groomed for leadership, did they discover the old beliefs to be more meaningful in captivity? No one can answer these questions. We do know Daniel remained true to the faith of his fathers.

Daniel becomes important in our study of families as the prototype of the son who leaves home, is tempted to forsake all the family teachings to gain pleasure for himself, but instead retains the truth and purity taught to him in childhood.

Daniel's courage won him great respect in the foreign court. His ability to say, "No," rubbed off on Shadrach, Meshach and Abednego. They, too, refused to bow down to worship the image. Their fiery furnace experience comes down to our time as a model of man's moral strength and God's protection. A parallel to it is Daniel's narrative of the lion's den.

For our study of families, we would like to know more of Daniel's ancestry. But we don't. So we must accept the fact that the story of Daniel is provided by God to teach us that moral determination and spiritual dedication are always rewarded in some way by God.

The book of Daniel also emphasizes the influence faithful people exert upon those around them. Even Nebuchadnezzar recognized the sovereignty of God because of the actions of faithful captives. What a victory!

27

FAMILIES IN THE MINOR PROPHETS

The Book of Hosea

Hosea is the first minor prophet as the books appear in the Old Testament. The twelve prophets designated as minor do not receive that identification through unimportance but rather because of brevity. The books are short compared with the four major prophets.

Hosea is the only minor prophet whose family rates much notice. In fact, we know very little about any of the others.

Hosea was the son of Beeri. He prophesied during the reigns of Uzziah, Jotham, Ahaz and Hezekiah, kings of Judah, and during the reign of Jeroboam II in Israel. His message was primarily to the northern kingdom.

When the Lord first spoke through Hosea, the Lord said to Hosea, "Go, take to yourself a wife of harlotry, and have children of harlotry; for the land commits flagrant harlotry, forsaking the Lord."

So he went and took Gomer the daughter of Diblaim, and she conceived and bore him a son (Hosea 1:2, 3).

For generations scholars have debated the question as to whether or not Gomer was a real person or simply a character in an allegory enabling the prophet to describe Israel's idolatry as harlotry in her relationship to God. We believe Gomer was real; that Hosea suffered as God suffered at the hands of His people; and that Hosea's final acceptance of Gomer stands as a prototype of God's forgiveness for His wayward nation.

Apparently Gomer was already a prostitute when Hosea married her. That God should command a man to marry a prostitute seems incomprehensible to most of us. That may explain why so many have been sure this is an allegory, not the true story of Hosea's life. While we may think of prostitution as the world's worst sin, perhaps God doesn't agree with us. Maybe there was value He saw in Gomer that we, with our lack of understanding, might miss completely. At any rate, Hosea was commanded to marry her. He obeyed.

One obvious fact emerges from the book. The prophet loved Gomer much more deeply than she was capable of loving him. Again we see the picture of God and His love portrayed in the life of the prophet.

Hosea is called the "weeping prophet of Israel" as Jeremiah was denoted the "weeping prophet of Judah." Hosea's personal life gave him enough cause for weeping without his constant dealing with the profligate people of God.

Hosea and Gomer's children were named symbolically to signify the tragedy of Israel. The first son was called

"Jezreel" to indicate the judgment of God upon that city, the capital during the bloody reign of Jehu. God declares, "I will punish the house of Jehu for the bloodshed of Jezreel" (1:4). The second child born to Hosea and Gomer was a daughter, "Loruhamah," meaning "unpitied." This signifies the end of God's pity for Israel. The third child, another son, they named "Lo-ammi," meaning "not my people." God says, ". . . for you are not My people and I am not your God" (1:9). Along with condemnation, however, the prophet offers hope for return to the land.

The book of Hosea is so filled with imagery that determining the thread of Hosea and Gomer's personal relationship becomes difficult. Apparently Gomer ran away to pursue her harlotry again, perhaps even bearing children to other men. But Hosea, always the true lover, bought her back. He refused to allow her to be with other men. He also observed a platonic role in his relationship with her for some time before finally forgiving and accepting her.

The entire book is tied up with the heartbreak of God over the faithlessness of Israel. Who could understand this better than Hosea? Who could better describe it to the people? We also see the eternal love and forgiveness of God as portrayed by Hosea in word and action.

We noticed quite a significant verse in the 4th chapter of Hosea. Throughout all the Scripture up to this point, women appear to meet much more condemnation than men for any form of sexual sin. The 14th verse of this chapter evens the score a bit.

"I will not punish your daughters when they play the harlot,
Or your brides when they commit adultery,
For the men themselves go apart with harlots,
And offer sacrifice with temple prostitutes."

God does not condone prostitution in this verse. It appeared to us rather to be a rebuke to men who expect women to be punished for actions they wink at in their own lives and the lives of other men. Is this the beginning of the end of the double standard of living?

The Book of Joel

Little is revealed of the personal life of the prophet Joel. He was the son of Pethuel. His family remains unknown since no information concerning marriage or children appears in the text. He speaks against the immorality of his day, predicting punishment from God.

The book of Joel contains no specific teaching for families except as all general Biblical warnings against immorality and forsaking worship of God apply to all of us.

The Book of Amos

Amos, one of the greatest of the prophets, fails to give any details of his background. We know nothing about him as far as lineage is concerned; also nothing about a marriage or family. He was a shepherd; his home was Tekoa.

Amos had a great effect upon the history of his people. He is designated as founder of the great prophetic school attended by Isaiah and Micah.

Amos prophesied doom when the nation appeared prosperous. His teaching was not specifically aimed at families except as all warnings against immorality and idol worship affect the family.

The Book of Obadiah

We know almost nothing about the prophet Obadiah. His prophecy was directed primarily toward Edom. Like all the others, it applies to families only as any teaching of morality and kindness would.

The Book of Jonah

The prophet Jonah was the son of Amittai. This is the sum total of family information concerning this important Old Testament character revealed by the text. However, the book contains valuable lessons for families.

From the beginning of this book, we have been studying families whose importance arose from being Jewish, plus many who formed part of the chain leading to the birth of the Savior. Here and there we have noted Gentiles who were loved by God. We also observed the fact that God was with Ishmael, the founder of the Arab nations.

In the Book of Jonah, the prophet, content with preaching to his own clans, receives a command from God to preach in Nineveh. Nineveh was the capital of Assyria, Jonah's nation's principal enemy. Jonah was determined not to go! Assyria was in the process of swallowing up Israel. Jonah should help them avert disaster? No way!

So Jonah took off on a ship to run away from God. After a tremendous storm threatened to sink the vessel, the sailors threw Jonah overboard. They were convinced he was the jinx causing all their trouble. When that great fish vomited Jonah out on dry land, he still didn't want to go to Nineveh. But he went anyway.

What a powerful preacher Jonah was! (We might note from this that not all powerful preaching originates from the right reasons!) Even the king repented in sackcloth and ashes! The people followed suit, turned to God and avoided destruction.

277

Jonah was furious! He had wanted annihilation for all those rotten Ninevites! He even asked God to let him die because he didn't want to live to see the great city's salvation.

Jonah sat outside Nineveh to observe exactly what would happen. There's no other way to describe Jonah's attitude. He was pouting. God tried to reason with him through a plant He caused to grow for shade for the prophet. Then God destroyed the plant with a great worm. Jonah grieved for the plant. But he still hated Nineveh!

This book holds an important message for families. God does not favor just one particular clan or people. He loves all His creation and yearns for them to return to Him. When we long for destruction of our enemies, no matter how evil they may be, our thoughts are not God's thoughts, certainly not in the Christian era.

Our families are most important to us. They are equally important with other families of the world with God. Yes, Russian families. Yes, Cuban families. Yes, Chinese families. We could name any nation. God loves them, too. We have never grown to the point of being able to separate ways of life from personalities. We often make our God too small.

The Book of Micah

Micah appears next in our catalog of minor prophets. He lived in Moresheth-gath in Judah. No details of his family or personal history are recorded in the text. He prophesied during the reigns of Jotham, Ahaz and Hezekiah, kings of Judah.

Some of Micah's warnings deal primarily with family relationships and the problems of families trying to survive in an evil environment. Micah condemns those who try to steal family homes and inheritances.

278

Woe to those who scheme iniquity,
Who work out evil on their beds!
When morning comes, they do it,
For it is in the power of their hands.
They covet fields and then seize them,
And houses, and take them away.
They rob a man and his house,
A man and his inheritance (Micah 2:1, 2).

This is a strong supportive statement for the sanctity of the home.

For son treats father contemptuously,
Daughter rises up against her mother,
Daughter-in-law against her mother-in-law;
A man's enemies are the men of his own household
   (7:6).

This statement aroused our interest especially. Our modern psychologists tell us sons have ambivalent feelings about their fathers, often longing to make them appear ridiculous and ignorant. The same experts declare that daughters upon entrance into puberty become contestants with their mothers for the attention of their fathers, often feeling they know more than their mothers have learned in all the years they have lived. We also know that conflict between mothers-in-law and daughters-in-law is much more widespread than any other type of in-law problem in our society today.

We speculated upon the meanings of the last sentence quoted from the prophet. There are many ways in which a man's worst enemies reside in his own household. Failure to have peace at home defeats many men in their career opportunities. We know from the study of David that his worst enemies were his own sons. Their jealousy and animosity toward their father almost destroyed David. This

279

same truth is mirrored in modern families. We have known preachers whose witness was completely destroyed by the impoverished souls of their families.

Again we must point out the contemporary quality of Biblical literature. Every one of the prophet's statements may be observed in modern life. The culture is different. The personal problems remain very much the same.

Perhaps no greater condemnation of family discord appears in Holy Writ than this statement in Micah. For the family to provide discipline, stability and courage to face the outside world, we must create a haven of peace at home. This becomes impossible if anyone living in that home wraps himself or herself in the robe of self-centeredness.

No clearer statement of upright moral and spiritual behavior may be found in the Old Testament than Micah's declaration of God's requirements for men in 6:8.

> He has told you, O man, what is good,
> And what does the Lord require of you
> But to do justice, to love kindness,
> And to walk humbly with your God?

Would that we might engrave these words on the hearts of family members! How improved our homes would be!

The Book of Nahum

The prophet Nahum, virtually unknown except for the book bearing his name, prophesied against Nineveh. He is called "the Elkoshite." There is said to have been a town called Elkosh on the Tigris River about twenty miles north of Nineveh. Nahum may have been an Israelite captive there.

Capernaum, one of the towns Jesus frequented regularly during his earthly ministry, means "village of Nahum." This may indicate that Nahum the prophet was either a resident or founder of that settlement.

It is interesting to note that Nahum and Jonah preached to the same city. Nahum may have enjoyed his mission a bit more. He got to tell the people they were doomed. Since Nineveh was a traditional enemy, his assignment might have been easier than Jonah's. Nahum preached approximately one hundred fifty years after Jonah.

At the time of Nahum's prophecy, Nineveh was classed as one of the most prosperous, if not the most prosperous, city in the world. She was mighty and brutal, capital of a military state, built upon the heartbreak and suffering of the families of many nations. God declared His determination to avenge the helpless by bringing about the decline of Nineveh's power and prosperity.

There is no special message for families in this book except the general message for all of the condemnation of God upon those who gain personal or national prosperity by inflicting heartache upon those it is possible for them to oppress.

The Book of Habakkuk

The text of the book of Habakkuk gives no personal information about the prophet. So it is impossible to present any details of his background or training.

The book itself contains some teaching referring particularly to families. It begins with the prophet's protests to God about his sinful surroundings. Then the prophet declares,

Thine eyes are too pure to approve evil.
And Thou canst not look on wickedness with favor.
Why dost Thou look with favor

281

On those who deal treacherously?
Why art Thou silent when the wicked swallowed up
Those more righteous than they? (Hab. 1:13).

We can identify with Habakkuk as we did with Job. We, too, see injustice and strive for understanding. We endure suffering in our families and shout, "Why?"

The Lord answered Habakkuk personally as He replied to Job. He tells the prophet that punishment for the wickedness around him will be forthcoming, to wait for its appearance.

In the midst of His reply to Habakkuk, the Lord makes a statement we might do well to ponder in regard to our family theme.

"Futhermore, wine betrays the haughty man,
So that he does not stay at home.
He enlarges his appetite like Sheol,
And he is like death, never satisfied" (2:5).

One is reminded in reading this Scripture of the modern treatments for alcoholism. None of the cure centers can help someone who will not admit to having a problem. Does the Bible say the same thing when the prophet asserts that "wine betrays the haughty man"? The haughty person admits to no problems. The continuation of the quotation is like a description of alcoholism where the appetite for the drug is never satisfied.

This is also a repeat of warnings against excessive use of alcohol because of its destruction of home life.

"Woe to him who builds a city with bloodshed
And founds a town with violence!" (2:12).

Several times in these later prophets we discover antipathy to bloodshed as a way of establishing themselves as a people.

We noted the difference between this teaching and the excursions into bloodshed such as we read in the story of Jehu. This dogma certainly applies to the families of that era.

One of the most vital doctrines of the prophet Habakkuk is discovered in one verse.

> "Behold, as for the proud one,
>   His soul is not right within him;
>   *But the righteous will live by his faith*" (2:4).

Our families live in very wicked times also. If we fail to live by faith and to teach our children to do the same, the might and power of America will disappear as surely as Chaldea's greatness did!

The Book of Zephaniah

"The word of the Lord which came to Zephaniah son of Cushi, son of Godaliah, son of Amariah, son of Hezekiah, in the days of Josiah son of Amon, king of Judah . . ." (Zeph. 1:1). Since Zephaniah declares himself a descendant of Hezekiah, that makes him a member of the royal family. He preached before Josiah's reforms began, so he probably was a mover and shaker in their inception.

We know nothing about any marriage or children for Zephaniah. It does appear that his branch of Hezekiah's family must have remained true to the faith of the righteous king.

The Book of Haggai

Haggai was the first post-exilic prophet. For our family study, there is very little in this book that fits our purpose except as any book of the Bible brings wisdom to those who study.

The Book of Zechariah

Zechariah was the son of Berechiah, the son of Iddo. His family was a priestly family. He, like Haggai, was post-exilic, serving during the return of Jerusalem and the rebuilding of the temple. We know nothing of any wife or children for Zechariah.

There are beautiful prophecies of the Messiah in this book and much moral teaching to be absorbed by families. However, the prophet's message is not specifically aimed at families.

The Book of Malachi

We know nothing of the personal history of the prophet Malachi. He was the last prophet of the Old Testament. His message was given in the middle of the 5th century B.C. He, like Haggai and Zechariah, was a contemporary of Ezra and Nehemiah. He does address family problems of that age to some extent.

One of the sins against which Malachi speaks strongly is mentioned in Malachi 2:14-16. The men were divorcing their Hebrew wives of long standing and marrying heathen women.

> . . . Because the Lord has been a witness between you and the wife of your youth, against whom you have dealt treacherously, though she is your companion and your wife by covenant. But not one has done so who has a remnant of the Spirit. And what did that one do while he was seeking a godly offspring? Take heed then, to your spirit, and let no one deal treacherously against the wife of your youth.

"For I hate divorce," says the Lord, the God of Israel, "and him who covers his garment with wrong," says the Lord of hosts. "So take heed to your spirit, that you do not deal treacherously."

How modern can the Bible get? Statistics of divorces among the middle-aged and beyond in America are staggering! Some advances have been made in legal protection for families since Old Testament days. However, wives, especially those who have been homemakers without additional careers, find the roving eyes of husbands almost beyond endurance. Divorce at that stage of life is particularly destructive of the woman with no job experience and no training for earning her own living and perhaps supporting children. Men try quite often to "deal treacherously" with such women in financial settlements. If this were not true in our society, there would have been no reason for the recent action taken by Congress to force support payment responsibility upon absentee fathers. As we have noted several times in the manuscript, we have constant reruns on marriage and family problems. This one existed 2500 years ago!

We found the prophet's statement, "But not one has done so who has a remnant of the Spirit" quite revealing. The Old Testament has no doctrine of the indwelling Spirit of God per se. References appear in Psalms that make us feel the psalmist believed in such a concept. However, for the most part, this is not a tenet of Old Testament dogma. That the prophet should accentuate it so deliberately in his statement of condemnation of men who mistreat those entrusted to their care struck us forcibly. We noted a similarity to our age. One who depends upon the indwelling Spirit

285

to rule and guide his or her life today will not "deal treacherously" with a marriage partner or anyone else either.

We also find condemnation of adultery in this book. " 'Then I will draw near to you for judgment; and I will be a swift witness against the sorcerers and against the *adulterers* and against those who swear falsely, and against those who oppress the wage earner in his wages, the widow and the orphan, and those who turn aside the alien, and do not fear Me.' says the Lord of hosts" (3:5).

We emphasized the word, "adulterers," because it applies particularly to families. But we want to point out that Christians have tended to single out this sin among all the others for condemnation while winking at things like swearing falsely and oppressing others.

The foundation stone of the home as far as the human side is concerned is absolute faithfulness to marriage vows. However, we cannot expect to rear good families unless the other parts of this Scripture are also observed. A neighborhood gossip who handles the lives of acquaintances recklessly cannot expect to bring up a child who has great regard for truth and sensitivity to the feelings of others. Business people who show little respect for employees and make a tremendous profit at the expense of others will not be exemplifying any form of godliness for the children reared in their homes. Parents that have no sense of responsibility for those who are not of their same color, nationality or even religion cannot expect their children to be inspired to develop understanding and empathy. Conviction is a sublime personality trait to pass on to our children, but that conviction must be colored by the love of God and the sacrificial spirit of Jesus Christ. Children spot a phony far off. It is even easier up close!

286

So we have no intention of setting up grades of sin by underlining the word, "adulterers." But, for our purpose of family study and because of the prevailing climate in our nation to say anything goes in sex relationships, we wanted to point out God's antipathy to faithlessness as expressed by the prophet. The sanctity of the house depends upon our reverent adherence to the marriage vows. That was true 2500 years ago. It still is.

Malachi closes his message with a prophecy of the coming of Christ and the difference he will make in families.

"And He will restore the hearts of the fathers to their children, and the hearts of the children to their fathers, lest I come and smite the land with a curse" (4:6).

Has Christ changed our homes? What about our nation?

THE NEW TESTAMENT

28

THE NEW TESTAMENT AND FAMILIES

As we perused the pages of the New Testament with the sole aim of family research, it soon became apparent that was not God's purpose in giving it to us. Many New Testament Scriptures form valid family guidelines. However, few intimate details remain of the family lives of our New Testament heroes.

We discovered in rereading, as we have known all along, that most New Testament emphasis is designated as individual rather than corporate. Salvation becomes personal. Even social consciousness appears individualistic rather than collective. No legal system emerges from its pages to control the citizen of the kingdom of God, or the society in which one lives.

The Old Testament, in its struggle to create a special nation, designates specific laws, a definite climate in which the family and nation must move. As the apostle Paul states, "Wherefore the law was our schoolmaster to bring us unto Christ, that we might be justified by faith. But after that faith is come, we are no longer under a schoolmaster" (Gal. 3:24, 25, KJV).

The Old Testament was more clearly national and provincial, an effort to establish His chosen people's loyalty to God, hence strong laws. The New Testament, international in scope, carries that established message plus the law of love in its Messianic context to the individual first, then to families and all nations, not just Israel.

Even while saying this, however, we must recognize the emphasis in the New Testament upon the Church as the Family of God. The Old Testament accentuates human bloodlines. The New Testament places the stress upon the bloodline of the Savior. When we accept that bloodline, are washed clean in His blood through baptism, we are adopted into the Family of God. Jesus becomes our older Brother, God our Father. Individualism in this setting must give way to family, God's Family, just as individualism in a personal family group must abdicate to the good of the whole.

The families of the Old Testament with their segregationist, nationalistic emphasis merge into one great New Testament family, brothers and sisters together regardless of national or racial origins, united in one great bloodline trickling down from Calvary.

Legal systems are unimportant in the New Testament because their major effect is external. Christ deals with motivations creating actions rather than the actions themselves.

Only in cleaning up reasoning can conduct be permanently improved. Personal purity of heart assumes precedence over traditional emphasis upon overt behavior. Christianity, thereby, becomes both more difficult and more rewarding.

Many Old Testament heroes are described with lengthy family data. The New Testament leaders concentrate upon their message with little recognition of themselves as individuals or their families per se. We observed this same phenomenon in the prophets. By the time of the prophets, it was evident to any thoughtful student that rites of worship and traditional observances of the Mosaic Law were not enough to keep mankind's heart true to God. So the prophets emphasized conditions of the soul rather than adherence to sacrifices and burnt offerings. We might mention Micah 6:8 again. "He has shewed thee, O man, what is good; and what doth the Lord require of thee, but to do justly, and to love mercy, and to walk humbly with thy God" (KJV). Concentration upon inner devotion rather than outward display had already assumed preeminence.

The New Testament continues in that vein. Thus personalities, except for that one great Personality, must take a backseat to heartfelt values and love of eternal God. Being part of the family of God gains precedence over membership in any earthly family.

In spite of this, we do possess, in a number of circumstances, enough data to help assess family influence upon New Testament leaders.

Religious tradition exists; some logical, some far out. Our topic is "What the Bible Say about Families," not what the fathers of the church might have said. So, except for occasional interesting references, we shall delete what we have learned in that area.

293

29

THE FAMILY OF JOSEPH AND MARY

Dominating the entire text of the New Testament is the birth of the Messiah, planned of God since the fall of the first human family, and described for us in the Gospels according to Matthew and Luke. Because the prophets had foretold His lineage, both Matthew and Luke record it. However, there is a difference in the two lists.

Both genealogies are similar from Abraham to David. Luke goes beyond Abraham to Adam. After David, Matthew gives a genealogy from Solomon. Luke records the descendants of David's son, Nathan. Matthew makes Jacob Joseph's father. Luke states Eli or Heli to have been the father of Joseph. (Cf. Matt. 1:1-16; Luke 3:23-28.)

As we read available material concerning these genealogies, one explanation seemed more logical than any other. Some scholars believe the Matthew genealogy to be that of Joseph, Jesus' legal father. They consider the Luke genealogy to be Mary's bloodline, calling Joseph Eli's son because he was Eli's son-in-law. Women are seldom mentioned in genealogies and sons-in-law were often designated as sons. Whatever conclusions we reach as to the variation, Jesus was from the line of David. Both Mary and Joseph descended from the tribe of Judah and the family of King David.

In discussing the ancestry of Jesus, a very interesting fact attracts our attention. In the Matthew account, four women are mentioned: Tamar (v. 3), Rahab (v. 4), Ruth (v. 4), and "the wife of Uriah" (v. 6). Tamar was the one who bore twins after she had disguised herself as a prostitute and had sexual relations with Judah, her father-in-law (Gen. 38:12-30). Rahab, a Gentile, was the prostitute who saved the spies sent by Joshua to Jericho (Josh. 2:1-21). Ruth, a Moabitess, had a clean reputation. But as a Gentile she would have been cast out had she lived in the time of Ezra. This would have eliminated Obed, Jesse, and even David himself from any sort of fame and honor. Finally, there was Bathsheba, "the wife of Uriah." She became the wife of David only after their adulterous affair and the murder of her husband (II Sam. 11).

Perhaps no significance should be attached to the presence of these women in the lineage of our Lord. We kept pondering, however, their inclusion and special mention when other women remained nameless. Did Rahab, the harlot, in the ancestry of Jesus presage the forgiveness and salvation He would bring? Was universality of the Gospel responsible for the mention of Ruth?

As we study families, we should consider God's method of sending the Messiah. Would it not have been possible for the omnipotent Father to send a full-grown Savior to carry His message for those three and one-half years? Is there family emphasis for us in God's plan to save mankind? He sent a baby, a helpless infant, to spend thirty years in the bosom of a dedicated, consecrated Jewish family before beginning His ministry.

Shall we examine the personalities of Joseph and Mary? Let us begin with Mary.

Jesus' mother may have been a teenager. Most Jewish families arranged betrothals early. Teenagers often find themselves plagued by insecurity, lack of self-confidence, fear of appearances, especially among their peers.

Mary, as described by Scripture, indicates none of these adolescent problems. When the angel Gabriel saluted her, he said, "Hail, favored one! The Lord is with you!" (Luke 1:28). The Gospel writer records no reaction such as one might expect from a young girl. Luke says she was troubled and pondered what it all meant. But she said nothing. She was as poised as if angels visited her every day.

When Gabriel announced she was to become pregnant with this very special Child, she responded, "How can this be, since I am a virgin?" (Luke 1:34). No hysterics. No protests. One can almost see her eyes widen she asserts her virginity.

Upon hearing Gabriel's explanation, Mary simply bowed in acquiescence. "'Behold, the bondslave of the Lord; be it done to me according to your word.' And the angel departed from her" (Luke 1:38). In one short conversation, a young girl's life changed radically. But there were no tears, no denials, just quiet faithful acceptance. Recorded in the same chapter, we read a beautiful song of praise attributed to Mary when she visited her kinswoman, Elizabeth.

Throughout this book, we have pointed to similarities of human nature from Biblical times to the present. Mary lived in Nazareth, a tiny village. The first chapter of Matthew informs us Joseph learned of Mary's pregnancy "before they came together" (Matt. 1:8). Mary might have told him herself. Perhaps her parents did. But he certainly did not know the whole story until the angel appeared to him. Would Mary not have informed him of Gabriel's visit?

It seems logical to us that the village gossips were having a field day. Can't you hear them?

"That sanctimonious Mary! Always at synagogue! Pretending to be so pure! Well, I always wondered about her. She seemed phony to me!" First century gossips would not have used the same lingo, but the thrust was the same.

What a heartbreaking experience for a young girl! No matter how many times she repeated her protests, would they believe? Would you? Yet we read nothing of rebellion or unhappiness on her part, only submission to the will of God.

Many of the ridiculous anecdotes recorded in some ancient literature remove this beautiful aspect of Mary's character when they try to deify her. One of the loveliest features of Mary's personality comes from the word picture of a flesh and blood young woman, hounded by scandal, facing rejection by the man she loved, hardly able to comprehend what was happening to her, yet submissive. When we read the story of Mary, "submissive" assumes beautiful, strengthening connotations.

Luke tells the story of the trip to Bethlehem to register as members of the family of David. Women coming to term

THE FAMILY OF JOSEPH AND MARY

in pregnancy often find automobile trips painful. Sometimes even sitting for long periods of time proves annoying. Yet Mary made this tiring journey either on foot or on the back of a donkey. The Scripture records no complaints.

We have mentioned the fact before that the Bible is often brutally frank about its famous people. Infamous statements and actions meet the light of day on its pages. But no nasty attitudes are mentioned for Mary. God selected His Son's mother carefully.

Joseph also bears up well under intense scrutiny. Matthew 1:19 says, "And Joseph her husband, being a righteous man, and not wanting to disgrace her, desired to put her away secretly."

The Old English had a word for Joseph's predicament. He thought he had been "cuckolded." No greater insult could be dealt to any man by his beloved. Yet Joseph, instead of making a public example of Mary as evidence of the rage of betrayal, decided to handle the whole thing quietly.

Then the angel appeared to him in a dream to explain Mary's pregnancy. Joseph, like Mary, submitted himself to the will of God. This certainly did not rescue his pride, except privately. From the moment he accepted Mary as his wife, he, too, would have been included as part of the gossips' daily headlines. That topic probably took two routes. "What a fool!" Or perhaps they said, "Well, I wondered if it was his. Now we know."

This latter statement is borne out in Luke 3:23. "And when He began His ministry, Jesus Himself was about thirty years of age, being supposedly the son of Joseph, the son of Eli."

We know very little about how the family lived. Joseph was a carpenter by trade. Mark 6:3 indicates Jesus probably learned the trade from him. At least seven children were brought up in the home: Jesus, James, Joseph, Simon, Judas, and sisters, unnamed (Matt. 13:55, 56).

Some traditions, in further effort to deify Mary, assert these were Joseph's children by a former marriage, insisting Mary remained a virgin until her death. Matthew 1:24, 25 might tend to deny this dogma. "And Joseph arose from his sleep, and did as the angel of the Lord commanded him, and took her as his wife; and kept her a virgin *until* she gave birth to a Son; and he called His name Jesus."

Teaching of perpetual virginity for Mary runs contrary to our knowledge of Jewish belief in regard to marriage. The depth of Joseph and Mary's loyalty to their faith is unquestioned. Faithful Jews considered marriage a duty with special blessings of God upon a prolific union. Failure to bear children was considered God's punishment upon a couple, usually the woman.

There appears little reason for keeping Mary a virgin throughout her lifetime unless one adopts the belief celibacy is superior to the setting in which God placed man and woman in that original idyllic garden. Assuming this premise to be true, God planned sexual relations in order to populate His world, placed these instincts within humanity, then condemned them. The complete lack of logic in such a position assails any thoughtful reader.

Celibacy is acceptable, but not superior. The sex relationship, blessed of God in the beginning, remains blessed if not abused. Jesus was God's Son, not Joseph's. The Savior had to be born of the Holy Spirit (Luke 1:35). But marital sex between Joseph and Mary following Jesus' birth was acceptable to God. Mary was not God, but human flesh. Any effort to make her anything else destroys the doctrine of incarnation. It also demonstrates the hang-ups of its originators.

Jesus was circumcised at eight days of age in accordance with the law (Luke 2:21). Joseph and Mary observed purification rites before taking the infant to Jerusalem to present Him to God (2:22). They offered the type of sacrifice legally demanded after the birth of a male child. God sent His Son to a faithful Jewish household. The comments of Simeon and Anna, and Mary and Joseph's reactions to them illustrate their personalities again (2:33). Apparently they failed to understand the full scope of Jesus' destiny.

Luke uses one sentence to describe the Lord's childhood. "And the Child continued to grow and become strong, increasing in wisdom; and the grace of God was upon Him" (2:40).

The Bible furnishes another glimpse into the kind of family that nourished Jesus in Luke 2:41. "And His parents used to go to Jerusalem every year at the Feast of the Passover." His family obeyed God's law.

We all recall Jesus' visit to Jerusalem at twelve when He confounded the elders with His wisdom and claimed God as Father. But how many of us have accented the last two verses of that second chapter of Luke?

And He went down with them, and came to Nazareth; and He continued in subjection to them, and His mother treasured all these things in her heart. And Jesus kept increasing in wisdom and stature, and in favor with God and men (2:51, 52).

From the standpoint of family study, several things emerge from these verses. Jesus at twelve thought Joseph and Mary should have understood what He was doing in the temple. He protested Mary's scolding, virtually saying, "You should have known I'd be here!" But He obeyed them and accompanied them back to Nazareth. Not only did He go home with them, but He remained "in subjection to them." In other words, God's Son needed careful discipline by God-fearing parents to bring about that increase in "wisdom, stature and favor." We found the statement of "favor with God and men" intriguing. We have never seen an undisciplined child who found much favor with anyone. If discipline was demanded and recorded for God's Son, how much more important is it for our children?

One wonders in reflecting on this home what the result might have been had Mary and Joseph shirked their responsibilities with Jesus. Jesus was divine. He also wore flesh and blood humanity. Most of us struggle with comprehension of the incarnation. At times, it seems almost beyond the ability of finite minds to embrace. So we often tend to believe Jesus could not have failed in His mission. If that were true, His period of temptation was nothing but image building. His heartbreaking prayer in the Garden of Gethsemane was sham.

The fact is Jesus could have failed. Had the human overcome the divine, He would have turned from the suffering demanded rather than bowing to God's plan when He said, "Not My will but Thine be done." So the human side of our Lord needed the same kind of loving discipline every child requires. That is why the type of home in which He grew to maturity assumes major importance. God selected Joseph and Mary with infinite care. Less dedicated people might have aborted their mission.

Another aspect of Mary's character is revealed in the statement of the Gospel writer that she treasured the things

He said and did in her heart. Is this not the way of mothers, especially sensitive, dedicated mothers?

Before we leave this family setting, some further observations should be made. Jesus attended the synagogue every week "as was His custom" (Luke 4:16). Habits like this are instilled by godly parents. In His case, it might have been like the temple visit, but we know at least two of his brothers were deeply committed men. So the family sowed seed.

James only accepted his brother's Messiahship after the resurrection. From then on, his loyalty was firm. He was a leader, the president of the Jerusalem Council (Acts 15:13). He was the oldest of Jesus' four brothers. James married (I Cor. 9:5), but we don't know about children. Paul consulted James after his conversion (Acts 21:18), and held him in high regard, considering him a pillar of Christianity (Gal. 2:9).

Matthew 13:55 and Mark 6:3 identify a man named Judas as the brother of the Lord. He, like James and the other brothers, did not believe in Jesus' Saviorhood until after the resurrection (John 7:5). He wrote the letter of Jude, describing himself in the first verse as the brother of James but a servant of Jesus. We believe this to indicate he considered spiritual ties to Christ more important than physical, an evidence of the depth of the man. I Corinthians 9:5 implies Jude was married. Tradition mentions his grandchildren during the reign of Domitian.

Information concerning Joseph and Simeon was unavailable to us. Whether or not they were believers or the Lord's sisters became Christians, seems impossible to prove either way. Acts 1:14 says, "These all with one mind were continually devoting themselves to prayer, along with the women, and Mary the mother of Jesus, and with his brothers." All his brothers? His sisters among the women? If they followed the Way, their role was supportive. Their names were not mentioned in leadership positions.

What a beautiful family! What an example for us! No sham or hypocrisy appears in the story. Joseph and Mary, excellent parents, created an exemplary family group.

What about us? Our children are not the result of incarnation. But is not every parental role a gift from God and very special? Do we pass the test?

30

THE FAMILY OF ZACHARIAS AND ELIZABETH

Zacharias, a priest of God, was a descendant of the priest, Abijah. Elizabeth claimed a priestly heredity also, with Aaron as an ancestor. Elizabeth was a kinswoman of Mary although the exact relationship is indeterminate. They were the parents of John the Baptist, the forerunner of the Christ.

Elizabeth had already passed child-bearing age when Gabriel announced John's conception to Zacharias. The angel even named the child for the old priest. Zacharias did not believe Gabriel. He was punished by inability to speak until after John's birth.

A modern Zacharias and Elizabeth might have hot-footed it to the nearest hospital for amniocentesis in view of their age bracket. Any discrepancy in the results of the test might have brought an immediate recommendation of abortion. After all, Elizabeth was past forty!

But, to continue our story, this older couple rejoiced in the impending birth of their son. While carrying him, Elizabeth uttered a beautiful prophetic message to Mary at the time of Mary's visit (Luke 1:42-45). Luke also recorded Zacharias' prophetic song of joy following John's birth (Luke 1:67-69).

What kind of persons were Zacharias and Elizabeth?

"And they were both righteous in the sight of God, walking blamelessly in all the commandments and requirements of the Lord" (Luke 1:6). What a commendation! Righteous and blameless! Not only that but the kind of people who observed both the requirements and the commandments. Are not sins of omission and commission both covered here? Zacharias and Elizabeth carefully avoided committing sin. However, by fulfilling requirements of the Lord, they also did their share of the Lord's work. Luke introduces us to a committed and dedicated married couple when we meet this priestly pair.

What type of son did they produce?

John the Baptist personally refrained from the use of all intoxicating beverages. He was filled with the Holy Spirit. John successfully preached a message of repentance. He gained many converts and became so well-known, religious leaders frequented his services. When Jesus embarked upon His ministry by asking John to baptize Him, John was the most famous preacher of their world. The Billy Graham of the first century in popularity and prominence!

But John the Baptist had been given a special assignment from God. He was to prepare mankind for the Messiah. At the coming of the Savior, John's ministry must take second place to that of his Lord. Anyone who has experienced the headliness of fame understands the difficulty of relinquishing it. Yet John said, "Behold, the Lamb of God!" (John 1:36). Two of his own disciples, hearing the statement, immediately switched their allegiance.

"Then Jesus arrived from Galilee at the Jordan coming to John, to be baptized by him. But John tried to prevent Him, saying, 'I have need to be baptized by You, and do You come to me?'" (Matt. 3:13, 14).

How many important preachers do you know who would have said that?

> And they came to John and said to him, "Rabbi, He who was with you beyond the Jordan, to whom you have borne witness, behold, He is baptizing, and all are coming to Him."
>
> John answered and said, "A man can receive nothing unless it has been given him from heaven. You yourselves bear me witness that I said, 'I am not the Christ,' but, 'I have been sent before Him.' He who has the bride is the bridegroom; but the friend of the bridegroom who stands and hears him, rejoices greatly because of the bridegroom's voice. And so this joy of mine has been made full. He must increase, but I must decrease" (John 3:26-30).

What an opportunity these disciples afforded for John to make a snide remark about Jesus! People did that sort of thing back then, too, you know, when motivated by jealousy. But this great man not only bowed to the Lord's divine mission, but said his joy was made full in Christ's ascendancy.

John was a rare human being indeed. He possessed such deep conviction of his assignment from God that even loss of personal popularity failed to sway his commitment both to God's purpose for his life and to the Savior he had come to announce.

Not only was John single-minded in his devotion to the purpose of God, but he also refused to ignore wickedness to save his own skin. He made a vicious female enemy similar to Jezebel of the Old Testament.

> For Herod himself had sent and had John arrested and bound in prison on account of Herodias, the wife of his brother Philip, because he had married her. For John had been saying to Herod, "It is not lawful for you to have your brother's wife."
>
> And Herodias had a grudge against him and wanted to kill him; and could not do so; for Herod was afraid of John, knowing that he was a righteous and holy man, and kept him safe. And when he heard him, he was very perplexed; but he used to enjoy listening to him (Mark 6:17-20).

We see here another proof of the unchanging personalities of people. All around us in our society today, we may observe this major difference in personal reaction to criticism. Herod had been equally judged with Herodias. He did not change his way of life, but still enjoyed hearing the man who said those things about him. He also protected John. Herodias was out for blood. She could not take criticism without severe emotional reactions to it. Are not human beings pretty much the same today?

As we know, Herodias had her way. Through the lowest possible means, she achieved her own ends. Herod ordered John beheaded. Even facing death, the great prophet refused to forsake his God.

Only once did John's faith in his mission seem to waver. While suffering imprisonment, he sent word to Jesus, a questioning word. "Are You the Coming One, or shall we look for someone else?" (Matt. 11:3). Jesus answered immediately. "The blind receive sight and the lame walk, the lepers are cleansed and the deaf hear, and the dead are raised up, and the poor have the Gospel preached to them" (Matt. 11:5). Was John crying out, "Reassure me that I have not lived in vain"? If so, that assurance was forthcoming from the compassionate Jesus.

Then Jesus said, "Truly, I say to you, among those born of women there has not arisen anyone greater than John the Baptist; . . ." (Matt. 11:11).

What sort of parents produced such a remarkable son? "Righteous, blameless, keeping both the commandments and the requirements." From what type of home did he come? One that put God first. John's great strength of character and purpose was no accident of fate.

31

FAMILIES OF THE APOSTLES

In studying families recorded in the Gospel accounts of the life of Jesus other than the families that nourished Jesus and John the Baptist, perhaps the most important ones involve the apostles, the Lord's closest friends, the men who established the church. Very little information remains in regard to their family life. They concentrated upon service to the Master rather than family ties.

Peter (Simon) and Andrew

These men were brothers, sons of Jonas (or John). Tradition makes Joanna their mother. Their native city was Bethsaida of Galilee. They were fishermen by trade.

We know nothing of any marriage for Andrew. Peter, however, married (Matt. 8:14; Mark 1:30; Luke 4:38).

Peter's wife appears as his companion on missionary journeys, assuring us she was intimately involved in his work for the Lord (I Cor. 9:5).

Apparently Peter and Andrew moved to Capernaum, for "the house of Simon" located there is mentioned in the Gospels (Matt. 8:5, 14; Mark 1:21, 29; Luke 4:31, 38). It seems Andrew made his home with Peter and his wife along with Peter's mother-in-law.

Peter and Andrew were partners with James and John in a fishing business (Luke 5:10). There is reason to believe they were prosperous, for they hired employees. They were not educated men, but they certainly had some knowledge of the world and of business because of their shipping involvement on the Sea of Galilee.

A significant statement of Andrew in John 1:41 makes us realize the familiarity of both men with the Messianic hope of the Jewish people. That indicates some education, at least in the laws and ideals of the people of God. "He found first his own brother Simon, and said to him, 'We have found the Messiah.' (which translated means Christ.)"

The New Testament records no children for Peter and his wife. Tradition mentions a son and a daughter.

We may draw some logical conclusions about the home of Jonas and Joanna because of the actions of their sons.

It was a traditional Jewish home. Peter and Andrew had been taught Jewish law and Messianic tradition.

It was a loving home, fostering deep affection in the children. Andrew longed to share his newly discovered faith with his brother. Simon listened to his brother's pleas. The two men worked well together in business. They lived happily in an extended family situation. Not only the brothers shared with each other, but all of them cherished Peter's mother-in-law enough to ask Jesus to help her (Matt. 8:14, 15; Mark 1:30, 31; Luke 4:38, 39).

Peter and his wife were close. Instead of remaining at home in those days of difficult travel, she chose to journey with her husband, offering all possible sustenance as he worked.

The home of Jonas and Joanna produced two outstanding sons. Peter's home exemplified extended family love plus a good marriage.

Two pictures emerge here. A loving, quietly sharing Andrew, less volatile than his brother, but the kind of man who served his Lord well, one who would make a worthy friend.

Peter, blustering, impetuous, the shirt-off-his-back kind of man! A man's man. But a warm son-in-law, a good husband, a fine servant of Christ, loving and kind.

Two totally different personalities produced by the same set of parents. Both men became stalwarts of the cross. Did the strength of the home result in the strength of the men?

James and John

These two men were brothers, sons of Zebedee and Salome. They were fishermen on the Sea of Galilee, partners with Peter and Andrew. There is evidence indicating Salome may have been a sister of Mary, the mother of Jesus, making James and John first cousins of the Lord. Jesus called these two apostles, "Boanerges," meaning "Sons of Thunder." This family also originated at Bethsaida but moved to Capernaum for the sake of their fishing business.

In examining the home from which these two apostles came, we realize they lived in prosperity as compared to most families of their era.

313

> And going a little farther, he saw James the son of Zebedee, and John his brother, who were also in the boat mending the nets. And immediately He called them; and they left their father Zebedee in the boat *with the hired servants*, and went away to follow Him (Mark 1:19, 20).

James and John were not penniless street people. Along with Andrew and Peter, they sacrificed a prosperous business to follow the Lord. We note an interesting point here. Zebedee made no protest although he was present at the call. Again we observe a family familiar with the Messianic promise. James and John were uneducated men as far as the concept of education of their day. To be considered learned among the Hebrew people of that time, one needed a Rabbinic education. Although these two apostles lacked this, they certainly were acquainted with Jewish law and with the prophetic assurances of a Savior.

Quite often families more prosperous than their neighbors consider themselves superior. We haven't changed so much, have we? This same attitude may be found in the family of James and John.

> Then the mother of the sons of Zebedee came to Him with her sons, bowing down, and making a request of Him. And He said to her, "What do you wish?" She said to Him, "Command that in Your kingdom these two sons of mine may sit, one on Your right and one on Your left."
>
> But Jesus answered and said, "You do not know what you are asking for. Are you able to drink the cup that I am about to drink?" They said to Him, "We are able."
>
> He said to them, "My cup you shall drink; but to sit on My right and on My left, this is not mine to give, but it is for those for whom it has been prepared by My Father." And hearing this, the ten became indignant at the two brothers (Matt. 20:20-24).

FAMILIES OF THE APOSTLES

We gain much insight into the home of Zebedee and Salome by this single story. No wonder James and John were called "Sons of Thunder" by the Lord. They were probably spoiled rotten! No one else's mother interceded with the Master to plead the case of her ambitious sons. And this lady had clout; or, at least, she thought she did. Perhaps the Lord could call her, "Aunt Salome."

Looking at the situation from her point of view, however, we see more evidence of emphasis on family. After all, was this kingdom going to be a family affair or not? They were all descendants of King David. Who had more right to chief seats, Jesus' cousins, or those with no blood ties?

In Salome, we see the typical matriarch. Zebedee was silent when his sons left to follow the Lord. There was nothing quiet about Salome. If her boys were going to leave the family business, she intended to see to it they exchanged it for something profitable, handsome seats in the government.

Another angle to her thinking might enter into the picture. Did she believe her sons had given up more than the rest and therefore deserved more? Obviously, none of the triumvirate had any concept of a spiritual kingdom at this point.

Salome grew in her understanding. Her loyalty remained unquestioned, even when she did not get her own way. In the account of the crucifixion, Salome appears. "And many women were there looking on from a distance, who had followed Jesus from Galilee, ministering to Him; and among whom was Mary Magdalene, along with Mary the mother of James and Joseph, and the mother of the sons of Zebedee" (Matt. 27:55, 56). "And when the Sabbath was over, Mary Magdalene, and Mary the mother of James, and Salome bought spices, that they might come and anoint Him" (Mark 16:1). Salome braved the Roman soldiers to see that her Lord was properly prepared in burial.

Salome was not a fair weather friend. She adored her sons, considered them abler than the rest, and longed for positions of importance for them. But when the tide of popular opinion turned, she was right there to endure defeat as she had hoped for and supported victory. She was a brave, strong woman; probably too much of a doting, ambitious mother, but also one from whom her sons derived endurance and resolve.

What do we know of these two men?

They were hot-tempered in the beginning, inclined toward rash decisions, often as a demand for proper treatment for themselves as well as the Lord. These men were wharf rats, accustomed to the rough waterfront!

> And it came about, when the days were approaching for His ascension, that He resolutely set His face to go to Jerusalem; and He sent messengers on ahead of Him. And they went, and entered a village of the Samaritans, to make arrangements for Him. And they did not receive Him, because He was journeying with His face toward Jerusalem.
>
> And when His disciples James and John saw this, they said, "Lord, do You want us to command fire to come down from heaven and consume them?" But He turned and rebuked them (Luke 9:51-55).

This fits the image of two spoiled boys expecting special treatment. Yet we see growth.

John was the only apostle with enough courage to remain at the foot of the cross with the women. His genuine affection, kinship and personal loyalty caused the Lord to commit His mother to John's care.

James, although wavering at the time of the crucifixion, was the first apostle to meet death as a martyr for the cause of Christ (Acts 12:2).

316

John lived to be an old man. The image of thunderous self-assertiveness of his youth disappeared as he concentrated in His Gospel upon Christ's love; and in his letters upon the theme of love for each other. John's letters accent familial love in the Family of God, the Church.

As far as we know, neither of these apostles married.

What sort of home produced these giants of the cross? A prosperous home dominated by an ambitious mother with many sterling qualities. There is much food for thought in this family story.

Philip

The New Testament contains no evidence as to Philip's family, either the one into which he was born or the one he may have established in adult life. We know he was a native of Bethsaida.

We did find some meager information in the writings of the church fathers. Eusebius quotes Polycrates, Bishop of Ephesus in the latter part of the second century.

> Polycrates states that Philip, "one of the Twelve," lived as one of the "great lights of Asia," and is "buried at Hierapolis along with his two aged virgin daughters"; and he adds that another daughter, who "lived in (fellowship with) the Holy Spirit," was buried at Ephesus. (*Hastings Dictionary of the Bible, Volume III*, page 835)

Clement of Alexandria mentions Philip's daughters, but says they married. (Ibid.)

If either of these references is reliable, Philip passed on his faith in his family as well as in his missionary endeavors.

Bartholomew or Nathanael

This apostle probably was Nathanael, Bar-Talmai, meaning "son of Talmai." He came from Cana where the first miracle of Christ was performed. Aside from this, we discovered nothing of his origins or family ties.

Thomas

We know of no family relationship for Thomas. The New Testament gives no facts except that he was a twin. Tradition appears contradictory. We do note something was certainly done properly in his rearing. He was loyal, even willing to die with Jesus (John 11:16). His deep love for the Master surfaced again at the Last Supper when he faced the thought of separation (John 14:5). His insistence upon seeing and touching the Lord's wounds following the resurrection never should have evoked the epithet, "Doubting Thomas." The others had already had that privilege.

Whoever his parents might have been, they should be praised for the success of their labors.

Matthew or Levi and James, Sons of Alphaeus

As far as we were able to discern, these two men were brothers. Nothing is recorded for this James in the New Testament except that he was listed among the apostles, the James whose father was Alphaeus. Mark 2:14 also records Matthew or Levi as the son of Alphaeus. So, in all probability, the two men were brothers. Some traditions identify Alphaeus with Clopas.

Since very little can be learned about this James, we may assume, at least, that he had done nothing to invoke the hatred that surrounded his brother Levi, the tax collector. Some scholars believe the name "Matthew" was assumed after Levi's conversion, just as Simon became "Peter."

The New Testament records a dinner in Jesus' honor at the home of Levi (Matt. 9:9, 10; Mark 2:14, 15). The

318

indications are that Matthew was married, but we don't really know.

The account of these two apostles is an example of two sons reared in the same Jewish home. One apparently did nothing to embarrass the family. The other, Matthew, collaborated with the enemy, the Romans, by tax-collecting.

This happens in homes today. Two youngsters brought up by the same set of parents, with even the same set of hereditary genes, turn out to follow totally different loyalties. Many times, however, later years bring them to much more similarity of thought and ideals.

Was a rebellious Matthew searching for something the staid religious leaders failed to provide? Who knows? Once he met the challenge of the Master, he faithfully followed. He even wrote the first Gospel in His honor. The black sheep seems to have had more ability than his brother, especially after turning his life around. Should we search for the reason for black sheep?

Thaddaeus

Many scholars seem convinced this man is the same as Judas, the son of James, and Lebbaeus. He is named in both Matthew and Mark as one of the twelve. We know nothing of his home or family.

Simon the Zealot

All we learned of this man involved his politics. He was a Cananaean, or Zealot, a member of a political party determined to overthrow Rome by force. The inclusion of Matthew and Simon in a small group attests to the Lord's ability to heal animosities. Jesus spoke to all types and classes of people, enabling them to identify with each other no matter how diverse their original thought. He created the Family of God through the *agape* love He both taught and lived.

We could discover no data about Simon's antecedents or his family.

Judas Iscariot

Judas' name identifies his residence as Kerioth, which means Judas came from South Palestine. All the other apostles hailed from Galilee. This may explain some of Judas' actions. Judaeans tended to denigrate Galileans. He was the son of a man named Simon.

One may only speculate as to the type of home that produced Judas. His betrayal of the Lord was obviously premeditated and calculated. No one knows his real motive, but we do know the premeditation. He persisted in malevolent thought in spite of all the Master's teaching. After realizing the enormity of his actions, he committed suicide rather than turning in adject repentance to God. We believe the text lays the way open for a change of Judas' destiny had he pursued the same course of action that Peter did.

As we search for family data in the Bible, we long to know what sort of people produced Judas. From what kind of environment did he come?

One final statement about the twelve seems imperative. Each of these men grew up in some sort of family. However, in their acceptance of Christ as Savior, they became instant members of the Family of God. Except for Judas Iscariot, it is evident from the New Testament that their membership in God's Family gained precedence over all human loyalties, provided their personal identity, and demanded their all.

Were this not true, they would have discussed their personal human relationships more in their writing.

What about us? It is possible to be born into a family that will hurt rather than help us. If we can find ourselves in Christ Jesus, become part of His family through accepting His bloodline offered on the cross, human identity becomes secondary. Being born on the wrong side of the tracks pales by comparison. Is this why the common people heard Him gladly? Many of them became martyrs rather than forsake the security of this new identity. History records the fact that they died joyfully.

Christianity is not only "pie in the sky by and by." It also includes loving fellowship here and now with the Family of God!

32

JESUS AND FAMILIES

Many of the Lord's miracles, social encounters, and teachings arose from family concerns. Let us consider some of these.

John 2:1-11 tells the story of a wedding feast in Cana of Galilee. Mary, the mother of Jesus, attended; also the Lord and His disciples. Jesus performed His first miracle of turning the water into wine to save a family from embarrassment.

We observe Jesus in the fourth chapter of John resting by a well in Samaria. As a woman approached the well, He requested a drink. We know the story. It is a family story, dealing with the problem of divorce as they knew it in the first century.

Most of us consider this woman terribly evil. She had been married five times. She was living with a man who was not her husband. (Did we say this was first century, not twentieth?) Since only men possessed the prerogative of divorce in that period, had those five husbands discarded her with little reason? History of that era divulges petty excuses for shedding wives. Since women received little or no training for anything but homemaking, the Samaritan woman might have been living with that sixth man only to preserve her own life.

Granted she had a poor track record. No matter what the background for the story may be, some facts are clearly evident. Jesus did not reject the disgraced woman. He even revealed His Messiahship to her. Then He enlisted her to witness to her community, a challenge other men of His era considered women unable to meet. This story in no way places Jesus' stamp of approval on the woman's lifestyle. It displays His *agape* love for troubled souls and His confidence in the ability of the downtrodden to rise to positions of capable service. In other words, one can overcome one's family situation, for the Lord will help and encourage.

In John 4:46-54, we read of Jesus' healing the nobleman's son. In this account, we realize our Lord's compassionate understanding of the love of a father for his seriously ill child. The Master honored parental devotion.

All three of the Synoptic Gospels record the healing of Peter's mother-in-law. The first chapter of Mark and the fourth chapter of Luke tell us the family united in requesting the Lord's help. He granted their plea. She was healed to rejoin her extended family.

The Sermon on the Mount applies to all phases of our lives, of course. We might note the Beatitudes, dealing with

324

particular attributes of character that would bless our homes. In this sermon, Jesus takes adultery beyond commission to motivation as He condemns lust. What would He say about the pornographic literature rampant in our culture and the tendency of many Christians to ignore the problem?

In Matthew 5:31, 32, we read,

> And it was said, "Whoever divorces his wife, let him give her a certificate of dismissal; but I say to you that every one who divorces his wife, except for the cause of unchastity, makes her commit adultery; and whoever marries a divorced woman commits adultery."

Many of us have interpreted this as a legal system. One may get a divorce if married to an adulterous mate; otherwise, no way! We determined generations ago that adultery was the only unforgivable sin against the marriage vows. Everything else is to be tolerated. Was this the Lord's aim?

In the light of the one-sided character of first century divorce laws and the tremendous compassion of Jesus, might these statements have been made to protect women? Was He saying to husbands of His day, "If you discard your wives, you are responsible for their relationships with other men"? Remember that first century women did not train for the business world. Most had no preparation for independent living. There were no court cases in which they could sue for alimony and child support. Does this teaching tie in with His attitude toward the Samaritan woman? Men of the Master's time needed discipline about divorce and their responsibility toward the women they married. Women required protection from uncaring men. He offered both by attacking the male concept of divorce in the sermon.

Some translations of Matthew 6:14, 15 state that we must forgive our brethren. For our study, we can apply this to members of our own families as well as to the Family of God. Jesus asserts failure to forgive others results in the heavenly Father's refusal to forgive us. Harsh words, are they not? Yet unforgiving spirits create havoc not only in families but throughout the entire field of human relationships. Such attitudes destroy the harmony of the Family of God. Harboring malice and anger within also wrecks the individual personality.

Jesus honored another family need in Matthew 8:5-13, this time in a Gentile family. He granted the centurion's request for healing of his servant, a member of his household. The man was cured. This showed respect for home again, keeping it intact by restoring a valued worker.

A beautiful story in Luke 7 tells of the widow of Nain whose only son had died. The writer notes Jesus' feeling of compassion. Knowing the desperate need of a widow for a supportive son, especially in that culture, Jesus raised the son. The Scripture says, ". . . And Jesus gave him back to his mother" (Luke 7:15).

The Lord also raised Jairus' daughter and restored her to her father. Jairus was a synagogue official, but apparently a believer (Matt. 9; Mark 5; Luke 8).

The story of the woman with the twelve-year issue of blood may not appear as family related, but it was. Leviticus 15 states the rules of uncleanness and impurity for such conditions. Not only was the woman unclean, but anyone who touched her, her clothing or her bedding became unclean also. What would this do to family and marital relationships? The Lord restored her to normal family life when He healed her.

In Matthew 15 and Mark 7, a very difficult story appears. A Syrophoenician woman approached Jesus begging help for her demon-possessed child. The disciples urged the Master to send her away. Jesus appeared insulting when He said, "It is not good to take the children's bread and throw it to the dogs" (Matt. 15:26). The mother persisted, protesting even dogs could eat crumbs that fell from the children's table. He healed her daughter.

One may wonder about the Master's attitude, the compassionate Jesus who dealt kindly with other Gentiles but sharply with this one. The explanation for His apparent insult lies in the particular word for "dog." Jesus used the diminutive form of the word, which could be understood as "pet puppy." The mother was quite willing to see herself as someone allowed to come into the house and have the crumbs falling from the table.

Two things do surface from the account. The woman testified to a power so great even the left-overs accomplished miracles. She also loved her child so deeply nothing deterred her from her purpose, the healing of that child. Jesus respected both attitudes. Both characteristics need to be incorporated into the Christian family.

In all three Synoptic Gospels we read of the father who brought to Jesus his son, apparently a victim of epilepsy caused by an unclean spirit. At the request of the father, Christ cured his son. In the account in Mark 9, a thought-provoking interchange takes place.

> And He asked his father, "How long has this been happening to him?" And he said, "From childhood. And it has often thrown him both into the fire and into the water to destroy him. But if You can do anything, take pity on us and help us!" And Jesus said to him, "If you can! All things are possible to him who believes."
>
> Immediately the boy's father cried out and began saying, "I do believe; help me in my unbelief" (Mark 9:21-24).

327

This father had endured years of emotional suffering. Evidently this was a last ditch attempt to help his son. In a spirit of defeatism, almost negativism, he said, "*If* You can do anything, please do it!" Jesus rebuked him. Yet, He honored the pathos in the father's cry, "I do believe; help me in my unbelief."

At some time in the lives of most families, this protest is wrenched from heartsick souls. God may rebuke. He often does. But He will understand. Did Jesus not say, "If you have seen Me, you have seen the Father?" (Paraphrase of John 14:9). The presence of the man at the feet of Jesus indicated faith, even if that faith were wavering at the moment. Our presence at the throne of God in prayer shows the same thing. We must not fear being honest with God. He knows what we think anyway. What's the point? People may insist we should always keep a stiff upper lip. God understands.

Perhaps it is stretching the theme a bit to include the story of the woman who was caught in adultery mentioned in the 8th chapter of John. But illicit sex between married people is the definition of adultery. Anything involving this sin affects teaching on family.

Conspirators created this episode to catch Jesus in disobedience to the law, or perhaps to thwart His influence upon the common people by making Him appear either heartless or immoral. The scribes and Pharisees believed they had Him no matter how He handled the situation. The result was fascinating.

After writing on the ground, He straightened up with a penetrating comment. "He who is without sin among you, let him be the first to throw a stone at her" (John 8:7). Then He wrote on the ground again. One by one the crowd melted away.

It is interesting to note in verse nine that the older ones left first. Why? We have often discussed the things we thought about older people when we were young. Anyone who is so shortly removed from childhood tends to believe age means criticism. Motivations for adult discipline are seldom understood by children. All they see is an authority figure breathing down their necks.

The years have taught us how mistaken we were in our judgments of the elderly. We are less critical now than we were in youth, largely because we know more about life's difficulties. We also remember how wrong we personally were many times even while possessing the very best intentions.

Had the older people in Christ's story grown more tolerant? Were they more conscious of a lifetime of mistakes?

This story illustrates the low esteem for women of that era. Our Lord's reaction clearly indicates His attitude toward such oppression. Since committing adultery alone is impossible, what happened to her partner? Was he off somewhere stocking the rock pile? Is this question one of the things Jesus wrote in the sand? No one knows, but we may observe the terribly slanted approach of the religious leaders. We also know our Lord disapproved of their attitude.

What can we get from this account for the family? Jesus called adultery sin. He was not broadminded about her actions. He commanded her not to get involved again. These are vital stresses for our permissive society where the philosophy of many is, "If it feels good, do it!" We may read articles often in magazines and books about the possibility the marriage relationship may be helped instead of hurt by an extra-marital affair. The Lord called adultery sin. That does not change even if all the psychologists and marriage counselors in the world consider it outmoded. Certain truths are eternal. This is one of them.

A second point is the Lord's forgiveness. He was the sole member of that crowd qualified to throw rocks. Does the Lord imply even adultery should be forgiven? Does this story grant insight into the fact that Christ considers other sins its equal? Are there sins that contribute to a marriage partner's infidelity in spite of the apparent innocence of the offended spouse? This story certainly provides food for thought.

What would Jesus say about the wife abuse problem of our day? What about rape? Would He condemn the victim for the enticing way she might dress or walk while excusing the rapist? Many courts do just that. No doubt Christ would rebuke such modes of dress and behavior, but would he condone men's reactions to them? No way! Our Lord never advocated one set of moral requirements for men and a contrasting group of demands for women.

We meet an unusual family numerous times in the ministry of Jesus, the Bethany family of Mary, Martha and Lazarus. This family was unusual because no parents are mentioned and none of the three family members seems to have been married. Love filled this household, love and hospitality. Families do not have to fit a set pattern for the Lord to dwell there.

In the 9th chapter of John, we read of the man blind from birth whom Jesus healed. From the standpoint of family, one very significant statement emerges from the story. "And His disciples asked Him, saying, 'Rabbi, who sinned, this man or his parents that he should be born blind?'" (They must already have been toying with the concept of original sin. Otherwise, how could they discuss the man's blindness as

330

his sin when he was born that way?) "Jesus answered, 'It was neither that this man sinned nor his parents; but it was in order that the works of God might be displayed in him'" (John 9:2, 3).

How comforting this assurance becomes to suffering families! The Master plainly said heartache and physical disability are not always the result of sin! Jesus healed the man, showing the works of God. If we trust even while suffering, will this not display God's works to the world also?

In Luke 12:16-21, the parable of the rich fool illustrates the Master's opinion of total emphasis upon material wealth to form a life support system. What a modern problem!

In Luke 11, Jesus compared the heavenly Father to the good earthly father. Again we see the importance our Lord places upon family. He used the same analogy in the parable of the lost or prodigal son in Luke 15. The good father forgave and accepted his foolish son who had squandered his inheritance.

What about us? Do we love our children completely only when they please us? If so, we have lost the major quality of the revered father of the parable.

It appears to us that students of Scripture have misnamed this parable. Each son lacked an important quality. Is misuse of money worse than an unforgiving and selfish spirit? Doesn't our name for the parable indicate our emphasis upon material things? Perhaps no one is harder to live with than a self-righteous, self-centered person like the older brother. Neither of these sons would have won any blue ribbons at a loving home contest. Either could have destroyed the family without the beautiful character of the father at the apex of the home.

There is a double message for us in this story. Without the heavenly Father at the center of our lives, we, too, annihilate peace and happiness in our families.

Another parable speaks to the family in Luke 16, the story of the rich man and Lazarus, the beggar. Jesus gave the beggar a name while the rich man remained nameless. In first century society, as in ours, would not the opposite have been true?

In Hades, the rich man, although in torment, asked for help to be sent to his family on earth. He wanted them to change their ways before it was too late. The parable teaches the eternality of familial love, even beyond the grave.

Jesus revived the divorce question in Matthew 19, Mark 10, and Luke 16. Most of us are not students of history. We do not realize what a vital question this was in the time of Jesus. Some first century men had divorced so many wives they make Elizabeth Taylor look like a school girl with her first crush!

In Matthew 18, the Master accented settling disputes before they snowballed out of proportion to their importance. He recommended openness in personal relationships, talking things over. This certainly is excellent advice for families.

Care of and respect for children form a strong part of Christ's teaching. He found children so charming and winsome He even said one must become as a child in order to enter the kingdom of heaven. What would He say about the prevalence of child abuse in our society? "But whoever causes one of these little ones who believe in Me to stumble, it is better for him that a heavy millstone be hung around his neck, and that he be drowned in the depth of the sea" (Matt. 18:6).

In considering child abuse, we must recognize it as one of our culture's greatest tragedies. However, in the Christian community, we may participate in a form of this barbarism without thinking deeply about it at all. Physical and sexual abuse are not the only modes it takes. Mental and emotional persecution may wreak havoc, devastating human personality. It is possible to engage in this type of mistreatment with little thought. Adults who were abused as children fill our prisons. This appears to be a vicious cycle, affecting far more people than we know.

Adults who belittle every opinion children express, designating their thoughts as ignorant or stupid do permanent damage. Permitting an older sibling to humiliate a younger one may have the same effect. Parents who make children feel unwanted and unloved abuse those children if they never lay a hand on them physically.

At one point, we participated in community work at a school for delinquent boys. The superintendent of that school said many boys assigned there by the courts were loved. However, not even one believed he was. Our parental love must be visible, openly expressed. A truly Christian home protects the sensitive feelings of the little ones who live there as well as those who visit. This does not mean wrapping them in cotton batting. It indicates creating healthy self-respect by making them valued, contributing family members.

The other side of the coin demands honor to parents. Jesus emphasized the Old Testament commandment ordering this (Matt. 15:4). For practical purposes, that includes teenage and young adult respect for parents who appear completely out of step with society as the young people know it. It means honoring aged parents suffering with some physical or mental disability. In addition to this command from God, never forget your time is coming! Your example may return to haunt you.

333

A few years back, we asked an aged woman her opinion on a national issue. She replied, "I don't know what my opinion is. No one pays any attention to my opinions anymore, so I guess I don't bother to have any." She was not complaining. She was simply stating a fact. Some of her children considered her senile, not because of her actions but because of a prevalent belief among those with little real knowledge of the aging process that senility is a natural part of it.

Is senility always genuine and unavoidable? Is it sometimes caused by families who cancel out the old folks' ability to contribute worthwhile thought? Most cultures in the world revere age. The American culture worships at the fountain of youth. The changing age of our population may alter this concept; in fact, is already beginning to do so. Statistics reveal most aged people remain mentally alert even if a bit slower on the draw. Reflecting upon our past, we wish we had been a bit more hesitant to speak when young. Haste creates so many word-eating banquets!

Before leaving this part of our manuscript, let us consider a parable of Jesus recorded in Matthew 7:24-27 and Luke 6:47-49. Jesus used common knowledge as His greatest teaching tool. Palestinians were familiar with deceptively solid sands upon which people built homes only to watch helplessly as those sands shifted in gully-washing rains. So He recommended rocky foundations, comparing those rocks to His teaching.

We use 20th century deceptive sands as home foundations; material wealth, secular knowledge, and community prestige. Jesus suggested treasures in heaven, knowledge of God, and prestige with His Father. Many of us value deceptive sands more than solid rock. Confusion and disillusionment overtake us when our homes crash around our heads.

No doubt our Lord taught other definitely family-related subjects we have failed to consider in this section. All His teaching relates to us as individuals. Individuals compose families. So everything He said applies to our study. The ones we mentioned seem particularly important to us.

33

THE FAMILY OF HEROD

The dynasty of the Herods runs throughout our New Testament. Since their characters and personalities seem inextricably tied to a study of New Testament families, perhaps we should discuss this family.

Information regarding their origins is limited. Some think they originated from Jewish captives who returned from Babylon. Josephus believed Antipater to have been Idumaean, therefore half Jewish. Detractors of the dynasty attempted to make them Philistines. Whatever their roots, the ability of this family makes its mark on history.

For our purposes, the first member of Herod's line to demand our attention is Herod the Great. He reigned from 37 B.C. to 4 B.C. Tradition tells us Herod the Great was a magnificent physical specimen, handsome and a skillful warrior. He defended Jewish religious rights, but was certainly no true worshiper of Jehovah. Historians are a bit kinder to him than New Testament writers.

Herod the Great was considered a second Solomon by many of the people. He rebuilt the temple. He practiced polygamy, although he was a novice compared to Solomon. He only had ten wives while Solomon had 700 wives and 300 concubines. Herod the Great sired eight sons and six daughters. Like other Jewish kings before him, he ordered the deaths of some of his sons for trying to usurp the throne.

In his later years, this Herod suffered intense pain due to chronic illness. As his pain increased, so did his cruelty. Matthew records the visit of the Wise Men to Herod's palace in his second chapter. We read of the slaughter of the babies of Bethlehem in the last part of that same chapter. Herod died soon after this barbaric decree.

Archelaus, the elder son of Herod the Great by Malthace, a Samaritan woman, receives mention in Matthew.

> But when Herod was dead, behold, an angel of the Lord appeared in a dream to Joseph in Egypt, saying, "Arise and take the Child and His mother, and go into the land of Israel; for those who sought the Child's life are dead."
>
> And he arose and took the Child and His mother, and came into the land of Israel. But when he heard that Archelaus was reigning over Judea in place of his father Herod, he was afraid to go there; and being warned by God in a dream, he departed for the regions of Galilee, and came and resided in a city called Nazareth; that what was spoken through the prophets might be fulfilled, "He shall be called a Nazarene" (Matt. 2:19-23).

Archelaus outraged the Jews by marrying Glaphyra, widow of his brother Alexander, even though she had children by Alexander and had another husband, Juba of Mauritania, living. Archelaus' wife also still lived at the time.

Archelaus was the worst of Herod the Great's sons. After nine years of suffering under his tyranny and cruelty, the Jews protested to Augustus who ordered Archelaus to Rome, heard the case, and banished him. Augustus replaced the evil king with a procurator from Rome.

We meet Herod Antipas in the Gospels also. He, too, was Herod the Great's son by Malthace. This Herod appears in Matthew 14:1ff.; Mark 6:14ff.; and Luke 3:19 where the story is told of John the Baptist's denunciation of Herod Antipas for stealing Herodias, his brother Philip's wife.

Any informed parent reading such a tale of debauchery becomes aware immediately of the tragic influences exerted upon Salome, the daughter of Herodias. Doubtless many people of her time envied Salome. She lived in a palace. She had everything money could buy. Yet her bloodthirsty, depraved mother instigated Salome's lewd dancing in the midst of a drunken brawl. Then she dictated the young girl's request for the head of John the Baptist on a platter.

If Herodias wanted her husband seduced to the point of such degradation, why didn't she do it herself? Had debauchery made her old before her time, thus physically unattractive to that mob? Or did the bored, undisciplined Herod only respond to new challenges? To force one's daughter into that type of compromising situation indicates a depth of depravity almost impossible to comprehend. Salome was an abused child even if no one recognized the problem at the time.

Herod Antipas, learning of the ministry of Jesus, suffered a serious attack of conscience. He thought John the Baptist had arisen from the dead and come back to haunt him. The king, frightened by his own guilt, was quoted as desiring to kill Jesus (Luke 13:31).

Apparently Herod Antipas had never seen Jesus until Pilate sent Him to the king at the time of His trial (Luke 23:7-15). Neither Herod or Pilate considered Jesus worthy of death, but they were politicians first and human beings second. So personal conviction fell before political expediency. This examination of Jesus before Herod is also mentioned in Acts 4:27.

Herod Antipas, although not so cruel as Archelaus, eventually suffered banishment to Lugdunum in Gaul. His downfall came through Herodias.

Herodias, burning with ambition, coaxed Antipas into a confrontation with Caius because of her jealousy over the status of Agrippa. Agrippa, who held the ear of Caius, brought charges resulting in banishment.

Another son of Herod the Great, this one by Cleopatra, a woman of Jerusalem, was named Philip. He is mentioned as tetrarch of Iturea and Trachonitis in Luke 3:1. He ruled from B.C. 4 until A.D. 34, the year of his death.

Philip seems the one moral man of Herod the Great's family. He married only once, to Salome, dancing daughter of Herodias, with no children. No cruelty, excessive ambition or lust appears in the record for him. Salome married twice. Her second husband was Aristobulus, son of Herod of Chalcis by whom she had three children; Herod, Agrippa and Aristobulus.

Herod, called Philip, was another son of Herod the Great by Mariamne, daughter of Simon the high priest. Through his mother's treachery, this son was omitted from Herod the Great's latter wills. He lived and died privately in Rome.

He was the first husband of Herodias, whose ambition drove her into the arms of his brother Herod Antipas who seemed to be going somewhere. The reader must be impressed with this man's great stroke of fortune in losing Herodias and all close association with the rest of Herod the Great's corrupt children.

Agrippa I, born about 10 B.C., was the son of Aristobulus, son of Herod the Great and Mariamne, granddaughter of Hyrcanus Agrippa I's mother and Bernice, daughter of Salome, Herod the Great's sister, and Costobar. Herod the Great had Agrippa's father executed and sent Bernice and Agrippa to Rome.

Agrippa I's wild living made him run up huge debts. Tiberius imprisoned him because of his extravagance. When Caligula ascended the throne, Agrippa I was released from prison and presented the tetrarchies of Philip and Lysanius and the title of king. After accomplishing the banishment of Herod Antipas, he received the tetrarchy overseen by Antipas also. When Caligula died and Claudius succeeded him, Agrippa was presented with Judea and Samaria in addition to all his other possessions. This made him ruler over all the territory claimed by Herod the Great.

Agrippa I befriended the Jews, adhering scrupulously to their rites of worship and respecting their traditions. He used his considerable influence to spread Judaism. When his daughter, Drusilla, became engaged to Epiphanes, son of Antiochus, king of Commagene, Agrippa I tried to force the young man's circumcision to please the Jews.

In Acts 12, we read of Herod's persecution of the church and the death of James at his order. This Herod was Agrippa I. The chapter records Peter's miraculous release from imprisonment. Herod Agrippa I had the guards executed.

Acts 12 also records Herod Agrippa's death in the 23rd verse. He had maintained his throne and expanded his influence. The persecution of Christians appears to have formed part of his Judaizing policy. It pleased the religious leaders.

Agrippa I married Cypros, daughter of Phasael, who was the son of Phasael, Herod the Great's brother. Cypros' mother was Salampsio, daughter of Herod the Great by Mariamne, granddaughter of Hyrcanus.

The intermarriage in this family was astounding and bound to be weakening, establishing tragic immorality and opening the way for recessive genes to assume prominence.

To Agrippa I and Cypros were born five children: Agrippa II; Drusus, who died young; and three daughters, Bernice, Mariamne, and Drusilla.

Claudius did not give Agrippa II his father's territory upon the king's death because Agrippa II was only seventeen years old. Agrippa II traveled to Rome and used his influence there for Judaism. Eventually he came into power in most of the areas his father had controlled.

All the Herods tended to combine Judaism and Hellenism, and Agrippa II pursued the same course. He attempted to spread Judaism among the surrounding kings. He finished the temple at Jerusalem.

In Acts 25 and 26, we find an extensive account of the meeting between Festus and Agrippa; also Paul's sermon before Agrippa II, Bernice and Festus, the Roman governor. Paul referred to the king's great knowledge of Judaism. History upholds the apostle's compliment. Acts 26:28 reports, "And Agrippa replied to Paul, 'In a short time you will persuade me to become a Christian.'" This statement may have been made in sarcasm or as a simple statement of truth. However the young king intended the remark, the sermon provoked no change in his life.

Agrippa II was the last of the Herods. He died about 100 A.D. His relationship with his sister Bernice prompted all sorts of incest rumors, probably with a basis in truth, for morality of any kind seemed unimportant to most of the Herod dynasty.

Bernice, too, was flagrantly immoral. History records her intimate relationship with the Roman Titus whom she never married although she lived with him as his wife.

Drusilla, the youngest daughter of Agrippa I, wallowed in depravity. She had been betrothed to Epiphanes, but he eventually refused circumcision, so they never married. She married Azizus, king of Emesa. The marriage was miserable. Drusilla's beauty attracted Felix, procurator of Palestine. She deserted her husband and married Felix by whom she had a son, Agrippa, who died in the eruption of Mt. Vesuvius during the reign of Titus.

Acts 24:24-26 relates Paul's sermon before Felix and Drusilla.

> But some days later, Felix arrived with Drusilla, his wife, who was a Jewess, and sent for Paul, and heard him speak about faith in Christ Jesus. And as he was discussing righteousness, self-control and the judgment to come, Felix became frightened and said, "Go away for the present, and when I find time, I will send for you."
>
> At the same time, too, he was hoping that money would be given him by Paul; therefore he also used to send for him quite often and converse with him.

In leaving this family, so tied to New Testament history, we felt the need to assess their character and life in regard to modern thought. The story of the Herods sounds like a television soap opera; intrigue, violence, incest, adultery, complete amorality. The Herods were defeated and destroyed by their own depravity. Roman civilization was not far behind. Self-destruction came as a result of their gross immorality, resulting in weakness.

Before any culture or civilization falls, the families must collapse.

What about America?

34

THE FAMILY OF PILATE

Before we leave this section from the Gospels, one other family should be mentioned. Pilate, the Roman governor to whom the Jews delivered Jesus at the time of His trial, remains an enigma. Traditions are mixed. Some legends make him the illegitimate son of a king. Others infer because of the name Pontius Pilate he belonged to a noted Samnite family whose name appears frequently in Roman history. Still others insist he came from the region of Pontus, thus making area not family the source of the name. No one appears to know definitely.

Tiberius appointed Pilate to office in 26 A.D. He held the office for ten years in spite of his intense cruelty. So many complaints reached Rome that Pilate was summoned to court, banished and eventually appears to have committed suicide.

In the light of his notorious cruelty, Pilate's treatment of Jesus is thought-provoking, to say the least. He wanted to release the Lord. The only thing that made him decide otherwise appeared to be fear he would be considered a traitor to Caesar. Christ's effect upon this blasé, inhuman, sadistic officer bears witness to the stance of the Savior.

Pilate's wife played a role also. She begged him to "have nothing to do with that righteous Man; for last night I suffered greatly in a dream because of Him" (Matt. 27:19). Pilate's wife was named Claudia Procula or Procla. Christian tradition makes her a Jewish proselyte who embraced Christianity. Some identify her with the Claudia mentioned by Paul in II Timothy 4:21.

Some traditions declare Pilate himself became a penitent Christian before his death. Some Coptic tradition elevates Pilate to martyrdom and sainthood.

This much we know. The cruel, often merciless Pilate was impressed by the dignity of our suffering Savior.

35

INDIVIDUALS AND THEIR FAMILIES FROM THE BOOK OF ACTS

Luke, Author of the Third Gospel and Acts

The parentage of Luke remains unknown. Tradition says he had neither wife nor children. He apparently was a Gentile by birth. Luke and Titus may have been brothers (II Cor. 8:18; 12:18). Both men were Greeks. Authorities dispute the question as to whether or not Luke was a Jewish proselyte or one of those who skipped Judaism entirely in his acceptance of Christianity. The apostle Paul characterized him as "the beloved physician" (Col. 4:14). Tradition asserts he died in Bithynia at the age of seventy-four. His writing evidences culture and education. Attention to minute detail in his Gospel might support the idea of a superior medical education; superior, at least, for that day.

Barnabas

Barnabas, a Levite of Cyprus, appears to have been a prosperous man. He was a cousin of John Mark (Col. 4:10); no other family facts are given. He was a remarkable man. His generous spirit led him to sell a field which belonged to him and lay all the money at the apostles' feet (Acts 4:37). He saw the tremendous capabilities of the apostle Paul (Acts 9:27), and willingly took a back seat to one he considered a more outstanding servant of the Christ.

Barnabas apparently was tall and impressive looking since the people of Lystra identified him as Jupiter or Zeus, thought to be one of the handsomest of the Greek gods (Acts 14:12).

Had Barnabas not been such an understanding man, one who was willing to sacrifice his own needs for the good of the cause he represented, John Mark might have fallen by the wayside after Paul's harsh treatment of him. Barnabas, one of the New Testament's unsung heroes, used his family loyalty in a positive context. This was an outstanding family with a great potential for the cause of Christ.

Ananias and Sapphira

We know little of this couple whose story is recorded in the fifth chapter of Acts except for their hypocrisy and covetousness. Some have interpreted the account as pro-communist or at least supportive of communal type living in the first century church. It seems to us the apostle Peter's statement belies that approach.

> But Peter said, "Ananias, why has Satan filled your heart to lie to the Holy Spirit, and to keep back some of the price of the land? *While it remained unsold, did it not remain your own? And after it was sold, was it not under your*

348

control? Why is it that you have conceived this deed in your heart? You have not lied to men, but to God" (Acts 5:3, 4).

No communistic system was enforced in the early church. Those who gave their money and property volunteered. Ananias' sin lay in his lie prompted by a desire to appear unselfishly sacrificial while feathering his own nest quietly on the side.

Another fact emerges from this story, that of personal responsibility for one's own actions, Sapphira, given an opportunity to tell the truth, supported her husband's lie and met the same fate.

Our culture abounds with Biblical interpretations of the wife's position in the Christian home. In an effort to combat the rising tide of women's liberation, some fundamentalists have promoted a philosophy teaching that the sole responsibility of a wife is obedience to her husband even when he is wrong. In the minds of some sincere Christian women, their function according to Biblical doctrine is praying for a husband's conversion and obeying him completely even if that obedience involves forsaking public worship for themselves and their children and participating in unwholesome lifestyles. These women convince themselves, supported by some Christian leaders, that their husbands will be held accountable for the wrong because they are the heads of the house.

Perhaps no Scripture combats that foolish dogma more than the fifth chapter of Acts. Had Sapphira told the apostle Peter the truth, she might have considered her actions defiance of her husband and threatening to their relationship. She cooperated with Ananias. No one said, "You were a proper wife for supporting your husband even in his lie. It's not your fault. Don't worry about it." Instead, she died.

Stephen

Stephen, named first among the seven men chosen as deacons when the dispute arose in the church concerning care of Greek widows (Acts 6:5), was also the first Christian martyr (Acts 7:55-60). He was an amazing man, exemplifying the spirit of Christ even while being assassinated. Obviously, his trial was a farce.

We were unable to learn anything reliable of his ancestry or family connections, only of his utter sacrificial devotion to the bloodline of the Family of God.

Philip the Evangelist

Philip, also one of the seven deacons chosen to minister to the Christian widows and other poor of the group (Acts 6:5), was probably a Hellenist Jew. He preached to the Samaritans (Acts 8:5), most hated of all peoples by the Jews. He also baptized the Ethiopian eunuch (Acts 8:26-38), a man who would have been anathema to orthodox Jews both as a black man and as a eunuch. This is one of the first instances in which a Christian preacher declared differences of race and disabilities of physical function were to have no detrimental effect upon a person's ability to accept Christ.

Tradition says Philip's birthplace was in the area of Caesarea. Acts 21:8 tells us he made his home there. Acts 21:9 states the fact he had four virgin daughters who were prophetesses.

We know nothing of Philip's ancestry or marriage. He appears to have carried into his home the same open-minded stance he applied to his missionary work among the Samaritans and the baptism of the eunuch. He preached an unsegregated Gospel. Thus his daughters were permitted to prophesy, which might be translated, "preach" or "proclaim a divine revelation."

Cornelius and His Family

Cornelius, a Roman centurion stationed at Caesarea, was a devout Gentile. He and his family are generally considered the first entire household of Gentiles admitted to membership in the Christian Church. (Acts 10)

No description appears of the family itself, so we know nothing about them, of whom the family was composed, or any other pertinent facts. The text fails to support using this family as a means to promote infant baptism. "Now there was a certain man at Caesarea named Cornelius, a centurion of what was called the Italian cohort, *a devout man, and one who feared God with all his household*" (Acts 10:1, 2). Infants possess no fear of God, or as another possible translation, no "reverence" for Him either.

Since Cornelius commanded an important post in the city housing the Roman governor and the military headquarters of the province, he probably was an older man with years of military expertise.

Mark, Author of the Second Gospel

John Mark is the full name of this young man. His father's name fails to appear in the New Testament or in reliable tradition. Acts 12:12 designates his mother as Mary, apparently a woman of some wealth since she had a house large enough to accommodate big groups.

Mark was a cousin of Joseph Barnabas (Col. 4:10). Mark probably was a native of Cyprus. He was a Levite, a "Hebrew of the Hebrews" like Paul.

351

Acts 13:5 might lead us to believe John Mark ministered or assisted in evangelistic work at Salamis in Cyprus. Some interpret this Scripture as meaning John Mark was the minister of the synagogue there.

Mark's desertion on the first missionary journey with Paul and Barnabas (Acts 13:13) may have resulted from familial devotion. The young man, obviously very fond of Barnabas, may have resented Paul's gradual ascendancy to greater prominence than his beloved kinsman who had championed Paul when other leading Christians feared him. He also may have resented the inclusion of Gentiles in the movement since he was so thoroughly indoctrinated in Jewish segregationist principles.

At some point, Mark's rift with Paul was healed. Paul mentions Mark's comforting presence in Colossians 4:10 and Philemon 24. Paul described Mark as "very useful in serving me" in II Timothy 4:11. Mark also enjoyed a close companionship with the apostle Peter. Peter seems to have made the home of John Mark and his mother Mary his own headquarters when visiting Jerusalem (Cf. Acts 12:12.)

We have no knowledge of any wife or family for John Mark except for his devout mother Mary, and his committed cousin, Barnabas, who must have been older than John Mark. For purposes of family study, we may easily see the Christian influence upon the young by dedicated family members, as well as profound effects of close association with visitors in the home such as Peter and Paul. When we practice Christian hospitality, we lay the groundwork for Christian stability in the youths growing up in our homes.

Manaen

Manaen, mentioned in Acts 13:1, as one "who had been brought up with Herod the tetrarch," is worthy of our notice.

Josephus mentions a Manaen (*Ant.* XV. x. 5) as a notable Essene who became acquainted with Herod the Great when Herod was just a lad (about 50 B.C.). Manaen saluted the boy as a future king of the Jews. When Herod the Great assumed power, he sent for Manaen, treated him as a friend, and showed favor toward the Essenes. Some believe this older Manaen entered service as a Rabbi in the royal palace.

The Manaen of Acts 13 may have been a grandson or grandnephew of the prominent Rabbi, brought into the palace as a playmate and companion for the young Herod Antipas. He was educated with Antipas, probably traveling to Rome with Antipas and Archelaus when they completed their education in the capital city.

When Antipas became tetrarch, Manaen would naturally have assumed a prominent position in the household of Antipas. Luke's great knowledge of the Herodian family may have come from his intimate association at Antioch with Manaen (*Hastings Dictionary of the Bible,* Volume III, page 228).

Details concerning Manaen's acceptance of Christ remain unknown. We do know several members of the household of Herod were converted to Christianity, proving the appeal of the Gospel to prominent families as well as to the common people.

Since we have already mentioned the degradation of most of the Herods, it might be well to call attention to this man Manaen, educated in the same way, yet espousing the teachings of Christ and enjoying respect and reverence of the Christian community for his wise and kind leadership. Was this a case of egotistical membership in a family as a ruinous factor in the human personality of most of the Herods, while Manaen, with no such concept of prominence, could be trained in much the same manner without a detrimental result?

Sergius Paulus

Sergius Paulus was the Roman proconsul at Paphos in Cyprus (Acts 13:7-12). Little is known of this man except that he came from a Roman patrician family. We mention this to show how all types of families were attracted to the message of Christ when it was presented in simplicity and power as the apostle Paul did on his missionary journeys.

Timothy

Timothy became a convert to Christianity during Paul's first missionary journey at Lystra, Timothy's home (I Tim. 1:2; Acts 14:8; 16:1; I Cor. 4:14-17).

Timothy was the child of a mixed marriage. His mother Eunice was a Jewess. His father, unnamed in the Scriptures, was a Greek (Acts 16:1). Timothy had been schooled in the Jewish faith by his mother Eunice and his grandmother Lois (II Tim. 1:5), both of whom had obviously converted to the Christian faith. Timothy had not been circumcised. Whether this resulted from objections of his Greek father or rejection by the Jewish community due to his mixed heritage, no one knows. Some ancient writings refer to Eunice as a widow and Acts 16:3 has been interpreted by some as indicating his father was already dead at this point in Timothy's life.

Paul's fatherly love for the young Timothy fills his letters. Timothy's health caused worry (I Tim. 5:23). He showed great affection for the aging apostle (II Tim. 1:4). Paul describes the young man as timid (I Cor. 16:10), and inclined to withdraw from any assertion of his own authority

(I Tim. 4:12). Paul warned Timothy about the lusts of youth (II Tim. 2:22), and tried to buoy up his spirits in facing shame for the Lord (II Tim. 1:8).

Paul also describes Timothy as loyal (II Tim. 3:10), his "genuine" son (I Tim. 1:2), his loved son (II Tim. 1:2), his loved and faithful son in the Lord (I Cor. 4:17), possessing the same mind with Paul (Phil. 2:20), working as Paul did (I Cor. 16:10), Paul's "fellow-worker" (Rom. 16:21), "our brother and God's minister" (I Thess. 3:2), "the slave of Jesus Christ" (Phil. 1:1), and one who "seeks the things of Jesus Christ" (Phil. 2:21).

Our reason for devoting so much space to Timothy arises from problems in Timothy's family experienced by many modern families. We hear all the time about single parent families and the difficulties of their children. Timothy, apparently, was the product of a single parent home. He also profited from the extended family, for the apostle Paul mentioned the influence of both a godly mother and a godly grandmother.

We also may observe the potential influence of a fine Christian leader, the apostle Paul, acting as a substitute father in the life of a young man who apparently was fatherless.

Timothy exemplifies the outstanding success of a godly single parent, bolstered by a loving grandmother, and supported by a caring Christian community. It can be done!

Silas (Silvanus) and Judas Barsabbas

Silas, along with Judas Barsabbas, represented the Jerusalem Church on a trip to Antioch (Acts 15:22). There they presented the decisions of the Jerusalem Council to the congregation at Antioch. They were both called prophets. They remained in Antioch for a period to strengthen the converts there. Silas accompanied Paul on his second missionary journey.

Judas Barsabbas may have been a brother of Joseph Barsabbas, mentioned as a possibility to replace Judas Iscariot as an apostle in Acts 1. Except for this possibility, we learned nothing of family relationships for either man.

Lydia

Lydia, a purple-seller from Thyatira, baptized along with her household when Paul visited Philippi, was probably Christianity's first convert in Europe. A church was established in her home.

We know nothing of Lydia's family nor of her ancestry. We do know she acted as hostess for the entire missionary team, emphasizing the importance of hospitality in the Christian home (Acts 16:14, 15).

Lydia lends a modern concept to New Testament women. She was obviously career-oriented, rather than exclusively a homemaker. No condemnation appears for her way of life. In fact, she was respected as a leader.

Paul did not salute Lydia in the Philippian letter, indicating she had either died or moved.

Priscilla (Prisca) and Aquila

The names of this couple appear in six places in the New Testament. Luke mentions them three times in the eighteenth chapter of Acts, the second, eighteenth and twenty-sixth verses. The apostle Paul talks about them in three of his letters: Romans 16:3-5; I Corinthians 16:19; II Timothy 4:19. In four of these references, the name of Priscilla appears first, indicating a very special prominence for her in the first century Christian community.

356

Actually, some historical evidence exists for outstanding family heritage for each of them. Some historians believe Priscilla, a member of a prominent Roman family, married the Jew, Aquila. This might appear confirmed by the fact that one of the oldest catacombs of Rome is the "Coemeterium Priscillae." There seems some evidence connecting her with the Acilian gens, for members of that family were buried there. (*Hastings Dictionary of the Bible,* Volume IV, page 103). There is a church in Rome that bore her name from the 4th to the 8th century. The name was later changed during the tenure of Pope Leo III to include the name of Aquila with his name appearing first.

Some scholars believe Priscilla was always the more outstanding of the two, but that scribes of the 2nd century attempted to change the order of names in Acts 18:26 because the culture of the 2nd century objected to the prominence accorded women in the beginning of the church.

Aquila, also, may have descended from an important family. Some scholars connect him with the Pontians of Rome. A distinguished member of that family bore the name Pontius Aquila. However, this, along with some of the suppositions concerning the family of Priscilla, is another of those vague references with similarity of names that history neither proves nor disproves.

There are some things we may know for sure in our pursuit of families of the Bible. This couple possessed qualities of life worthy of our study, especially in this era when roles of women are changing.

Priscilla and Aquila worked together in their occupation, tentmaking. This made them somewhat unusual for their time since male/female roles tended to be clearly defined. When Paul left Athens for Corinth, "he stayed with them and they were working; for by trade they were tentmakers" (Acts 18:3). This was a family business.

Another fact emerges here. Priscilla and Aquila opened their home, their lives and their business to Paul. These people loved others and shared.

Priscilla and Aquila lived in an atmosphere of kindness and good will. The young preacher Apollos was mixed up. In spite of his eloquence, he needed correcting. The older couple refused to make a public spectacle of the young man. Instead, "they took him aside and explained to him the way of God more accurately" (Acts 18:26). Notice that both of them taught Apollos, not just Aquila. The text lends itself to no other interpretation.

Priscilla and Aquila exemplified stability in all their dealings with people. They were 1st century rocks of Gibraltar. They felt no need to parade their superior knowledge. In Apollos, they saw a gifted young preacher, mistaken but outstanding nonetheless. So their purpose became the salvation of that young man, not the elevation of their own status in the Christian community.

When Paul greeted Priscilla and Aquila in the Roman letter, he described them as "fellow-workers in Christ Jesus, who for my life risked their own necks, to whom not only do I give thanks, but also all the churches of the Gentiles; also greet the church that is in their house. . ." (Rom. 16:3-5).

This 1st century couple combined their talents, cooperating and collaborating in the service of Christ, not only as tentmakers, but also teachers and leaders in the church. They risked their own lives to save Paul. By hosting a congregation in their own home, they exposed themselves to possible persecution daily at the hands of authorities in that fearful early period of the church. In fact, they appear as nomads; first because of prejudice against Jews, and then as a result of hatred for Christians. Everywhere they moved, they established a church in their house.

The New Testament describes valiant, faithful people with few words. Priscilla and Aquila may be numbered among 1st century heroes and heroines, leading out in the infant church.

So, does it matter who was more prominent or whose heritage more outstanding? It obviously didn't to them. Their lives centered in the Lord Jesus Christ, His bloodline flowing from Calvary, and their teaching, establishing churches and living abundantly in support of the glorious Family of God.

Where should the emphasis be placed in today's Christian family? Would we be so concerned about defined roles were our complete emphasis upon witnessing for our Lord? Would we waste time asserting our rights and demanding our privileges were Jesus reigning completely in our lives? Pray about it.

Crispus

Crispus was the chief ruler of the Jewish synagogue at Corinth (Acts 18:8). Here again we note an entire household accepting Christ together. We find no basis for infant baptism in a family conversion in the text. "And Crispus, the leader of the synagogue, *believed in the Lord with all his household* . . ." (Acts 18:8). Infants lack the knowledge to make conscious decisions such as belief.

Felix

We dealt with Felix briefly in the section concerning the family of Herod because he married Drusilla, Agrippa's sister. The New Testament contains no accolades for Felix (Acts 24). However, Luke is almost complimentary compared to some of the other historians of the era. Felix was a brother of Pallas, a well-known favorite of Claudius Caesar. Some believe Felix to have been a freedman of Antonia, Claudius Caesar's mother. Pallas and Felix claimed ancient kings of Arcadia as ancestors. Thus the procurator asserted his royal heritage although no proof exists for his claims.

Moral and spiritual depravity marked the lifestyle of Felix and Drusilla, as might be said of most of those whom the family of Herod touched.

Publius

Luke writes in the twenty-seventh and twenty-eighth chapters of Acts of the shipwreck experienced when Paul was being transported to Rome to appear before Caesar. All two hundred and seventy-six persons on board were saved, marooned on the island of Malta. In the seventh and eighth verses of the twenty-eighth chapter, we meet Publius.

> Now in the neighborhood of that place were lands belonging to the leading man of the island, named Publius, who welcomed us and entertained us courteously three days. And it came about that the father of Publius was lying in bed afflicted with recurrent fever and dysentery; and Paul went in to see him, and after he had prayed, he laid his hands on him and healed him (Acts 27:7-8).

Publius headed a hospitable family, touched by the needs of shipwrecked strangers. Apparently no thought was given to any recompense when they helped Paul and his companions. Paul repaid them with a more important commodity than money, health.

360

Luke never says the family converted to Christianity. Tradition names Publius as first bishop at Malta and later bishop of Athens. It seems noteworthy that Paul healed many folk on the island with no record of any preliminary demand for faith.

Other Prominent Characters in the Book of Acts

We shall devote the next section to the apostle Paul, his ancestry, and his teachings on family. So we did not include him in this section, choosing instead to pursue the other course.

Of the seven deacons chosen by the Jerusalem Church, we concentrated upon Stephen and Philip, first due to their prominence, but also because we were unable to locate any details about the families of Prochorus, Nicanor, Timon, Parmenas and Nicolas (Acts 6:5). A legend exists concerning Nicolas and his beautiful wife, but it appears more fictional than factual.

One family we did not mention was that of the Philippian jailer. His conversion along with that of his entire household is recorded in Acts 16:26-34. Again the entire group believed, eliminating infant baptism (Acts 16:34).

We mentioned Apollos only in connection with Priscilla and Aquila because no family details appear in the Scriptures about this young man. He was an Alexandrian Jew, well educated and eloquent. Some appear to have preferred his polished style to the more rough preaching of Paul. Apparently Apollos backed away from the controversy at Corinth by remaining absent from the city where he had been a prominent preacher until the division was somewhat healed. Although this has little to do with family behavior, we might say to modern preachers, "Go thou and do likewise if you have become controversial!"

361

Throughout the entire book of Acts, we observed a group of primarily Jewish Christians strangely disinterested in the genealogies deemed a focal point of their Old Testament History. First century Christians had altered their entire list of priorities. Ancestral blood had bowed its head to redeeming blood. Roots from which they had come were abandoned for routes in which they were traveling through life. Family status moved aside to permit eternal destiny to occupy front stage center. Personal family relationships, although still valued among them, made them even more conscious of their membership in the Family of God. What a committed people!

Is commitment the theme of our families today? Or do we major in minors?

36

THE APOSTLE PAUL: HIS BACKGROUND AND TEACHING ON FAMILY

Paul the apostle was born in Tarsus of Cilicia of the tribe of Benjamin, and inherited Roman citizenship from his father. He described himself in Philippians 3:5, 6 as follows: "circumcised the eighth day, of the nation of Israel, of the *tribe of Benjamin, a Hebrew of the Hebrews,* as to the Law, *a Pharisee;* as to zeal, a persecutor of the church, as to the righteousness which is in the Law, found blameless."

Again in Galatians 1:14, from Paul's own pen, "And I was advancing in Judaism beyond many of my contemporaries among my countrymen, being more extremely zealous for my *ancestral traditions.*"

When the apostle defended himself against a mob in Jerusalem, he made the following statement: "I am a Jew, *born in Tarsus of Cilicia*, but brought up in this city, *educated under Gamaliel*, strictly according to the law of our fathers, being zealous for God, just as you all are today" (Acts 22:3).

When the commander threatened Paul with scourging following this mob reaction, Paul asked, "Is it lawful for you to scourge a *man who is a Roman* and uncondemned?" (Acts 22:25). The commander then informed Paul he had bought his citizenship. The apostle replied, "But I was actually *born a citizen*" (Acts 22:28).

We may infer Paul's father was wealthy. Education under Gamaliel, the most prominent Jewish teacher of the day, could not have been cheap. The fact that Paul learned a trade along with His Rabbinic education only accents the family's emphasis upon Jewish tradition. Most well-to-do Jewish families combined the teaching of some handcraft along with academic qualifications. Such attitudes were born of necessity for a group of people often forced to move around due to prejudice.

Paul's mother's piety seems implied in Galatians 1:14 just as he extols Timothy's grounding in the faith at the feet of his mother in II Timothy 1:5 and 3:15.

It seems strange that Paul's parents are not identified since the astute apostle had to be aware of the profound influence exerted upon his life by his heritage. Yet, they remain nameless. We don't know about siblings except for a sister mentioned casually in Acts 23:16-22 because her son warned Paul of a threat against his life. Obviously, the apostle's relationship with his sister's family must have been at least partly amicable, or the warning would not have been given.

With such a strong Pharisaic background, was Paul's conversion to Christianity resented by his kin? Is that why he never refers directly to his parents? No one knows, but it certainly enters the realm of possibility thinking.

Paul bore an interesting mixture within his personality: Jew, Greek and Roman. The apostle carried strong Jewish emphases in his thinking, probably centered in Pharisaism. We might describe him as bordering on fanaticism in any belief he embraced. He showed a severity of temperament that could have been a direct result of this type of inheritance. Since Gamaliel appears extremely broad-minded, ready to assess motives and allow time to heal problems (see Acts 5:34-39), the apostle did not gain his bombastic approach at the feet of the great Rabbi. One wonders if Paul might have inherited his strong determination that sometimes cost him so dearly at the knee of a Pharisee father. If so, his father might have resented Paul's becoming a Christian unless he, too, converted. Perhaps his father was already dead.

At any rate, Paul carried in the depths of his personality many of the aspects of his Pharisaical training. He knew the chaining effect of this background and constantly struggled against it. No other New Testament writer assails the futility of law in regard to salvation in the manner Paul does. His very understanding of this because of the education his family had provided made Paul the greatest proponent of Christianity the world has ever known. He knew, because he had studied so thoroughly, that legalism lacked redemptive quality. His education made him a trained jurist, a skilled Rabbinical scholar, and a magnificent logician in debate. This demands mention in our family study because the sort of family from which Paul came determined his type of education.

But Paul did not possess only Hebrew learning. He was versed in Greek literature and philosophy as well. Whether this is due to the influence of the great university in Tarsus might be questioned. However, Tarsus was the capital of Cilicia and a prominent trade city. All sorts of people passed in and out through the ships of all nations docking there. This kept Paul from provincial attitudes that might have hampered his missionary endeavors. Versatility of the Greeks united with the tenacity of the Jews in the personality of the great apostle, making him a citizen of the world with a Rabbinic education. His background also made him an effective witness to the cities. They were his "turf."

Paul knew Roman law also. Evidence of this knowledge appears in his questioning of the scourging already mentioned and also as he appealed to Caesar for a hearing. All Roman citizens had this right. Paul obviously knew it. His respect for Rome shows itself in his planting churches in Roman colonies. His bearing commanded respect from Roman governors and the centurion, Julius, who took charge of Paul on the voyage to Rome to appear before Caesar. Yet he must have been a somewhat sickly man, driven by zeal for the Savior to ignore and rise above his "thorn in the flesh" (II Cor. 12:7).

He quotes his enemies in II Corinthians 10:10. "For they say, 'His letters are weighty and strong, but his personal presence is unimpressive, and his speech contemptible.'" A first century document describes him as, "bald-headed, bowlegged, strongly built, a man small in size, with meeting eyebrows, with a rather large nose, full of grace, for at times he looked like a man and at times he had the face of an angel" (*Hastings Dictionary of the Bible*, Volume III, page 700).

Paul's hearers either loved or hated him. Nothing in his personality evoked a "take it or leave it" reaction on the part of his audiences. The driving force of his fanatical love for Christ, for his own people, and for God's creation as a whole came across in full measure everywhere. One might assess him as crude or rude, but ignore him? Never! Oh, for some 20th century fanatics like Paul!

How we would have liked more information about his parents! The fact is he lived a devout and moral life before he met Christ on the road to Damascus. His parents must have been outstanding people in their dedication to their personal beliefs. Their son reflected that commitment.

Paul's Teaching on Family

Romans

This book is not placed in the canon in chronological order, but more properly as to importance for the Christian community. Paul wrote this letter to the church at Rome, the greatest city of the ancient world. The epistle itself also merits first place. Its excellence of Christian depth is surpassed in no other part of the New Testament.

Searching for references specifically applicable to families in this book presents a problem. However, the letter contains so much wisdom that all of it pertains to a personal walk with the Lord, and, therefore to family pursuit of excellence.

Some of the Bible's strongest condemnations of homosexuality are recorded in Romans. Since this sexual lifestyle, if engaged in by all people, would end the family, in fact the whole human race, in one generation, this teaching applies to family study.

> For this reason God gave them over to degrading passions; for their women exchanged the natural function for

that which is unnatural, and in the same way also the men abandoned the natural function of the woman and burned in their desire toward one another, men with men committing indecent acts and receiving in their own persons the due penalty of their error (Rom. 1:26, 27).

Paul also lists personality traits that are the result of a "depraved mind." All of these apply to the family, but some seem particularly devastating to family peace. ". . . disobedient to parents, without understanding, untrustworthy, unloving, unmerciful" (Rom. 1:30, 31). Since discipline, understanding, trust, love and mercy must form the bulwark of Christian family life, the apostle's description of the depraved mind illustrates the importance of Christian thought to the Christian home.

Romans 5:1 speaks of faith bringing justification and peace. Nothing is more necessary for happy home life than peace. Peace among family members comes only from inner peace derived from faith and trust, not only in God, but also in each other.

What family has not experienced trouble? How may we deal with it? ". . . we also exult in our tribulation; knowing that tribulation brings about perseverance; and perseverance, proven character; and proven character, hope; and hope does not disappoint; because the love of God has been poured out within our hearts through the Holy Spirit who was given to us" (Rom. 5:3-5).

Without the ability to persevere, what family survives trouble? Without character, proven character, what family can face crises with an aura of hope? Without the indwelling Spirit, filling individual members with love, can Christian families long remain Christian? Whether Paul aimed this passage at families or not, it certainly fills a deep need.

368

In Romans 7:2, 3, Paul defines the strength of marriage vows.

> For the married woman is bound by law to her husband while he is living; but if her husband dies, she is released from the law concerning her husband. So then if while her husband is living, she is joined to another man, she shall be called an adulteress; but if her husband dies, she is free from the law, so that she is not an adulteress, though she is joined to another man.

Paul is using this to illustrate the Christian's death to the Law and union with Christ. Still it shows the morality necessary for marriage.

The entire 12th chapter of Romans should be pursued by the Christian family as a statement of ethical behavior within the family unit. Practiced at home, this set of rules could reach out and leaven the entire community.

"Therefore let us not judge one another any more, but rather determine this—not to put an obstacle or a stumbling-block in a brother's way" (Rom. 14:13). This, although written to Christian brethren in the Family of God, certainly applies to the human family.

"Now we who are strong ought to bear the weakness of those without strength and not just please ourselves" (Rom. 15:1). One of the secrets of a successful marriage is complementing or completing each other. We all have weaknesses and strengths. Marriage counselors often suggest marriages must be 50-50 endeavors. It has been our experience that all marriages present complicated periods when one must be willing to say, "For this time, we will make it 90-10." Good marriages and good families concentrate upon uplifting all the members, not just pleasing ourselves. People who are interested only in self-satisfaction should stay single

369

and avoid inflicting themselves upon the rest of the world as much as possible.

Again in chapter 15, advice Paul offers the Roman church may be applied with significant importance to family life. Our first quotation is a prayer. "Now may the God who gives perseverance and encouragement grant you to be of the same mind with one another according to Christ Jesus; that with one accord you may with one voice glorify the God and Father of our Lord Jesus Christ" (Rom. 15:5, 6).

When we were young, many Christian couples hung plaques on the wall saying, "Christ is the head of this house, the unseen Guest at every meal, the silent Listener to every conversation." Sometimes just looking at that was a conversation stopper! And some conversations need stopping. If we really believe what the plaque said, would not our families glorify the God and Father of our Lord Jesus Christ with one voice?

Paul continues with wisdom so needed in families. "Wherefore, accept one another, just as Christ also accepted us to the glory of God" (Rom. 15:7).

Anyone who enters marriage with the idea of changing the partner may expect disappointment. Interestingly enough, acceptance of another human being, warts and all, often effects changes for the better. Everyone wants and needs acceptance first. Then, with the assurance of being loved, we frequently long to improve ourselves for the one who appreciates us, even in our weakness. If Christ had demanded perfection before we were permitted to become Christians, how many Christians would there be?

The problem of acceptance often affects families when personalities of children differ greatly. This hurdle presents marked difficulties when the first child is easy to handle, tractable and cooperative. Then along comes one who swings from the chandelier before walking. But acceptance provides the foundation for a stable personality.

For parents with learning disabled or exceptionally gifted children, or perhaps crippled ones, this presents an even greater hazard. Acceptance at home makes such a difference when one must meet a world showing curiosity at best and rejection at worst. We need to accept each other in the Family of God as Paul advises, but even more so in the personal family situation.

Romans 15:14 finds the apostle complimenting his readers. "And concerning you, my brethren, I myself also am convinced that you yourselves are full of goodness, filled with all knowledge, and able also to admonish one another." In a family situation, we certainly need to admonish one another. Acceptance does not indicate lack of discipline. However, we frequently correct without complimenting. We human beings need assurance that someone thinks we are great. Vinegar repels. Honey attracts. Dishonesty must not form part of this way of life. But everyone acts beautifully at times. How often do we mention this to those we love most? Grandparents can function well as confidence builders. Little ones are sure Grandma and Grandpa think they are great. That is good.

1st and 2nd Corinthians

These letters were written to the church in one of the richest, largest and most important cities of the Roman Empire. The commerce of the world made its way to Corinth's harbor. Along with that commerce came much that was evil. Vice ran rampant. Some of this wickedness had invaded the church. Paul aimed his correspondence at removing worldly cultural influence from the Family of God. Several parts of these letters apply to our own families as well.

In I Corinthians 5:1, we read, "It is actually reported that there is immorality among you, and immorality of such a kind as does not exist among the Gentiles, that someone has his father's wife." Paul scolds the church for appearing to condone such action by fellowshiping the offender.

Leviticus 18:8, Deuteronomy 22:30 and 27:20 condemn such behavior. Webster defines incest as "sexual intercourse between persons too closely related to marry legally." Whether this incident qualifies as incest might be debated, but the relationship was strictly forbidden and certainly could result in nothing but heartbreak for all concerned.

Since the man's conduct evoked such a negative reaction from the inspired writer, what would he say about the statistics of our society that most sexual abuse of children occurs with close friends of the family or relatives? Paul recommended removal of the offending church member at Corinth. What would he say about our knowledge of this evil in our society with little or no action on our part to change it?

"But actually, I wrote to you not to associate with any so-called brother if he should be an immoral person, or covetous, or an idolater, or a reviler, or a drunkard, or a swindler—not even to eat with such a one" (I Cor. 5:11). Harsh words, are they not? But they are there. It has been our experience that we as God's Family frequently apply Paul's teachings in this verse until we come to "covetous." Then, since our culture considers the person who makes and hoards a large amount of money smarter than others, we forget all about the New Testament concept of covetousness, preferring to espouse the materialistic way of life and

372

teaching our children to do likewise. We have met church officers who wept when their sons dedicated their lives to the ministry because "they would never have anything!" How do we reconcile this to Christian commitment in our families?

What about our families? Do we know where our children go, who their friends are? Do we wink at immoral behavior ourselves for fear of the sneering crowd? If we want to rear devout Christian families, we must live what we profess. Generation gaps are unavoidable. Credibility gaps need not exist.

In the 6th chapter, the apostle criticizes dragging Christian brothers into court (Rom. 6:5, 6). Would he not advise the same attitude about siblings?

In I Corinthians 6:9, Paul again reprimands sins that deny admission to heaven. Sexual sins affecting families are listed: fornication, adultery, perversion, and homosexuality. He treats fornication and adultery in a uniquely spiritual manner in verses 15 and 16. "Do you not know that your bodies are members of Christ? Shall I then take away the members of Christ and make them members of a harlot? May it never be! Or do you not know that the one who joins himself to a harlot is one body with her? For He says, 'The two shall become one flesh.'"

Our permissive society rejected these strong teachings long ago. But Paul wrote them. They were Spirit inspired. We cannot call our families Christian if we ignore them. We must take them into account.

The apostle Paul recommended celibacy in different places in his writing. I Corinthians 7:1 is one of those quotations. However he opens the door to marriage for those who might succumb to immorality.

Then Paul discusses the sex relationship in marriage. This discussion places Paul far ahead of his time. He, in spite of his Pharisaical background where doubtlessly he learned to pray, "I thank Thee, Lord, that I was not born a Gentile, a slave, or a woman," accords women the conjugal rights husbands must not deny. Some mention of this appears in the Old Testament, but Paul makes husband and wife equal in this chapter.

> Let the husband fulfill his duty to his wife, and likewise also the wife to her husband. The wife does not have authority over her own body, but the husband does; and likewise also the husband does not have authority over his own body, but the wife does.
>
> Stop depriving one another, except by agreement for a time that you may devote yourselves to prayer, and come together again lest Satan tempt you because of your lack of self-control (I Cor. 7:3-5).

Lack of fulfillment in the sexual realm has caused many problems in marriage and laid the groundwork for the dissolution of families. Paul warns against it.

"But to the married I give instructions, not I, but the Lord, that the wife should not leave her husband, (but if she does leave, let her remain unmarried, or else be reconciled to her husband), and that the husband should not send his wife away" (I Cor. 7:10, 11).

The apostle goes on to assert unbelieving spouses may be saved by the faithful spouse. In verse 15, he says, "Yet if the unbelieving one leaves, let him leave; the brother or sister is not under bondage in such cases, but God has called us to peace."

We pondered over the last clause in that sentence. Is the apostle suggesting a battleground in the home is not worth

374

the price one pays? We also meditated upon Paul's statement in I Corinthians 7:7. "Yet I wish that all men were even as I myself am. However, each man has his own gift from God, one in this manner, and another in that." Does Paul mean some people simply cannot live alone and that his celibacy is a gift from God in order that he might be free to travel in the service of the Lord?

Since this is a family book, we have not dealt with singleness to any great extent. At this point, it might be well to discuss single lifestyle, so prevalent in our society today. The thoughtful Christian must deal with Paul's recommendation of singleness. Since he considers his celibacy a gift from God, why have we who wear the name Christian so long hung labels on people who choose this lifestyle? Why have we considered such individuals weird, or at least a bit different? Have we, with our denigration and labels, precipitated divorces by encouraging marriages that never should have taken place?

In I Corinthians 7:32, 33, Paul speaks of pressures to please one's spouse rather than the Lord, thus making the unmarried more single-minded in service to God. We all know this is often the fact and many times defeats the career of a dedicated Christian servant. We might counter, of course, with a married witness who understands more about family problems. However, the fact remains, singleness is an acceptable, worthy way of life and much to be preferred to double harness where the two pull in opposite directions.

Some of the persons we have considered magnificent servants of God and life-builders in those around them enjoyed and opted for the single life. We have observed teachers and youth workers who filled in the gaps thoughtless parents left in the lives of children and young people. Being single does not indicate second class citizenship in the Kingdom of God or anywhere else. But note this one warning. Single life-style in New Testament terms includes celibacy. Fornication, as well as adultery, carries New Testament condemnation.

The 39th verse of the 7th chapter arouses questions also. "A wife is bound as long as her husband lives; but if her husband is dead, she is free to be married to whom she wishes, only in the Lord." We spend much time discussing Scriptural teaching on divorce and remarriage. Too few of us emphasize marrying "only in the Lord" in the first place. The sin of some divorces comes from the original marriage. We need to do more teaching in our homes and churches about this issue. What a difference it would make in family life!

Some very strong, somewhat unusual teaching appears in I Corinthians 11. "However, in the Lord, neither is woman independent of man, nor is man independent of woman. For as the woman originates from the man, so also man has his birth through the woman; and all things originate from God" (I Cor. 11:11, 12). The apostle, it seems to us, recommends two attitudes here. First, we are to accept each other as important and irreplaceable, different but equal. Second, the stability of marriage relationships may be established through a sense of interdependence; neither is to dominate, for men and women need each other.

Certainly one of the most beautiful chapters of Holy Writ is found in this letter, I Corinthians 13, the "Love Chapter." Every family needs to discover this chapter and incorporate it into the family agenda. How important this is in our day when many define love as crawling from one bed to an-other and in and out of marital relationships as though the marriage ceremony came equipped with revolving doors!

Read all of I Corinthians 13 right now. Consider with us the apostle's definition of love in compact form.

Love is patient, kind, not jealous, not conceited or arrogant, courteous, unselfish, not easily provoked, doesn't hold grudges, appreciates righteousness, rejoices in truth, bears all things, believes all things, hopes all things and endures all things. What is the length of service demanded of this quality of personality? "Love never fails."

A family filled with this kind of true emotion will not fail either. Achieving this type of love is not for the faint-hearted or fearful. It is a tall order, never accomplished in a hurry, never successfully adopted without God's help. But it is certainly worth the effort.

Hope comes to a grieving family in I Corinthians 15 where Paul brings an encouraging chapter on death and resurrection. The Christian family should familiarize itself with Paul's treatise in this chapter before death strikes a loved one.

II Corinthians is probably the most personal letter Paul wrote. Much of it is devoted to explanation of his feelings about the Corinthian Church, their reactions to his first letter, defense of his own dedication as a servant of Christ and request for their contributions to help the poor saints in Jerusalem. So, not too many teachings specifically for families appear in the letter.

However, a very important family concept may be found in II Corinthians 1:3, 4. "Blessed be the God and Father of our Lord Jesus Christ, the Father of mercies and God of all comfort; who comforts us in all our affliction so that we may be able to comfort those who are in any affliction with the comfort with which we ourselves are comforted by God."

Paul applies this to all Christians. Let us narrow it particularly to the family circle. Any troubled, suffering family member should be guaranteed sympathetic understanding along with a listening ear. Many parents consider childhood's problems small and insignificant. A good memory changes that attitude. Each age carries insurmountable difficulties to the inexperienced sufferer. When someone is enduring pain, even if it is self-inflicted by stupidity or sin, understanding should come first, discipline second. All we need to reinforce this concept is a mental picture of the heavenly Father loving, comforting and disciplining His erring children. We meet this attitude in chapter 2 where Paul urges the church to reinstate the man who sinned with his father's wife. Forgiveness must form an integral part of a Christian family, just as the apostle recommends it to the Family of God at Corinth.

II Corinthians 6:14 urges Christians to be careful of being "bound together with unbelievers. . . ." Some have interpreted this as pertaining to marriage. We are not sure the context justifies that exclusive interpretation, but warning against partnerships with unbelievers certainly would include marriage, the life partnership having the greatest effect upon personal lifestyle.

Galatians

This was a "circular" type of letter, written to no particular church, but rather to a group of churches in Galatia. Paul emphasized his opposition to a prevalent doctrine that Gentiles must become Jewish proselytes before being acceptable to the church. Since it is a short letter with the one main thrust, not too much applies specifically to family study. Yet certain teachings may be helpfully integrated into the family scene.

In Galatians 3:28 we read, "There is neither Jew nor Greek, there is neither slave nor free man, there is neither male nor female; for you are all one in Christ Jesus." This recalls the Pharisaic prayer mentioned earlier in our book. It appears the apostle, in his effort to identify Christianity as a separate religion, proceeding from the fulfillment of prophecy for God's people, rising from the tutoring of the law but not demanding obedience to such tenets as circumcision, seeks to throw off the bonds of Pharisaism for all time. One of those fetters was second class citizenship for women.

This applies to our families. If sexism is not part of the Gospel of Christ, it must not reign in our homes. Many women work outside the home today. Statistics indicate the majority of those so employed not only help support the family materially but also are expected by their husbands to shoulder most of the domestic duties of the household as well.

If one opts for defined male/female roles in this manner, the male role becomes complete material provision; the female responsibility, the household duties. If material support is divided, so should household duties be! Otherwise, the family fails in the Christian teaching that "there is neither male nor female; for you are all one in Christ Jesus." Oneness demands love, not discrimination.

Strong concentration upon the Family of God idea appears in the 4th chapter of Galatians.

But when the fulness of the time came, God sent forth His Son, born of a woman, born under the Law, in order that He might redeem those who were under the Law, that we might receive adoption as sons. And because you are sons, God has sent forth the Spirit of His Son into our hearts, crying, 'Abba! Father!' Therefore you are no longer a slave, but a son; and if a son, then an heir through God" (Gal. 4:4-7).

The "Family of God" theme runs throughout all Scripture. First we see it in the Garden of Eden, the family whose association God sought. Then we observe a chosen nation, a list of genealogies. Finally a bloodline flows from Calvary. Genealogical inheritance is by chance. We do not become members of Calvary's bloodline by chance but rather by choice. God placed such importance upon family concepts that He carried the theme into redemption.

Perhaps we should say something about the idea of adoption since the term is used to signify our membership in the Family of God. Adoption is not a derogatory term either in the Family of God or in earthly families. We have two blood children, born to us with our own personal inheritance of genes. We have one child by the process of adoption. Since three of our grandchildren come from our adopted daughter and two of our other grandchildren are adopted, with only one bloodline grandchild so far, we understand not only intellectually, but also emotionally, what the adoption process involves. Legally and lovingly, the adopted members of our family are inheritors equally with those of the bloodline.

The New Testament should teach Christians not to discriminate between adoption and natural birth in personal families. Parents who adopt children love them equally with those who give birth to them. Caring for children cements that love, not the physical process of birth itself. There may be accidental conceptions, but there are no accidental adoptions. God dignifies adoption by using the term in connection with salvation and our being heirs with Jesus Christ.

380

Galatians 5:15 says, "But if you bite and devour one another, take care lest you be consumed by one another." Congregations may be destroyed by such behavior. It also invades our families. We know each other so well we know how to injure family members. How tragic family life becomes when we reserve courtesy for strangers! The apostle declares such behavior indicates we walk by the flesh, not the Spirit.

"Now the deeds of the flesh are evident, which are: immorality, impurity, sensuality, idolatry, (of money and things?) sorcery, enmities, strife, jealousy, outbursts of anger, disputes, dissension, factions, envyings, drunkenness, carousings, and things like these . . ." (Gal. 5:19-21). How many 20th century homes mirror these character traits? The authors of most of the soaps might well have been reading the apostle before creating the plots!

Then Paul lists fruit of the Spirit: "love, joy, peace, patience, kindness, goodness, faithfulness, gentleness, self-control . . ." (Gal. 5:22, 23). Should this not form a word portrait of the Christian family?

In chapter 6, Paul urges the church family to be gentle while restoring an erring brother, being conscious of one's own frailty (6:1). He also tells us to bear one another's burdens (6:2). If this is an essential quality for the Family of God, is it not also necessary for the human families who make up the larger group?

A good warning for each Christian family is recorded in Galatians 6:7. "Do not be deceived, God is not mocked; for whatever a man sows, this he will also reap."

Discouraged parents may draw strength from, "And let us not lose heart in doing good, for in due time we shall reap if we do not grow weary" (6:9). Seed sown in child-hood may appear wasted. Fruit often comes when one's hopes are almost gone.

Ephesians

Ephesians is another circular letter, this time to the churches of Asia, primarily to combat Gnosticism that appeared to be making inroads into the church. The book contains some important family teaching.

In chapter 2:19, Paul uses the analogy of the household to describe our relationship to God.

The prayer of the apostle in the 3rd chapter again uses family as an important part of God's creation.

> For this reason, I bow my knees before the Father, from whom every *family* in heaven and on earth derives its name, that He would grant you, according to the riches of His glory, to be strengthened with power through His Spirit in the inner man; so that Christ may dwell in your hearts through faith; and that you, being rooted and grounded in love, may be able to comprehend with all the saints what is the breadth and length and height and depth, and to know the love of Christ which surpasses knowledge; that you may be filled up to all the fulness of God.

This prayer might well be incorporated into family devotions. Family problems could easily disappear overnight were the conditions of this prayer manifested in the lives of family members, especially in those responsible for the young lives God has entrusted to their care.

Ephesians 4:15 recommends an attitude for church mem-bers that certainly would provide peace and tranquility in homes. ". . . speaking the truth in love, we are to grow up

382

in all aspects into Him, who is the head, even Christ." It is possible to be truthful and quite nasty at the same time. But truth spoken in love heals instead of wounding.

The advice of Ephesians 4:26, 27 needs to be heeded by family members. "Be angry, and yet do not sin; do not let the sun go down on your anger, and do not give the devil an opportunity." Marital quarrels should be settled before bedtime. Anger opens the door for the devil to take over if we allow it to simmer and burn within our hearts.

Let us quote Ephesians 4:32. "And be kind to one another, tender-hearted, forgiving each other, just as God in Christ also has forgiven you." Who can offer perfection in human relationships? Only if we give it dare we to expect it. Forgiveness forms the main axle upon which family wheels turn, for there is no love without forgiveness.

Perhaps no New Testament Scripture is quoted more often in regard to marriage than Ephesians 5:22-31. Let us begin with verse 21 this time, "and be subject to one another in the fear of Christ."

In a discussion group someone mentioned this verse in conjunction with verse 22. A man remonstrated. "Oh, that applies to Christians, not husbands and wives!" One of the women in the group immediately asked, "Aren't husbands and wives Christians?"

How often we search Scriptures to prove what we already thought rather than to search for eternal truth! The fact is that Christian husbands and Christian wives are Christians first, then husbands and wives. Were we to zero in on this simple truth, many of the male/female controversies would simply vanish!

The concept of Christian servanthood, so uniquely accented by our Lord, equips us for subjecting ourselves to others if the situation requires it, male or female notwithstanding. If our main emphasis is placed upon our Christian responsibility in any human relationship, arguing about who is top dog becomes totally unnecessary. Most who create an issue over this problem seldom quote, "But Jesus called them to Himself, and said, 'You know that the rulers of the Gentiles lord it over them, and their great men exercise authority over them. It is not so among you, but whoever wishes to become great among you shall be your servant'" (Matt. 20:25, 26). Or if the Scripture is quoted in their hearing, they reply with that same inane statement that Jesus was speaking to spiritual leaders, not husbands and wives. Spiritual truths apply to anyone who longs for depth of spirituality. Male/female struggles indicate yearning for human power, not spiritual depth. Such depth enables families to accept the rest of Paul's advice in Ephesians 5:22-31.

> Wives, be subject to your own husbands, as to the Lord. For the husband is the head of the wife, as Christ also is the head of the church, He Himself being the Savior of the body. But as the church is subject to Christ, so also the wives ought to be to their husbands in everything.
> Husbands, love your wives, just as Christ also loved the church and gave Himself up for her; that He might sanctify her, having cleansed her by the washing of water with the word, that He might present to Himself the church in all her glory, having no spot or wrinkle or any such thing; but that she should be holy and blameless. So husbands ought to love their own wives as their own bodies. He who loves his own wife loves himself; for no one ever hated his own flesh, but nourishes and cherishes it, just as Christ also does the church, because we are members of His body.

For this cause a man shall leave his father and mother, and shall cleave to his wife: and the two shall become one flesh.

If husbands followed Paul's advice, would wives need to struggle for their own place in the sun? If a couple maintains such a close relationship that loving one's wife is actually loving one's self, would either of them attempt to denigrate the other? No wife so cherished as the apostle describes the marital love of a husband feels so downtrodden she has to instigate male/female battles. No man who loves that way assumes the role of despot or tyrant in his own household!

Verse 33 deserves our notice also. "Nevertheless let each individual among you also love his own wife even as himself; and let the wife see to it that she respect her husband." This is a most thought-provoking statement. Paul commands husbands to love their wives four times in just a few verses here. Then he follows that last urgent statement to husbands by insisting wives should respect their husbands. Why not "love" their husbands? Why urge love upon the men and respect upon the women?

Men who consider women only sex objects know little of real love as I Corinthians 13 describes it. Very little teaching about the responsibility of husbands in this regard appears before the teachings of Jesus and the writings of Paul. It was a society of "Macho" males.

On the other hand, anyone who has attended women's clubs discovers they sometimes turn into "roast husband" sessions. No two people always agree. No relationship is everything we would like it to be all the time. Respect demands we not discuss the faults of our beloved thoughtlessly in a group.

Another concept appears here. Respect should be earned and deserved. The husband who fulfills the requirements laid down by Paul in this chapter seldom needs to worry about the respect of his wife and family. Paul has been interpreted as stern with women in this Scripture. We believe his instructions for men much more difficult to fulfill.

> Children, obey your parents in the Lord, for this is right. HONOR YOUR FATHER AND MOTHER (which is the first commandment with a promise), THAT IT MAY BE WELL WITH YOU, AND THAT YOU MAY LIVE LONG ON THE EARTH.
> And, fathers do not provoke your children to anger; but bring them up in the discipline and instructions of the Lord (Eph. 6:1-4).

Many times we provoke our children to anger by jumping to conclusions. Improper behavior should always be discussed. Discipline involves teaching as well as punishing. "Just because I said so" usually frustrates and angers children. Someone must be the authority, of course, and that someone is the parent. However, respect for a child's intelligence demands explanation. How else will they learn to control emotion with reason when they are no longer under our wings? Yet one must be careful not to allow the psychologists of all time, our children, to gain the upper hand in these discussions nor to turn them into a shouting match.

How much of the Lord's discipline and instruction finds its way into your family calendar? Some rebellion is an inevitable part of growing up. It lessens as credibility gaps shrink.

Philippians

The entire tenor of this letter accents joy in being Christian, the importance of concentration upon the positive

386

aspects of one's life in Christ. Considering Paul's status as a prisoner at the time of the writing, the book should arouse a sense of shame in us for our complaints. The Philippian church appears to have been one of the purest on record.

"Do nothing from selfishness or empty conceit, but with humility of mind let each of you regard one another as more important than himself; do not merely look out for your own personal interests, but also for the interests of others" (Phil. 2:3, 4). What would the pursuit of the excellence of this verse provide for family peace and tranquility?

"Do all things without grumbling or disputing" (Phil. 2:14). Bill's mother lived to be ninety, a productive member of society almost to the end. Her philosophy helped. She said, "I have learned never to have to do anything I don't want to do by wanting to do what I have to do." Grumbling and disputing waste much energy that could be applied to worthwhile tasks.

The entire 3rd chapter of Philippians sets a life standard that would make our homes a preview of heaven were we to absorb the teaching.

Several verses from the 4th chapter should be noted in family study. Anxiety plagues our society. Fears impede our spiritual growth. "Be anxious for nothing, but in everything by prayer and supplication with thanksgiving let your requests be made known to God. And the peace of God which surpasses all comprehension, shall guard your hearts and your minds in Christ Jesus" (Phil. 4:6, 7). Prayer life enables us to survive peacefully in a nuclear, threatening society, even if that peace is only internal.

"Finally, brethren, whatever is true, whatever is honorable, whatever is right, whatever is pure, whatever is lovely, whatever is of good repute, if there is any excellence and if anything worthy of praise, let your mind dwell on these things" (Phil. 4:8). Every home and family needs improvement. No lifestyle rewards without occasional longing for greater fulfillment. But concentration upon negatives makes us lose sight of positives. We must look for the good points in our marriages, families and homelife. Everyone's happiness will be greater. Improvement often accompanies change of attitude.

"I can do all things through Him who strengthens me" (Phil. 4:13). Walking hand in hand with Christ makes crises turn into challenging spiritual growth. Just as exercise of physical muscles strengthens, so may we develop spiritual tone through crises.

Colossians

Colossae was listed as an important city at least 500 years before the time of the apostle Paul. The apostle did not establish this church and had not been there. The letter appears to have been written primarily to correct false doctrines taught by Judaizers and Gnostics. This is another prison letter.

"Set your mind on the things above, not on the things that are on earth" (Col. 3:2). How many families have been ruined by concentration upon earthly values and possessions? We must live in this world, but determination to grab material things makes us *of* it and not just *in* it.

Paul reiterates warnings against earthly passions in Colossians 3:5. Verses 8 and 9 in chapter 3 assume tremendous importance in family living. "But now you also, put them all aside: anger, wrath, malice, slander, and abusive speech from your mouth. Do not lie to one another. . . ." How deeply we wound those we love when we explode with careless anger, saying things we can never recall! Are "stupid," "klutzy," and similar epithets part of our family conversations? What about "Shut up"?

A gossipy family produces gossipy children. Gossip becomes a malicious weapon destroying many innocent lives. We often wink at such antics. The Bible does not. Such behavior degrades the object of the malice, but destroys those who engage in it even more.

We sometimes categorize lies as important or unimportant, white lies or big black ones. No such connotation appears in Scripture. Lies divide, sow discord and degrade the liar. Parents must endeavor to help children be truthful. Threats often create lies in frightened little ones.

". . . put on a heart of compassion, kindness, humility, gentleness and patience; bearing with one another, and forgiving each other, whoever has a complaint against any one; just as the Lord forgave you, so also should you. And beyond all these things, put on love, which is the perfect bond of unity" (Col. 3:12-14). Does the apostle describe our homes here? Are they united or fragmented? If fragmented, why? We need to search for answers in the Bible, not in the world around us.

Colossians 3:18-21 repeats the teachings of Ephesians 5 and 6 in less detail. Prayer life appears in Colossians 4:2, 3, also the need for an attitude of gratitude. Although the apostle is writing to the congregation of Colossae, we should always remember individuals and families form churches. Proper Christian training in the home builds strong churches.

1st and 2nd Thessalonians

The first letter seems aimed at correcting false teachings concerning the second coming of Christ as well as strengthening the faith of the young church. The second letter followed soon because some of the church members preferred misunderstanding to truth. Some may have even forged a letter confirming their own thoughts, pretending it came from Paul. (See II Thess. 3:17.)

Paul uses the analogy of a mother to indicate proper care of new Christians. "But we proved to be gentle among you, as a nursing mother cares for her own children" (I Thess. 2:7). Again he refers to family. ". . . you know how we were exhorting and encouraging and imploring each one of you as a father would his own children, so that you may walk in a manner worthy of the God who calls you into His own kingdom and glory" (I Thess. 2:11, 12).

These verses give us insight in two ways. First, since Paul had no family of his own, he must be reflecting the love and guidance offered by the parents to whom he was born. The second insight comes from realization of our responsibility to care for our own children the way the apostle describes.

Chapter 4 of I Thessalonians exhorts Paul's readers to sexual purity; then, "and that no man transgress and defraud his brother in the matter because the Lord is the avenger in all these things, just as we also told you before and solemnly warned you" (4:6). There are many ways in which we may transgress and defraud our brothers. Remember Cain and Abel? Jacob and Esau? Joseph and his brothers? We could go on. In each Old Testament case, God made the transgressor pay. That moral law still prevails.

In I Thessalonians 5:11 we read, "Therefore encourage one another, and build up one another, just as you also are doing." Lives may be strengthened or destroyed within the confines of the home. Encouragement provides sustenance for the aching heart as well as for the youngster trying to discover strength within. However, we must be tuned to each other's deepest needs before we are able to provide that encouragement.

> . . . Live in peace with one another. And we urge you, brethren, admonish the unruly, encourage the fainthearted, help the weak, be patient with all men. See that no one repays another with evil for evil, but always seek after that which is good for one another and for all men. Rejoice always; pray without ceasing; in everything give thanks; for this is God's will for you in Christ Jesus (I Thess. 5:13-18).

It has been our experience that prayer life undergirds all the other things the apostle mentions. Rearing a Christian family is impossible without prayer.

> For even when we were with you, we used to give you this order: If anyone will not work, neither let him eat. For we hear that some among you are leading an undisciplined life, doing no work at all, but acting like busybodies. Now such persons we command and exhort in the Lord Jesus Christ to work in quiet fashion and eat their own bread (II Thess. 3:10-12).

Many Americans downgrade what they have misnamed "The Protestant Work Ethic." A better title would be "The Biblical Work Ethic." Workaholics can destroy themselves, and, sometimes, those around them. A happy medium is better. But the Bible teaches in both testaments that work blesses and rewards the conscientious worker.

Accepting responsibility begins with family. Even toddlers may be assigned easy work details such as picking up toys and clothes. Tasks increase with maturity. Children can learn the satisfactions of a job well done. However, youngsters seldom accomplish this if they have complaining, griping parents. Freeloaders are the world's most dissatisfied people. The joy of achievement, the rewards of successfully completed work evade them. Labor blesses the laborer and those who observe the toil.

We don't think it was accidental for the apostle to declare non-workers busybodies. It is very easy to be critical when one is uncommitted and uninvolved!

1st and 2nd Timothy

These letters, addressed to the young preacher Timothy, are called "Pastoral Epistles" because they contain instructions for church government and membership training. Included in that teaching are some family helps.

The 2nd chapter of 1st Timothy has created a furor because of Paul's command that a woman must not usurp authority over a man (I Tim. 2:12, KJV). The Greek word translated "usurp authority" could be better translated "to acts on one's own authority; to domineer over someone." The position of teacher in the early church was a position of authority and responsibility. Paul seems to be excluding women from this, indicating that a woman who puts herself into the position of teaching men is acting on her own authority and is unacceptably domineering. However, before we decide the apostle was organizing a legal system to deny all right for women for time and all eternity, we must deal with all the statements he made in regard to women.

We have already discussed the freedom he accorded women when he wrote of interdependence in I Corinthians 11. We noted his statement of "neither male nor female" in Galatians 3. He led into his subjection paragraph in Ephesians 5 by insisting Christians be subject to one another. He named Priscilla before Aquila and we have Scriptural evidence that both of them taught Apollos. Sapphira suffered death because she refused to maintain a moral stature of her own in what might be termed opposition to her husband. The Christ Paul loved and served refused to make vassals of women. He protected them in a male-dominated society. Paul did the same thing when he commanded men to love their wives, considering those women part of themselves. We could go on but space forbids.

So why did he say these things in 1st Timothy? It seems obvious to us that some women had been abusing their new freedom, seizing power that did not belong to them and creating havoc in the church. Considering their male-dominated culture and a persecuted church, rebuke for such actions served a worthy purpose. Usurpation should always bring rebuke. However, our interpretation of these statements as a law for Christians for all time in all cultures seems strange since Paul found legal pronouncements out of tune with Christian love.

In the same chapter, Paul commanded the men to pray. Then he urged the women to dress modestly, not in the way worldly women did. He suggested good works and quiet learning for women (I Tim. 2:8-11). In a society where mostly wicked women were outspoken, was this not wise advice? If he intended to indicate only silent women to be worthy Christians for all time, would that not condemn Philip's daughters and Priscilla, probably also Phoebe? If so, would he have mentioned Priscilla and Phoebe as worthy workers? And the many women he cited as fellow laborers with him, did they do so in complete silence or only function at the dishpan and the washboard? Perhaps this is another of those Scriptures we read to prove what we already thought.

Paul had spent too much time in his various letters commending outstanding and involved women for us to believe this. Certainly he never intended to make the home an absolute monarchy with the husband as king. The husband is the head of the house. Scripture teaches that. But, it is a household where that husband walks beside one whom he loves as he loves himself, a definite part of himself. In such surroundings, no one "usurps" anything. But love and respect give what no one needs to seize.

"But she shall be preserved through the bearing of children if the women continue in faith and love and sanctity with self-restraint" (I Tim. 2:15). We have certainly twisted this statement out of all reason also.

Any thoughtful mother understands what children have done for her. Bearing and caring for children make a woman more responsive than she might be without them. A family teaches responsibility and selflessness. One learns the value of cherished beliefs in longing for one's children to possess them. One sees beauty in God's creation as one observes a child's reactions to things adults long ago took for granted. In all these ways, children increase our depth, teach us humility, and make us fit citizens for the kingdom of God. Of course, these attitudes hinge upon our "faith," "love," "sanctity" and "self-restraint." Without those, children are often resented and neglected. That must have been particularly true in the society in which Paul wrote for all child care fell upon the shoulders of the mother.

Are we not shallow when we decide the apostle meant only the physical process of birth in this statement?

Writers flood our society with literature dedicated to ways and means to juggle careers. How does one cope with a family and a time-consuming job? Most of these articles tend to downgrade the woman who chooses to buy fewer material things in order that she might give herself to homemaking and mothering.

In a recent interview, Jane Pauley, one of the hosts on the Today Show on NBC, stated that pressures from the boss cause most women to try to combine mothering with a demanding career to neglect babies who cannot force issues the way employers do. Anyone knows there are only twenty-four hours in the day. Especially during a child's pre-school years, conscientious mothers must be torn, even if it is only because the closeness they long for must go to some other woman who occupies the center of the child's life during the working hours of the mother.

Although we are sure Paul did not mean the physical process of birth saves the mother, but rather the developmental process of depth achieved through nurturing, resulting in greater Christian maturity, we must agree that the apostle places his blessing upon homemaking and mothering as valid careers, demanding and fulfilling for Christian women. We must not allow ourselves to be propagandized by our society.

When the women's liberation movement began in full swing many years ago, a woman wrote an article published in a national women's magazine. She stated that an eight-year-old child could do any of the things demanded in a homemaking career, even to the care of children. I found myself wondering how her house looked and what her concept of child-rearing was if her brand of it could be accomplished by an eight-year-old child! Mothering, perhaps we should say parenting, of intelligent children demands every ounce of wisdom and creativity the human mind can produce. Anyone who says otherwise has been an utter failure at the job!

Our purpose in the above paragraphs is not condemnation of the working mother, simply validation of homemaking and mothering as a career choice, one of the most rewarding anyone could possibly select. When a woman opts to devote her life to family pursuits, each child who contributes to the welfare of the kingdom of God and the uplifting of the community testifies to the mother's vision.

The apostle commends family relationships in I Timothy 3 when he uses the family as a criterion for church officers. We have labored "husband of one wife" endlessly in our interpretation of I Timothy 3:2 as though the verse contained nothing else. We even know of one church that removed an aged elder when his wife died because he no longer was the "husband of one wife." Divorced officers are anathema in some churches. In fact, our desire to enforce our own ideas of what the apostle meant has turned Paul, the essential non-legalist, into the greatest legalist of all time.

It is not our purpose to add our voices to the controversy. But, in fairness to the text, we must point out the family-related instructions for church officers. The word "hospitable" is a qualification. "Gentle and uncontentious" are mentioned, also "free from the love of money." Then comes the punchline for family relationships.

"He must be one who manages his own household well, keeping his children under control with all dignity (but if a man does not know how to manage his own household, how will he take care of the church of God?)" (I Tim. 3:4, 5).

A disciplined family life surfaces as a requirement for church leaders. Why do we zero in on one requirement while ignoring the others?

We once knew an elder who divided a church over the election of a divorced man as a deacon. That elder had an undisciplined teenage son. His wife feared his anger over money to such a degree she went to work to have decent clothes to wear. Other board members catered to him to avoid his wrath in meetings. But he considered himself fully qualified as an elder, and some agreed with him although quite familiar with his lifestyle.

Scholars debate verse 11 in the 3rd chapter. Women are urged to "be dignified, not malicious gossips, but temperate, faithful in all things." The argument arises over whether Paul referred to deacon's wives or deaconesses. The use of the Greek word for deacon in Romans 16:1 in regard to Phoebe might tend to validate the office of deaconess in the early church. But, whatever we think about Paul's aim in giving the advice, it certainly applies to Christian homemakers.

Respect for older members of the family is taught in chapter 5, verses 1 and 2. Responsibility falls upon the family to care for its elderly members and upon the church when no family remains. "But if anyone does not provide for his own, and especially for those of his household, he has denied the faith, and is worse than an unbeliever" (I Tim. 5:8). In this day of divorce when so many women have difficulty collecting child support payments, this Scripture seems apropos, to say the least.

Another very significant verse for our time is found in I Timothy 6:10. "For the love of money is a root of all sorts of evil, and some by longing for it have wandered away from the faith, and pierced themselves with many a pang." Many families have fallen apart for this reason, too. Pangs are bound to come from loving money. When is enough enough?

We have already noted the faithfulness of Timothy's grandmother Lois and mother Eunice as mentioned in II Timothy. How important this is to children!

Perhaps we should quote two more verses before leaving these letters. "For among them are those (false teachers) who enter into households and captivate weak women weighed down with sins, led on by various impulses, always learning and never able to come to the knowledge of the truth" (II Tim. 3:6, 7).

How much easier it is to captivate those who are governed by impulse! How simple it became to mislead women of that day, most of whom could neither read nor write! We have a responsibility in our homes and families to use our brains, not just our emotions. Some have interpreted this Scripture to mean Paul considered women incapable of knowing truth. The modifying adjective "weak" rules out that interpretation. The many women Paul saluted can never be defined as weak women, but rather as stalwarts of the faith. They learned and witnessed for Christ. Paul's reference here does not refer to all women for all time, but rather to weak women of all time. Our responsibility becomes building spiritual strength, so that no one can ever call us weak Christians, male or female.

Titus

This, too, is a "Pastoral Epistle," addressed to Titus, a Gentile and a Christian minister. The apostle's theme in the letter, as in the letters to Timothy, is church government and training for the membership.

"To the pure, all things are pure; but to those who are defiled and unbelieving, nothing is pure, but both their mind and their conscience are defiled" (Titus 1:15).

A Christian friend who accepted Christ late in life once described the rationale for what his daughter defined as unreasonable rules for her dating. "A father is a fellow who tries to prevent what he used to try to promote." Sometimes, even in a family, what we believe about others depends upon our own spiritual state or background.

The apostle Paul commends Christian behavior in older men as an example. They must be "temperate, dignified, sensible, sound in faith, in love, in perseverance" (Titus 2:2). What a difference a godly grandfather makes in a family!

Paul also suggests older women be "reverent in their behavior, not malicious gossips, nor enslaved to much wine, teaching what is good, that they may encourage the young women to love their husbands, to love their children, to be sensible, pure workers at home, kind, being subject to their own husbands, that the word of God may not be dishonored" (Titus 2:3-5).

It is impossible to estimate the moral and spiritual influence of dedicated grandparents. In our culture where both parents work outside the home in so many families, grandparents may be the recipients of cherished secrets, dreams and hopes when parents do not have time to listen. What a boon for everyone! Grandparents feel wanted and needed. Some of the pressures are removed from parents. Children are assured of a sympathetic ear, something childhood desperately needs to achieve stable adulthood.

"Likewise urge young men to be sensible; in all things show yourself to be an example of good deeds, with purity in doctrine, dignified, sound in speech which is beyond reproach, in order that the opponent may be put to shame, having nothing bad to say about us" (Titus 2:6-8). Where did generations before us get their ideas that young women must be pure but young men could be expected to "sow their wild oats"? Certainly not from the New Testament! Our society, however, tends to say girls should be permitted to lower their morals rather than attempting to raise the standards for men. What should we be teaching in our homes?

Paul advises both Timothy and Titus to avoid endless genealogies. This reiterates the precedence of Calvary's bloodline over pride in family bloodlines.

Philemon

Paul wrote this letter to a family. It is a private letter, not specifically written for circulation among the churches. Philemon, a member of the Colossian Church, had accepted Christ through Paul's efforts. Apphia appears to be Philemon's wife, Archippus their son. So this letter is unique, the only one in the New Testament sent to a family, with a message to the church in their house as an apparent after-thought.

Paul commends them for the love expressed by the family toward all those around them. Would that this might be said of us today!

In this letter, Paul involves a Christian family in two issues. The first is practicing forgiveness, one of Christ's strongest teachings. The other is slavery; a social issue accepted in that culture, which must be dealt with in the light of Christian doctrine.

Onesimus, a runaway slave from the household of Philemon, had accepted Jesus in Rome and ministered to the needs of the apostle Paul. In writing this letter, Paul asks Philemon to forgive Onesimus and take him back into his household as a Christian brother. The apostle even writes, "If then you regard me a partner, accept him as you would me" (Phile. 17).

When Paul sent Onesimus back to Philemon, was he placing his stamp of approval upon the practice of slavery? Hardly. In fact, the apostle writes, "For perhaps he was for this reason parted from you for a while, that you should have him back forever, no longer as a slave, but more than a slave, a beloved brother, especially to me, but how much more to you, both in the flesh and in the Lord" (Phile. 15, 16). Paul dared to pose a question to a Christian family. "Can my Christian brother be my slave?" That was an unheard-of inquiry in that culture. But for Christianity to be valid, social questions had to be asked.

Slavery no longer poses a problem in America. Many other issues do exist, however, to test the depth of our Christian commitment. How does the family deal with social problems?

Paul gives a persuasive answer in this letter. Is my Christian brother inferior to me because his skin is a different color? Is my Christian sister beneath my notice because her lifestyle differs from mine? Does my Christianity enable me to consider abortion, the death of an unborn child, a valid solution for an unwanted and inconvenient pregnancy? May I add more and more luxuries to my lifestyle while Christian brethren starve in other lands?

We could add many social issues. The Christian family must pursue Christian answers, not go along with the crowd. If Christianity changes nothing about the way we live and behave toward others, of what real value is it?

37

THE REMAINING EIGHT LETTERS AND FAMILIES

Hebrews

The traditional view on the authorship of Hebrews attributes the letter to Paul. Since no one knows, we chose to group it with the remaining letters rather than those generally accepted as Pauline. However, it seems to us that the orderly, logical and precise writing might well fit into Paul's education and temperament.

Hebrews praises Jesus continually, showing His superiority to the Mosaic Law and His fulfillment of it. Therefore the entire book assumes great value to the Christian family. There are some verses, however, we found especially fulfilling for those who long to build strong Christian families.

It is for discipline that you endure; God deals with you as with sons; for what son is there whom his father does not discipline? But if you are without discipline, of which all have become partakers, then you are illegitimate children and not sons. Furthermore, we had earthly fathers to discipline us, and we respected them; shall we not much rather be subject to the Father of spirits, and live? For they disciplined us for a short time as seemed best to them, but He disciplines us for our good that we may share His holiness. All discipline for the moment seems not to be joyful, but sorrowful; yet to those who have been trained by it, afterwards it yields the peaceful fruit of righteousness (Heb. 12:7-11).

Much may be gained from these verses, but is not the central theme that of discipline motivated by love? Our children suffer if deprived of discipline. The entire family suffers from an undisciplined child, but the child most of all.

Chapter 13 calls us to love. "Do not neglect to show hospitality to strangers, for by this some have entertained angels without knowing it" (Heb. 13:2). The letters all urge hospitality. Can we maintain Christian homes without it?

"Let marriage be held in honor among all, and let the marriage bed be undefiled; for fornicators and adulterers God will judge" (Heb. 13:4). Marital lovemaking is beautiful and rewarding; fornication and adultery, ugly and guilt-producing.

"And do not neglect doing good and sharing; for with such sacrifice God is pleased" (Heb. 13:16). Children brought up in homes where doing good and sharing are ways of life learn to give of themselves. Without this impetus, selfishness reigns supreme.

James

This general letter was written by James, the brother of the Lord. Tradition tells us the High Priest and rulers took

James to the roof of the temple and ordered that he deny Christ. He declared Jesus to be the Son of God. They hurled him from the temple in anger. According to the story, this took place about 63 A.D. The letter itself has no central theme, but contains many Christian precepts. It is a practical book, helpful for family life.

How many family quarrels might be avoided by observing James 1:19, 20. ". . . But let every one be quick to hear, slow to speak and slow to anger; for the anger of man does not achieve the righteousness of God." As an aged friend once reminded a youth group, "Don't forget that God gave each of us two ears and only one mouth!"

James carries the precept a bit further. "If anyone thinks himself to be religious, and yet does not bridle his tongue but deceives his own heart, this man's religion is worthless" (James 1:26). Many of us bridle our tongues for strangers while releasing the pent-up vitriol on family members.

"If a brother or sister is without clothing and in need of daily food, and one of you says to them, 'Go in peace, be warmed and be filled'; and yet you do not give them what is necessary for their body; what use is that?" (James 2:15, 16). We have a modern way of saying that. "Put your money where your mouth is." James refers to the church, but we have already quoted Paul on duty to family members. If we don't care for our own, we are worse than unbelievers!

In chapter 3, James emphasizes the dangers of a destructive tongue. All parents learn things they didn't know they said when toddlers begin mimicking their conversations. The apostle warns, "With it (the tongue) we bless our Lord and Father; and with it we curse men who have been made in the likeness of God; from the same mouth come both blessing and cursing. My brethren, these things ought not to be this way" (James 3:9, 10). Do we need to clean up our act?

Would we espouse wisdom in our families? "But the wisdom from above is first pure, then peaceable, gentle, reasonable, full of mercy and good fruits, unwavering, without hypocrisy" (James 3:17). That credibility gap again! The wise parent avoids it.

Read James. Every line bears important advice for abundant living.

1st and 2nd Peter

These letters, attributed to the apostle Peter, seem to be focused upon enduring under persecution. They were addressed to Christians in Asia Minor. 1st Peter was probably written around the time of the beginning of Nero's persecution of the church, the 2nd near the time of Peter's death. These epistles were born in a time of great suffering and reflect that in their content.

In I Peter 3, we meet again the theme of godly wives who save their husbands. "In the same way, you wives, be submissive to your own husbands so that even if any of them are disobedient to the word they may be won without a word by the behavior of their wives, as they observe your chaste and respectful behavior" (I Peter 3:1, 2).

This quotation recalls Ephesians 5:22 and I Corinthians 7:14. Before deciding submission means sacrificing one's own way of life completely, the Christian wife must remember Sapphira. We have seen many believing wives who won their husbands. We never saw one accomplish this either through constant nagging or by giving up her own moral and spiritual values to cater to his. "Without a word" and "chaste and respectful behavior" provide the clue.

We also pondered, in that day of widespread sexual immorality, how much being "submissive to your own husbands" meant the sex act; submission to them and to no other man. This interpretation must remain forever in the realm of conjecture, but seems to have some validity especially in the light of I Corinthians 7.

The apostle continues instructing women.

> And let not your adornment be external only—braiding the hair, and wearing gold jewelry, and putting on dresses; but let it be the hidden person of the heart, with the imperishable quality of a gentle and quiet spirit, which is precious in the sight of God. For in this way in former times the holy women also, who hoped in God, used to adorn themselves, being submissive to their own husbands (I Peter 3:3-5).

The thoughtful reader must wonder about the amount of New Testament advice given specifically to women when the Old Testament has greater male orientation. Had women abused their newly found freedom in Christ? Or had Christian leaders become increasingly aware of the influence of women upon future generations? Either way women should develop an understanding of their servitude to Christ, not as demeaning but uplifting; and their influential effect upon posterity.

"You husbands likewise, live with your wives in an understanding way, as with a weaker vessel, since she is a woman; and grant her honor as a fellow-heir of the grace of life, so that your prayers may not be hindered" (I Peter 3:7).

Some women get all bent out of shape about Peter's calling them "weaker vessels." The fact is that in some ways women are weaker than men. Women have less strength in the large muscle structure of the body, greater dexterity in the smaller ones. Women live longer, perhaps indicating greater strength in some ways. Peter's statement must be taken in the light of his culture. He was a traveling evangelist. Had he observed men forcing their wives to lift great loads, do tasks not proper for the body structures of women? Had he noted the complete lack of understanding accorded their wives by some men who thought of them only as pack horses and child bearers? Why must women decide the statement is degrading, not protective? Chips on our shoulders are easily knocked off!

Peter actually affords women equality when he instructs husbands to honor wives and consider them "fellow-heirs of the grace of life." What a compliment in a male-oriented society! Linking these attitudes of mind to the efficacy of prayer reveals much also. Self-centered superiority blocks prayer life.

"To sum up, let all be harmonious, sympathetic, brotherly, kind-hearted, and humble in spirit; not returning evil for evil, or insult for insult, but giving a blessing instead; for you were called for the very purpose that you might inherit a blessing" (I Peter 3:8, 9). What type of climate prevails in our homes, blessing or insulting?

"Above all, keep fervent in your love for one another, because love covers a multitude of sins" (I Peter 4:8). How does love cover sins? One way is found in I Corinthians 13. Love "does not take into account a wrong suffered" (I Cor. 13:5).

II Peter 1:5-7 describes Christian growth essential to the success of the Christian family. ". . . applying all diligence, in your faith supply moral excellence, and in your moral excellence, knowledge; and in your knowledge, self-control, and in your self-control, perseverance, and in your perseverance, godliness; and in your godliness, brotherly kindness, and in your brotherly kindness, Christian love."

Parents who concentrate upon developing these character traits in themselves generally produce them in their children; perhaps not immediately, but eventually.

1st, 2nd and 3rd John

These letters demonstrate the growth of the apostle John from one of the "Sons of Thunder" to the apostle of love. John writes to the churches to try to combat Gnosticism. But he also endeavors to teach Christians the importance of love above all other virtues. These letters are written evidence of the effect a genuine walk with Christ has upon the human personality. All three letters help families mature in Christ. We have selected a few verses.

> The one who says he is in the light and yet hates his brother is in the darkness until now. The one who loves his brother abides in the light and there is no cause for stumbling in him. But the one who hates his brother is in the darkness and walks in the darkness, and does not know where he is going because the darkness has blinded his eyes (I John 2:9-11).

Our language is filled with trite sayings. Most of them exist because they are true. One such descriptive expression is "blind hatred." As the apostle says, hatred blinds. Anyone who allows this emotion to control his or her lifestyle becomes blind to all good. Hatred may result in murderous action against its object (see I John 3:15); but, most of all, it destroys anyone who harbors it. Hatred burdens the strongest soul beyond endurance. Hateful attitudes tend to be hereditary and degrade families.

John warns against loving the world and its things (I John 2:15). This theme appears in all the New Testament letters.

This is certainly one of the most destructive forces impeding spiritual progress in the Christian family today.

"But whoever has the world's goods, and beholds his brother in need and closes his heart against him, how does the love of God abide in him?" (I John 3:17). Again we discover we are worse than unbelievers if we prosper and refuse to help others, especially family members.

"If someone says, 'I love God,' and hates his brother, he is a liar; for the one who does not love his brother whom he has seen, cannot love God whom he has not seen. And this commandment we have from Him, that the one who loves God should love his brother also" (I John 4:20, 21). Could anything be plainer? Brotherly love is not just suggested but commanded.

"If anyone sees his brother committing a sin not leading to death, he shall ask and God will for him give life to those who commit sin not leading to death . . ." (I John 5:16). Our prayers interceding for sinful family members may give life. Every family should engage in intercessory prayer for each other.

"If anyone comes to you and does not bring this teaching, do not receive him into your house, and do not give him a greeting; for the one who gives him a greeting participates in his evil deeds" (II John 10, 11). John was warning the church against false teachers. However, we should assess this for our families today.

Filling our homes with Christian friends develops our children in the faith. The reverse may be true. Going to church every Sunday will not erase the effects of a completely worldly environment the other six days. Entertaining friends who go against all we profess, especially if we fail to defend our commitments while they are in our homes,

410

may convince our children those commitments depend upon whom we happen to be with at the moment. Witnessing to unbelievers is one thing. Capitulating in a crowd that disagrees with us is quite something else again.

"I have no greater joy than this, to hear of my children walking in the truth" (III John 4). John is speaking to Gaius in this letter, commending him for his exemplary faith. Gaius appears to have been John's son in the Gospel.

As parents whose children have reached adult life, we can echo this statement. So many things considered important to youthful parents disintegrate into nothingness as we age. Aging Christian parents see John's statement as a reflection of priorities. When we come to the final years of life, we realize even more acutely that Christian faith, its acceptance and total commitment to it, is the only valid focus for life. Seeing our children growing in their dedication makes all past family sacrifice worthwhile.

Jude

This letter comes from the pen of Jude, one of the Lord's brothers. Little is known about him. The epistle warns against false teachers, Libertines and Antinomians of that day. The letter also tries to comfort persecuted Christians.

This book contains no reference specifically to families. Perhaps it would be well to quote two verses as a foundational premise for family living.

"But you, beloved, build yourselves up on your most holy faith; praying in the Holy Spirit; keep yourselves in the love of God, waiting anxiously for the mercy of our Lord Jesus Christ to eternal life" (Jude 20, 21). Isn't that what it is all about?

38

REVELATION

This book, attributed to the apostle John, was probably written during his banishment to the Isle of Patmos, a rocky spot in the Greek Archipelago, southwest of Ephesus. In such a barren place, the apostle experienced the necessary solitude for close communion with God producing the prophetic visions recorded in the book.

The language of Revelation is magnificent. Descriptions of the reigning Christ thrill our souls. Choice symbolisms, at times exciting and then again frightening, adorn its pages. It seems to us the purpose of the book is found in its symbolism. We are not expected to understand its veiled language completely. God is telling us there are amazing facts we are incapable of comprehending in their entirety. They belong to His infinite knowledge, but He opens the curtain and allows us a glimpse into eternity.

Throughout the Bible, facts needed for our salvation stand out in complete clarity. Prophetical visions challenge the reader, but were never aimed at total comprehension. As a child thrills to the prospect of parental rewards, or fears disobedience because of parental power, so the children of God must view the symbolic sections of Revelation.

We have always believed those who are sure they know this book's exact meaning—and their names are legion—possess an egotism not in accord with Christian humility. However, having said that, we also want to note the presence of quite understandable sections on Christian living. We would like to cite a few verses.

". . . To him who overcomes, I will grant to eat of the tree of life, which is in the Paradise of God" (Rev. 2:7). We return in this vision to the garden with its tree of life. Our lives possess unfair aspects. No family escapes this. But overcoming takes us back to the Paradise of God for eternity. How encouraging for the suffering family! Revelation is filled with such hope, more than space permits us to mention.

Another thought-provoking statement for families appears in Revelation 3:19. "Those whom I love, I reprove and discipline; be zealous therefore, and repent." If God reproves and disciplines because He loves, should permissive parenting dominate our thinking?

Just as the letters denote the futility of clamoring after things, so Revelation points out the impotence of earthly fame and fortune at the throne of God in the final day.

And the kings of the earth and the great men and the commanders and the rich and the strong and every slave and free man, hid themselves in the caves and among the rocks of the mountains; and they said to the mountains and to the rocks, "Fall on us and hide us from the presence of Him who sits on the throne, and from the wrath of the Lamb; for the great day of their wrath has come; and who is able to stand?" (Rev. 6:15-17).

So many of us strive for wealth and fame for our families. Of what value is it in the final analysis? When we stand at the judgment bar of God, there are no reserved seats for the rich and famous.

The serious quality of the Christian life overwhelms us when we read of God's Son in all His power. Our service to Him in our families assumes a glorious aspect when we pursue John's vision in Revelation 11. "And the seventh angel sounded; and there arose loud voices in heaven saying, 'The kingdom of the world has become the kingdom of our Lord, and of His Christ; and He will reign forever and ever'" (Rev. 11:15). The beauty of this thought makes it imperative our beloved families participate in such glory.

The grieving family may find comfort in this book. "And I heard a voice from heaven, saying, 'Write,' "Blessed are the dead who die in the Lord from now on!"' 'Yes,' says the Spirit, 'that they may rest from their labors, for their deeds follow with them'" (Rev. 14:13).

One of the most rewarding parts of Revelation from the family standpoint comes in the symbolism of Christ as the bridegroom and the church as His bride. What greater confirmation of the marriage relationship could be found anywhere? Even the new Jerusalem is described as a bride.

And I saw the holy city, new Jerusalem, coming down out of heaven from God, made ready as a bride adorned for her husband. And I heard a loud voice from the throne,

415

saying, "Behold the tabernacle of God is among men, and He shall dwell among them, and they shall be His peoples, and God himself shall be among them, and He shall wipe away every tear from their eyes; and there shall no longer be any death; there shall no longer be any mourning, or crying, or pain; the first things have passed away" (Rev. 21:2-4.

The glorious destiny of the Christian family!

"And one of the seven angels who had the seven bowls full of the seven last plagues, came and spoke with me, saying, 'Come here, I shall show you the bride, the wife of the Lamb'" (Rev. 21:9). The description of the holy city that follows defies imagination. Another tribute through analogy to the beauty of marriage!

Revelation teaches both heaven and hell, not just eternal bliss. "He who overcomes shall inherit these things, and I will be his God and he will be My son. But for the cowardly and unbelieving and abominable and murderers and immoral persons and sorcerers and idolaters and all liars, their part will be in the lake that burns with fire and brimstone, which is the second death" (Rev. 21:7, 8). Much as we desire to concentrate upon eternity's beauty, the warnings exist. Our families need a deep awareness of this teaching.

"And the Spirit and the bride say, 'Come.' And let the one who is thirsty come; let the one who wishes take the water of life without cost" (Rev. 22:17). If the bride of Christ invites those who thirst to come to Him, is that not the primary function of earthly brides who believe in Him? Especially for their families?

Throughout this book, praise of Jesus Christ rings. Hallelujahs resound. He is declared to be "King of Kings and Lord of Lords." If we center our families in Christ by making our lives personal "Hallelujah Choruses," joy will fill our homes, even if it must be a joy that smiles through tears. Our homes will be foretastes of heaven.

Our physician brother once delivered a baby to a black woman who feared she might die due to some complications. While on the delivery table, she suddenly called out, "Oh, Lordy! Oh, Lordy! Heaven's my home! Heaven's my home! But I just ain't a bit homesick!"

Is that the real problem with our families?

Index of Scriptures

419

420

INDEX OF SCRIPTURES

424

Index of People

431

Index of Topics

441

Christian Thought
Imperative in the Christian home, 368
Concentrate upon the things of God, 387,388
What we believe about others often depends upon our own spiritual state, 398,399

Church, the Family of God
New Testament emphasis, 292, 379,380
Bloodline of Christ on Calvary supersedes human genealogies, 292,320,321,362,400
Membership in God's Family gains precedence over membership in any earthly family, 293
Hospitality to members of God's Family influences children for Christ, 352
Effect of dedicated church members upon children in single parent homes, 355
Young Christians require nurture similar to parental nurture, 390

Circumcision
Commanded by God to Abraham, 54
Used as a ploy to kill Shechem, Hamor and their men, 83
Agrippa I's daughter, Drusilla, engaged to Epiphanes on the condition he be circumcised, 341; refused, 343

Complaint
Natural, not to be condemned, but not a central focus of one's life, 227
Constant complaint destructive to family peace, 250
Futility of excessive complaint; waste of energy, 387

Communication
Result of its lack in Isaac's family, 71

Consolation
Found in the Book of Psalms, 232
For the grieving family, 377

Cooperation
Requirement for church officers, 396

Courtesy
Component of love, 377

Covenant
Of God with Noah's family, 40
Always with families, 40
With Abraham, 47
With Isaac, 55

Covetousness
Forbidden in Hebrew Law, 106
Paul's condemnation of it, 372
Church officers must be free of it, 396

Curse
Upon Adam, Eve and serpent, 20, 21
Upon Cain, 25
Noah's curse upon Ham, 41
Cursing or striking either parent punishable by death in Hebrew Law, 108,109
Warning against cursing parents, 245
Warning against blessing God and cursing brothers with the same tongue, 405

Deception
Its effect for family destruction, 18, 19,20,68,69,70,75
Rachel and the household gods, 80
Forbidden among Christians, 390

443